D0269208

LANCASHIRE COUNTY LIBRARY

3011813304669 2

MY FIGHT YOUR FIGHT

My Fight
Your Fight

Ronda Rousey
with
Maria Burns Ortiz

CENTURY

LANCASHIRE COUNTY LIBRARY	
3011813304669 2	
Askews & Holts	18-Dec-2015
796.8092 ROU	£14.99
NHA	

Century is part of the Penguin Random House group of companies
whose addresses can be found at global.penguinrandomhouse.com.

Penguin
Random House
UK

Copyright © Ronda Rousey 2015

Ronda Rousey has asserted her right to be identified as the author of this
Work in accordance with the Copyright, Designs and Patents Act 1988.

First published by Century in 2015
First published in the USA by Regan Arts in 2015

www.randomhouse.co.uk

A CIP catalogue record for this book is
available from the British Library.

ISBN 9781780894904

Printed and bound in Great Britain by Clays Ltd, St Ives Plc

Penguin Random House is committed to a sustainable future
for our business, our readers and our planet. This book is
made from Forest Stewardship Council® certified paper.

For Mom and Dad,
I hope you're proud of me.

"There is no history of anything happening until it does.
And then there is."
—Mom

CONTENTS

FOREWORD

BY DANA WHITE, PRESIDENT OF THE UFC

Ronda Rousey is a game changer.

Of course I didn't know that in 2011, when I was in Los Angeles and was asked by TMZ when women were going to fight in the Ultimate Fighting Championship (UFC). I looked at the camera and said, "Never."

Back then, I meant it. I had no problem with women fighting and making a living doing it, but whenever the subject of having them compete in the UFC came up, I flashed back to this fight I had seen in a local show in Northern California. There was this woman who fought just like a guy, and she was in the ring with someone who looked like she took five Tae Bo classes. It was one of the worst, one-sided beatings I've ever seen, and I just didn't want to see that in the UFC.

Then Ronda showed up.

A few months after the TMZ interview, we had a show in Las Vegas, and someone was calling my name. It was Ronda Rousey. I had heard of her; I had been told that she was a good female fighter. I walked over, shook her hand, and she said, "I'm gonna fight for you someday and I'm going to be your first female world champion." Now you've got to understand, everybody—men and women—tells me that. They all say, "I'm gonna work for you someday and be your next world champion."

But she was persistent, and as I watched her compete in the Strikeforce promotion that we had bought, I knew that she was something special. Ronda asked to have a meeting with me at one of the UFC events. Fifteen minutes into the conversation, I was thinking to myself, *I think I'm gonna do this. She's the one who can kick-start this whole thing, and I believe every word that's coming out of her mouth.* She had such charisma and energy. And to watch her fight, she was unbelievable.

So I made my decision, Ronda came in, and I made her the main event of UFC 157 on February 23, 2013. That decision got a lot of heat from the media and the fans, but she went out that night in Anaheim and delivered an awesome fight against Liz Carmouche. It was exciting from the moment it started until it finished, just before the bell rang to end the first round.

That was just the beginning.

The level of talent among the women just skyrocketed. It took off so fast that I never saw it coming. And leading it all was Ronda. She really is the perfect storm. I knew it, I felt it, and I went with it. Talent, looks, determination, she has it all. And while she went from bartender to superstardom, the reality is that she was always this amazing athlete, a former Olympic medalist who finally found what it was she wanted to do. She realized that she was a competitor who wanted to go out there and prove that she was the absolute best. And once she came to that realization, she took over the world of mixed martial arts, absolutely dominated it, and became one of the biggest, if not *the* biggest, stars in the UFC.

When I call her a game changer, it's because she is one in every sense of the word. Not just for women, but for women's sports too. People always say, "Ah, women's basketball, it's the WNBA," "Women's golf, they hit from a shorter tee," "Women's tennis, they don't hit as hard as the men." Nobody says that about Ronda Rousey. She is one of the most intense, unbelievable athletes I've worked with in all my years in boxing and MMA, and I'm not alone in comparing her in the Octagon to a prime Mike Tyson. Watch her intensity, watch how she walks out and how she runs after her opponent. She's not messing around, and when she comes out to fight, you know bad stuff is going to happen to her opponent.

She just has this focus, not just in a fight or in training, but in her everyday life. This is a woman who doesn't party. All she does is wake up every morning and say, "How can I be better than I was yesterday?" That's literally how she lives her life.

Ronda is an incredible role model, empowering women and girls. When I was a kid, the boys played over here and the girls played over there; the boys do all the physical stuff and the girls play with dolls and play house. This past Halloween girls across the country dressed up as Ronda Rousey. That's because she's an amazing, beautiful, and powerful woman.

She inspires everyone. This past summer, the Little League World Series was going on, and Pierce Jones, a thirteen-year-old African-American boy from the South Side of Chicago, one of the stars of the series, comes up to bat, and underneath all his stats, it listed his favorite athlete. It was Ronda Rousey. That's groundbreaking. He could have picked anyone— LeBron James, Derek Jeter, there are so many male athletes to choose from— but his favorite athlete is Ronda Rousey.

Ronda has changed the world of sports, and by the time she's done, she may change the world as well. I don't put anything past her, and I almost feel like Ronda Rousey is writing her book too soon, because she's just getting started. What this woman is going to accomplish is going to be amazing, so get ready for Part Two of the Ronda Rousey story.

WHY I FIGHT

I am a fighter.

To be a fighter, you have to be passionate. I have so much passion, it's hard to hold it all in. That passion escapes as tears from my eyes, sweat from my pores, blood from my veins.

So many people assume that I'm cold and callous, but the truth is you need a big heart to fight. I wear my heart on my sleeve, and I have had it broken too. I can compete with broken toes or stitches in my foot. I can take a hit without batting an eyelash, but I will burst into tears if a sad song comes on the radio. I am vulnerable; that's why I fight.

It has been that way since I was born. I fought for my first breath. I fought for my first words. The battle to be respected and heard is one I'm still fighting. For a long time, I felt I had to fight for every little thing. But now, one big battle every couple of months makes up for all the minor ones I forfeit every day. Some lost battles are small. Getting cut off in traffic. Taking shit from a boss. The everyday slights that drive us up to the edge. Some lost battles are life altering. Losing someone you love. Failing to achieve the one thing you have worked hardest for.

I fight for my dad, who lost his battle, dying when I was eight years old, and for my mom, who taught me how to win every second of my life.

I fight to make the people who love me proud. To make the people who hate me seethe. I fight for anyone who has ever been lost, who has ever been left, or who is battling their own demons.

Achieving greatness is a long and arduous battle that I fight every day. Fighting is how I succeed. I don't just mean inside a 750-square-foot cage or within the confines of a 64-square-meter mat. Life is a fight from the minute you take your first breath to the moment you exhale your last. You have to fight the people who say it can never be done. You have to fight the institutions that put up the glass ceilings that must be shattered. You have to fight your body when it tells you it is tired. You have to fight your mind when doubt begins to creep in. You have to fight systems that are put in place to disrupt you and obstacles that are put in place to discourage you. You have to fight because you can't count on anyone else fighting for you. And you have to fight for people who can't fight for themselves. To get anything of real value, you have to fight for it.

I learned how to fight and how to win. Whatever your obstacles, whoever or whatever your adversary, there is a way to victory.

Here is mine.

FIGHT NIGHT

It is late afternoon by the time I get up. I have slept all day, waking up to eat and then going back into hibernation. I get dressed, pulling on the black shorts and black sports bra.

My hotel room is warm. I want my body to be warm, loose.

I stand in front of the mirror. I pull my hair back in sections. First the top, securing it with an elastic band. Then the left. Then the right. Until all my hair falls down my neck. I take another elastic and bring the three sections together, winding them tightly into a bun. My hair pulls at my scalp and opens my eyes wide. As I am standing in front of the mirror something clicks. Seeing myself prepared for battle I feel transformed; everything is different.

There is an hour before it is time to leave. I pull on my Reebok sweats and my battle boots—cheap, black, faux-suede Love Culture boots that are falling apart but that have seen me through almost every professional win.

My team is sitting in the living room of my hotel suite, spread out between the loveseat-sized sofa and a couple of chairs. Their voices are hushed, but the occasional muffled laugh comes through the closed door. I can hear them moving around. Edmond, my head coach, double-checks his bag to make sure

3

we are not forgetting anything. Rener, who trains me in Brazilian Jiujitsu, rolls and re-rolls the banner with my sponsors' logos that will be displayed behind me in the cage. He wants the banner to be just right, so it can be unfurled with a simple flick of the wrist. Martin, who trains me in wrestling, is unflappably calm. Justin, my training partner in judo and childhood friend, rubs his hands anxiously. They are decked out head-to-toe in my team's official walkout gear.

I open the door separating the two rooms, and everyone freezes. The room is silent.

Security knocks on the door; they're ready to escort us down.

When I walk out of the hotel room, I feel like Superman stepping out of the phone booth—chest out, cape billowing behind him. Unstoppable. Unbeatable. Only instead of an *S*, I have the UFC logo emblazoned across my chest. My mean face is on. From the minute I leave the room, I'm in fight mode.

Outside my door there are three men with earpieces tasked to take me down to my fight.

"Are you ready?" the head officer asks—he means to walk down to the arena.

"Ready," I reply—I mean to win the fight.

Edmond glances around the room, doing a final visual sweep. He hands me my Monster headphones and I slip them on around my neck.

The head security officer leads the way. My team surrounds me, and the other two officers take up the back.

We march through service elevators into tunnels of concrete floors, fluorescent lighting, and exposed pipes. The hallways are empty, and the sounds of our feet reverberate through the corridors. We pass underground rooms where concession workers clock in and rooms where the recycling is sorted. I hear the din from the employee cafeteria. The beeping of a forklift loading pallets fades into silence as we walk through the maze toward the locker room.

As we get closer, I see more signs of life. Production staffers weave through the halls. Cameramen, more security, coaches, athletes, athletic commission members, random strangers are popping in and out of doors. An official from the state athletic commission joins us as we enter the arena. From this moment until I leave the building at the end of the night, I will never be out of her sight.

On my locker room door there's a white paper printout with my name in black letters held up by electrical tape. "Good luck," the security officer says as I step into the windowless cinder-block room. The walls are light beige; the carpet is thin and dark. There's an athletic mat on the floor and a flat-screen TV on the wall plays the live broadcast of the undercard fights.

In other locker rooms, people bring stereos and play music. People joke and make light of things.

My locker room is serious. It is quiet. No one smiles. I don't like people telling jokes in my locker room. Now is not a time to tell jokes. From the minute we leave my hotel room, do not fuck around. The time for fucking around is over. Some serious shit is about to happen.

I am not looking to escape the pressure. I am embracing it. Pressure is what builds up in the chamber behind a bullet before it explodes out of the gun.

We walk into the locker room and settle in. My fifth corner-man, Gene LeBell, an MMA pioneer and longtime family friend, joins up with us. He sits clicking his stopwatch on and off. I lie down on the floor, my head on my bag. I close my eyes. I try to drift off to sleep.

I wake up and want to warm up, but it is too early and Edmond stops me.

"Relax, it's not time yet," he says in his thick Armenian accent. His voice is calm and reassuring. He rubs my shoulders briefly, as if trying to knead out the excess energy surging through my body.

I want to bounce around and do something. I want to be more ready.

"Even if you're cold, you're fine," Edmond says. "Just relax. You don't want to over warm up."

Edmond wraps my hands as the representative from the state athletic commission watches to make sure everything about the wrapping process is legit.

Gauze first. Then the white fabric tape that makes a ripping sound as it pulls away from the roll. I watch as the tape loops hypnotically between my fingers, around my hands, and down to my wrists. Then Edmond smooths the end of the tape along my wrist and I am one step closer to the moment I have been waiting for, the moment I have been training for, the moment I have never been more ready for.

The commission official signs my wraps with a black permanent marker. I start stretching, bouncing around a bit. Edmond holds the mitts for a few punches, but stops me before it goes too long. It feels like it's not quite enough. I am itching to do more.

"Relax, relax," he says.

Over the broadcast I can hear the crowd. As more people pour in the excitement builds until I can hear the noise pushing through the walls. The crowd's energy pulsates through the concrete into my body.

The clock ticks. Edmond sits me down on a folding chair. He leans in close.

"You are more prepared than this girl," he says to me. "You are better in every area than she is. You have fought for this moment. You have sweated for this moment. You have busted your ass for this moment. Everything we have done has led up to right now. You are the best in the world. Now, go out there and fuck this girl up."

Destroying my opponent is the only thing I want to do in that moment. It is the singular focus of every cell in my body.

In the hallway, I hear Burt Watson's gravelly voice. Burt is the official babysitter of UFC fighters, which means he handles so many random things that there's not a title for what he does other than to say he helps take care of us.

"We rollin', yeah!" he shouts. "This is what we do, and why we do it, baby. This is your night, your fight. Don't let them take your night, baby." His voice bellows along the corridor as he walks me out. I get excited.

My challenger always comes out first. I can't see her, but I hear her lame music blasting throughout the arena. I immediately hate her walkout song.

I hear the audience react to her. In the shadow of the tunnel, I can feel their applause pounding the air, but I know that their reaction to me is going to explode through the arena. People are going to lose their goddamn minds when I walk out. I can almost feel their roar in my bones, and I know that the noise will rattle my challenger.

Edmond presses my face hard. He rubs my ears and nose. My face tenses, preparing for possible impact. He pulls my hair back tighter on my head. My scalp tingles. My eyes widen. I am awake. I am alert. I am ready.

We get our cue. Security flanks me. My corner walks a step behind me.

Joan Jett's fierce guitar chords send a charge through me and, as "Bad Reputation" blares, I storm through the hallway, glaring straight ahead.

The crowd roars when I step out, but it is like the volume and brightness of everything around me has been turned down. I can see nothing but what is right ahead of me, the path to the cage.

At the steps of the Octagon I remove my headphones, take off the battle boots. I take off my hoodie, my T-shirt, my sweats. My corner helps me because it can be hard to remove a layer of clothes when your hands are taped and in padded gloves.

Edmond pats me down with a towel. I hug each member of my corner. Rener. "Uncle" Gene. Martin. Justin. Edmond kisses me on the cheek. We hug. Edmond pops my mouth guard in. I take a sip of water. Stitch Duran, my cutman, wipes my face with Vaseline and steps aside.

I hold out my arms and an official pats me down to make sure I don't have anything hidden on me. He runs his hands behind my ears, up my hair, and into the tight bun. He has me open my mouth. He checks my gloves. He directs me up the stairs.

I bow when I enter the cage, a slight nod that is a habit from my judo days. I stomp my left foot twice. Then my right. I jump and stomp them both. I walk toward my corner. I shake my arms. I slap my right shoulder, then my left, then my thighs. I touch the ground. My corner unfurls my sponsorship banner behind me. I bounce from foot to foot. I squat and pop back up. I stomp my feet once more. Then I stop.

The moment has arrived. My body is relaxed yet hyper-alert, ready to act and react. My senses are heightened. I am overcome with a single desire—to win. It is simply a matter of win or die. I feel as if I was just here, in this moment, in this cage, as if the time that has separated this fight from my last fight did not exist. My brain reverts to fight mode, and I enter a zone where nothing but fighting has ever existed.

I stare across the cage.

UFC announcer Bruce Buffer comes to the center of the cage. Bruce is the best in the game, but when he looks toward my opponent's corner all I hear is, "Wah wah wah wah wah wah wah." Then he turns toward my corner and says, "Wah wah wah wah wah wah wah."

I see the other girl. I lock in on her.

I always try to make eye contact. Sometimes, she looks away. I want her to look at me.

I want her to stare me in the eye. I want her to see that I have no fear. I want her to know she stands no chance. I want her to be scared. I want her to know she is going to lose.

The referee looks at my opponent and asks, "Are you ready?"

She nods.

He points to me.

"Are you ready?"

I nod and think, *Born that way.*

And then we begin.

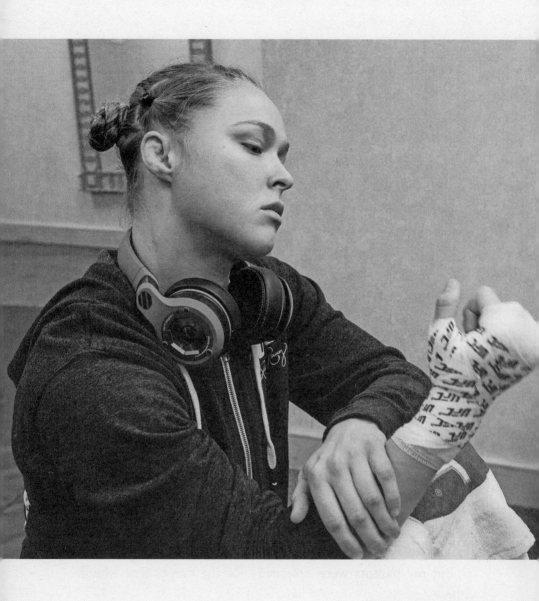

I WAS BORN READY

A lot of people get self-conscious about not being ready before a fight. They walk out feeling cold and unprepared, believing that feeling will disappear if they could warm up a little bit more. It gets into their head.

I was raised to be ready to fight at a moment's notice. I hardly warm up at all, and yet, I am so prepared to fight that at the beginning of a match, I am almost forcibly holding myself back, just waiting for that referee's hand to drop.

You never know if you'll have to be ready sooner than you expected.

When I was born, I almost died.

On February 1, 1987, my pregnant mother was rushing around the house trying to get everything in order before my parents left for the hospital.

"Ron, are you ready?" my mom asked my dad.

"Darlin', I was born ready," he answered.

But my parents were not ready for the events that would follow.

I was born with the umbilical cord wrapped around my neck, cutting off my air supply. My heart stopped. I came out blue and listless. On the 0–10 Apgar scale used to rate babies' health at birth, seven is considered good. My score was a zero.

Mom says that the doctors thought I was dead. Everything was movement and chaos. Doctors running in from all directions. The squeaking wheels of metal carts carrying equipment being rushed into the room. Cabinets slamming as the medical staff pulled items from the shelves. The lead doctor shouting orders as people poured into the room. Eventually, the doctors managed to get me some air. They cut the cord, unwrapped it from around my neck, gave me baby CPR and oxygen. Then after what my mom describes as an eternity—but was probably closer to a few minutes—I started breathing and my heart started beating.

The whole experience had my parents pretty freaked out. It was the only time my mom saw my dad cry.

My parents named me Ronda after my dad, whose name was Ron. Some people think there's some special reason I'm Ronda without an *h*, but it was unintentional. After all the panic died down and it was clear that I was going to live, the nurse asked my dad what they wanted to name me. He said, "Ronda." The nurse asked how to spell it. His name was Ron and he just assumed it was spelled the same, so he told her, "R-O-N-D-A." And that's what they put on my birth certificate. They might as well have put down "Ronda, no H" since I've had to go through my entire life correcting people on the spelling—and only recently have people started spelling it right more often than not—but I think it fits me better. *H* is a stupid letter anyway.

My parents were happy I was alive, but the doctor who saved me said that I might have brain damage and that it might not be evident right away. In fact, he told my mom it might take months or even years if the damage was in areas that control things like walking or speech since those delays aren't apparent until you get to those developmental stages.

Doctors don't usually sugarcoat the truth, but he offered my mom his nonclinical opinion.

"In most cases like this, she would not have survived," he said. "I can't tell you anything definitive right now beyond the fact that she's breathing, her heart rate is good, and her reflex responses are what they should be. I have no idea what the future holds, but babies are unbelievably resilient and this one is certainly a fighter."

WINNING IS THE GREATEST
FEELING IN THE WORLD

Winning was conditioned in me early on. When I was little, during judo tournaments, I would sit and play hand games with the kid I was about to fight. My mom would pull me away and say, "Sit there and think about winning. Stop messing around."

When I win, I'm euphoric. Nothing can bother me. Winning raises me up, above the fray. I float happily above all the things that make life messy and hard. After I win, for a little while, everything is right in the world. Winning feels like falling in love, except it's like falling in love with everybody in the room all at once—and it's amplified when you are in an arena of 18,000 people.

When I turned two and still wasn't talking, my parents started to worry. My pediatrician told my mom lots of things, like I'd just start talking when I was ready or that I wasn't speaking because I didn't see a need to talk. My two older sisters seemed to understand what I wanted and would communicate my desire for a cookie or to play with My Little Ponies. But my mom knew something wasn't right. She had two other daughters and was

14

taking classes in things like developmental psychology as she worked toward her PhD.

With my third birthday approaching, I had yet to say a single intelligible word. My mom took me to lots of specialists. They couldn't find anything in particular wrong with me, but the doctors seemed to believe that being cut off from oxygen at birth might have something to do with my difficulty learning to speak.

When part of your brain dies, it's dead forever. (OK, so that's pretty much the definition of dead.) However, babies are pretty amazing. Babies are super-resilient. Sometimes, baby brains can rewire themselves so that they still work. My developing brain just rewired itself. If you took one of those multicolored cerebral activity scans, you'd see the part that controls my speech is located in a different part of the brain than it is for most people. But until my brain got everything rewired, it was like I couldn't connect the words in my head with my mouth.

Speaking was a constant battle between what I wanted to say and what I said. It wasn't just about words, it was about everything. What I felt. What I wanted. What I meant. It was always a struggle. If I was asked to repeat myself too many times, I would get frustrated and kick the person I was speaking to. It is one thing to fight other people, but fighting yourself is different. If you're fighting yourself, who wins? Who loses?

On my third birthday, more than anything else, I wanted a WWF Hulk Hogan Wrestling Buddy. My sisters and I used to watch *WWF Superstars of Wrestling* on Saturday mornings after *X-Men*. During commercial breaks, we launched ourselves off the brown upholstered couch, attempting to submit one another on the itchy tan polyester carpet. One of the greatest toys to come out of the 1980s was Wrestling Buddy, a two-foot-tall pillow version of Hulk. You could body-slam it, wrestle with it, throw it to the ground. It was awesome. When my mom asked me what I wanted, I kept repeating one word, "Balgrin."

No one had a clue what I meant. But my mom took me and my sisters to the toy store to find my Balgrin. The guy who worked there showed me every toy that involved a ball. We left empty-handed. We went to another store. And another.

Each time I tried to explain what I wanted, sounds spilled out in a jumbled mess that no one understood. It was like the words I needed were pinned down, and I couldn't free them. I could see them. I could feel them. I just couldn't say them. I felt trapped. I burst into tears, snot ran down my face. The world closed in on me; I began to lose hope.

My dad met up with us when he finished work. We went to one last toy store and met the greatest toy store salesman that ever lived, deserving of enshrinement in the toy salesmen Hall of Fame.

As soon as we had made it through the doors my dad approached a clerk and said, "My baby girl wants a Balgrin. I don't know what the hell a Balgrin is, but we're not leaving here until we have one."

"Well, what does it do?" the guy asked me.

Afraid to speak, I slammed my body into the ground a few times.

The clerk didn't laugh. He thought about it for a moment. I looked up at him hopefully.

"Do you mean a Wrestling Buddy? It's like a pillow, and you wrestle with it."

I nodded slowly.

"Balgrin," I said.

"Right," he replied as if I'd spoken clear as day, "Hulk Hogan."

He got one from some back shelf. I did a happy dance in the aisle. My mother thanked the heavens.

The clerk placed the Wrestling Buddy box in my hands and I was flooded with joy. I refused to let my parents take Hulk Hogan for even a moment, not even to pay for him, so the clerk just rang up another box.

When we got home, Hulk and I were nearly inseparable. I jumped off the couch with an elbow to his chest. I'd pin him on the ground and make my mom count to three. In what was either complete coincidence or an eerie sign of things to come, I eventually ripped off his arm. Using an old trick to patch up judo *gis*, my mom sewed his arm back on with dental floss and then, as I did every night, I got into bed with him.

Yep, that's right. I slept with Hulk Hogan.

For a kid who couldn't communicate like all the other kids, being understood by a stranger on my third birthday was a major breakthrough. This was an early lesson on the importance of always believing that if I wanted something bad enough and tried hard enough, I could make it happen.

I have done a fair amount of things so far in my life. (I don't want to say a lot because I'm not even thirty, and I've got a lot left to do—let's say I'm at Gandalf-the-Grey level, post all the Hobbit drama, prepared to help destroy the ring and become Gandalf the White.) And often I've accomplished things people said were unrealistic, unlikely, or, my favorite, impossible. I never would have been able to do any of those things without hope.

The kind of hope I'm talking about is the belief that something good will come. That everything you're going through and everything you've gone through will be worth the struggles and frustrations. The kind of hope I'm talking about is a deep belief that the world can be changed, that the impossible is possible.

The day of my third birthday was an early introduction into never giving up hope, never giving up on myself, and surrounding myself with people who saw in me things I might not see in myself. It was the first time I felt like I had won.

EVERYTHING CAN CHANGE IN
A SPLIT SECOND

Anyone who watches fights has seen it happen: One second a fighter is looking dominant, unstoppable. Then he hits the canvas. One punch or split second of lost focus can change the entire direction of a fight. Life is like that.

One of the reasons I crave winning so much is that life is so uncertain, so volatile. When I win, there is that one little moment of time where I'm not worried about everything being taken away from me at any second.

There have been so many times when what I thought was real totally got turned upside down, sending my whole world into free fall. The knowledge that everything good can be taken away at any second is what makes me work so hard.

Los Angeles, California, to Minot, North Dakota, is not a traditional route for American migration. But when I was three, my sister Maria saw someone shot point-blank in the head while coming home on the school bus. My parents saw that as a sign that it was time to get the hell out. We moved to middle-of-nowhere North Dakota.

My mom had finished her PhD and one of the job offers she received came from Minot State University. Minot State had a solid speech pathology program and, as part of the job benefit the university would provide me with intensive speech therapy. My dad retired from his job as an aerospace plant manager when we moved. The cost of living in North Dakota was cheap compared to California, and my parents decided we only needed one income. So, in the summer of 1990, we moved into a house on a five-acre piece of farmland that was twenty miles outside of Minot.

My sisters and I had free rein. In California, we had never been allowed outside without a grown-up. But here, away from the peaking crime rates and smog levels that were plaguing L.A. at the time, we raced our bikes up and down the gravel driveway. We explored the small patch of woods behind our house. We gathered cocoons, until my mom barred that activity after one of them turned out to be a spider's egg sac and hatched in the house, sending tiny spiders in all directions. We set up a Slip'N Slide on the hill our house was built into and spent hours hurling ourselves downhill on the yellow sheet of plastic.

I was obsessed with collecting rocks and amassed an impressive assortment. My dad taught me how to identify quartz, pyrite, petrified wood, limestone, and flint. In August, my mom started going to town daily to prepare for her class. My sisters were not as enamored with country life as I was and usually joined her, leaving me and my dad alone. On these days, he would buckle me into the front seat of our brown and white Ford Bronco and take me off-roading in search of the perfect rock hunting spot. We would drive through the fields and between the trees planted as windbreaks, bouncing over rocks and roots. After a while, we would come to a clearing we had never seen before and my dad would say, "This looks like the place." I would spend hours digging in the dirt and bringing him specimens to examine as he leaned against the car, wearing aviator sunglasses and smoking a cigarette.

It was during one of these adventures that I discovered my father was the strongest man who ever lived. A thunderstorm had passed through the night before, and as we drove, mud flew everywhere. We came across a normally dry creek bed that had a few inches of water. My dad stopped and turned to me, "What do you think, Ronnie? Should we ford the river?"

I nodded.

"You got it, kiddo," he said, touching the brim of his hat in a mock salute.

He grinned and gunned it. Muddy water doused the windshield as if it had been thrown from a bucket. The Bronco jerked, then nothing. My dad pushed down on the gas again. There was a whir of tires moving, but we did not move. He thrust the car into reverse. We bumped backward, but the car didn't go anywhere. In the passenger side rearview mirror, I saw mud flying everywhere as the tires spun to no effect.

"Well, fuck," my dad said. He got out of the car; I slipped out of my seatbelt and climbed out after him. He was squatting down by the back tires.

"What we got here is a problem," he said. "Now what we gotta do is find ourselves a solution."

He surveyed the area.

"This looks like as good a rock hunting spot as any," he said as if it was all part of his plan. "But we're going to be looking for different rocks than usual. What I need is for you to find me some big rocks, like rocks the size of your head, OK?"

I nodded, and we both scanned the ground for large rocks. I found one the size of a large grapefruit. I reached down and put my hands around to lift it up. It wouldn't budge. I tried again, mustering all my three-year-old strength. Nothing.

"Here," I called to my dad.

He came over carrying two rocks the size of cantaloupes in one arm. My mouth just about dropped at the feat. I pointed to the rock I had been trying to lift. He scooped it up as if it was nearly weightless.

"Great eye," he said, with a smile. I beamed with pride.

He took the rocks and put them as close to under the tire as he could get them, and we spent the next half hour repeating the process—me pointing at rocks and watching, awed, as he lifted them as if they were nothing.

"Let's see if this works," he said.

We got back in the Bronco. He started the engine and pushed down on the gas. He shifted back and forth. The car lurched in both directions but didn't dislodge.

"Well, shit," he said. "It was a helluva try. I guess we're going to have to walk. I'll have to get John Stip to get his truck and help pull me out later." The Stips lived the next farm over from us. We got out of the Bronco again. It was hot and I was tired. I could still see the car license plate, when, red-faced and sweaty, I looked up at my dad.

"Can't make it," I said.

He scooped me up as effortlessly as he had the rocks. I put my head on his shoulder as he walked through the tall grass and I was soon fast asleep. I woke up to the crunching sound of my dad's footsteps on the gravel road that led up to our house. The Bronco was a barely visible speck in a faraway field.

As the sun set over the prairie, we ate dinner on the porch, overlooking nothing but fields for as far as we could see.

That evening as we made the quarter-mile walk down the unpaved road to check our mailbox, I looked up at my mom.

"I like North Dakota more than California," I said. It was the first complete sentence I ever spoke.

Summer in middle-of-nowhere North Dakota is beautiful. Winter in North Dakota is another story. There is nothing but subzero temperatures and snow. Lots of snow. But that first winter, the novelty of snow had yet to wear off. So, on a completely ordinary day in January, Mom and Dad bundled us up, and we waddled out into the snow. The Stips joined us.

My dad went down a completely ordinary hill on a completely ordinary orange plastic sled. He went down first to make sure it was safe for me and my sisters to follow. I laughed as I watched him shoot down the hill. He hit a bump, an ordinary log covered with some snow. The sled skidded to a stop at the bottom of the hill.

But my dad just lay there. Mom thought he was joking.

We waited.

He didn't get up.

My sisters and I sat at the top of the hill watching as Mom ran down the hill, then knelt beside Dad.

There was a blur of snow and flashing lights. An ambulance showed up but got stuck in the snow. Another ambulance came. It took about an hour before medical personnel got to my dad.

My mom rode with my dad in the ambulance. Our neighbors took us back to their house for hot cocoa. We waited for Mom to call.

The news was not good.

My dad, who was the strongest person I knew, I mean he had superhero-level strength, had broken his back. The first time I saw my dad after his accident, he was lying in a hospital bed, unable to move. I kept hoping that the next time we walked into his hospital room, he'd be up, standing in front of the bathroom mirror, slapping on Old Spice aftershave and looking at us with a smile as though nothing had ever happened and announcing— as he had every morning as long as I could remember—"It's showtime." I kept waiting for him to jump out of the bed. But he didn't. He was in and out of surgery, narrowly escaping death on the operating room table again and again.

The first time Mom took us to see him after surgery, the lights in his room in the intensive care unit were dim.

"You have to be quiet," she said as we stood outside the doorway. "Dad is very tired."

We nodded solemnly and quietly filed in behind her like baby ducks. The steady beeping of his heart monitor filled the room. Every thirty seconds or so, a machine whirred.

"Ron, the kids are here," my mom said in the soft voice she reserves only for when you are really sick.

My dad was lying flat on his back. He opened his eyes. He couldn't move his body, but he shifted his gaze toward us.

"Hey guys," he said, his voice a whisper.

I edged closer to the bed. My dad was bandaged around his torso, where the doctors had cut into him to operate on his broken spine. There was a large bag of blood next to an IV, dripping into his arm. Hanging from the side of the bed was another bag. A tube connected to some place beneath the blankets that I could not see was filling the bag with blood as it dripped out of his body.

A nurse came into the room and as she got close to Dad I launched myself at her. Mom caught me midair as I screamed at the top of my lungs, "Why cut my daddy in half?! Why you do?!" I hated her. Hated her for hurting my dad. Hated her for the pain he was going through. Hated her for the pain I was going through.

I swung my fists and kicked my legs as Mom carried me into the hallway and blocked my path to the door. I gulped for air. Tears streamed down my face as Mom tried to explain that they were helping Daddy.

"He got hurt," Mom told me. "The nurses and doctors are working to make him better. They are trying to help him."

I was not sure I could believe her.

"You can ask Daddy," she said. "But we need to try to help him too. That means we need to be quiet when we're in his room. OK?"

I nodded.

"OK then. Let's go." She led me back into the room. My dad spent more than five months in the hospital. Every day after school, my mom would pile the three of us kids into the car and we would make the 130-mile drive from Minot to Bismarck, since our local hospital wasn't equipped to deal with an injury as severe as my dad's.

There is not a lot to see outside of a car window in the North Dakota countryside during the winter, just endless stretches of white. White is actually what I remember most about that period of my life. The white hospital halls. White tiled floors. White fluorescent lights. The white bedsheets. I also remember the blood; there was a lot of blood.

My dad had a rare bleeding disorder called Bernard-Soulier syndrome, which makes it difficult for the body to form blood clots, and blood clots are an essential part of how our bodies stop bleeding. Minor injuries can result in bleeding complications, and major complications can result from traumatic injury. People with the disorder often suffer prolonged bleeding

during and after surgery. My dad had suffered a traumatic injury and major surgeries: There was so much blood.

Mom talks about how my dad would be crashing and how nurses would run into his room with the bags of blood you see hanging from IV stands, normally dripping into people's arms at a slow trickle. A nurse would connect the bag to his arm, place the bag on a table, and put all of her bodyweight on it so that the blood would shoot into his veins.

The nurses would usher us out of the room before they changed his sheets and dressings, hoping we wouldn't see it. But that much blood is impossible to miss. It would saturate his bandages, stain the sheets. I stared at the blood as it spread. Red dots blooming into huge circles. All that blood left me feeling helpless. Even as a four-year-old, I knew that much blood meant things were not going well.

There were lots more surgeries. Lots more bags of blood. The doctors inserted a metal rod in Dad's back. We spent a lot of time in the waiting room. The nurses would put cartoons on the TV for us. I ate a lot of soup from the hospital cafeteria. I drew a lot of pictures.

All through the winter and spring we made that long drive. On the way down, I would stare out the icy windows and draw pictures in the condensation on the windows. On the way home, my sisters and I would sleep while Mom drove in silence.

Dad was never quite the same after his accident. No one in my family was.

NEVER UNDERESTIMATE
AN OPPONENT

The moment you stop viewing your opponent as a threat is the moment you leave yourself open to getting beat. You start thinking you don't have to train as hard. You cut corners. You get comfortable. You get caught.

When I was little, people didn't take me seriously because I could hardly get a sentence out. When I competed in judo, I was discounted because I was the American and Americans suck at judo. When I got into MMA, people brushed me off, first as a girl, then as a one-trick pony who only had a single move. I have carried other people's lack of confidence in me around for my entire life. Even when I am the 11–1 favorite, I feel like I'm the underdog. Every single second of every day I feel I have something to prove. I have to prove myself every time I walk into a new gym, onto a new movie set, into a business meeting, and in every fight.

There have always been people who have written me off. They're not going away. I use that to motivate me. I'm driven to show them just how wrong they are.

My dad was released from the hospital at the end of the spring of 1991. Medical bills had mounted, so he needed to go back to work. He found a job, only it was at a manufacturing plant across the state. The arrangement meant he had to live two hours away and commute home on the weekends.

By this point, I was speaking relatively clearly. Well, clearly might be a stretch, but I was intelligible beyond my small family circle. Speech therapy had paid off and I advanced from being nearly two years behind (a pretty significant delay when you're not even four) to being on the low end of average. However, in my family, average wasn't going to cut it.

My speech therapist suggested I get more individualized attention to force me to work on my speech further. As people often do when they are faced with physical or neurological limitations, I found a workaround. Somehow my sisters always understood me, and they would step in and translate.

"Ronda is crying because she wants to wear the red shirt, not that blue one you put her in."

"Ronda wants spaghetti for dinner."

"Ronda is looking for her Balgrin."

My speech therapist thought this help was hindering my improvement. When I struggled speaking, I would just look to one of my sisters to jump in and assist. My therapist told my mom that I would be best served in a situation where I had no other option than to speak for myself.

As much as my parents hated the idea of having our family living on two different sides of the state, this arrangement would provide an opportunity for me to find my voice—literally. I hadn't started grade school yet, so I went to live with my dad, while my sisters stayed with my mom.

In the fall of 1991, my dad and I moved into a one-bedroom

house in the tiny town of Devils Lake, North Dakota. Our house was small and old, the carpets were thin, and the linoleum in the kitchen was coated in permanent grime. We had one of those TVs with rabbit ears that got four snowy channels, so we rented a lot of videos. We watched animated movies about talking animals and R-rated movies that my mom would have disapproved of because they involved a lot of swearing, a lot of people being shot, and a lot of things getting blown up. Every night before bed, we watched *Wild Discovery*, which explains why to this day I possess a wealth of random animal knowledge. There was a pullout couch in the living room that was my bed, but we only used it when my mom and sisters came to visit. Otherwise, I crawled into bed with my dad and fell asleep in my footy pajamas.

Domestic life wasn't my dad's specialty. The contents of our kitchen included milk, orange juice, a couple of adult frozen dinners, a box or two of cereal, and several Kid Cuisine TV dinners (the ones with a cartoon penguin on the front). My dad pulled back the plastic wrapper, popped the meals in the microwave, then mere seconds later handed me a small black tray containing compartments of soggy pizza, wrinkly corn, and dry brownie. Other nights, we got fast food, picking up a pizza at Little Caesars or a kid's meal at Hardees.

"I know your mom is worried about how you talk," my dad said one day as we pulled up to the drive-thru at Hardees.

I shrugged.

"But don't you worry about it. You are going to show everyone one day. You're just a sleeper. You know what a sleeper is?"

I shook my head.

"A sleeper just waits and when the time is right, they come out and wow everyone. That's you, kiddo. Don't you worry."

He turned to me.

"You're a smart kid. It's not like you're some fucking moron. You think you got problems because you're a little slow to talk. Let me show you what stupid looks like."

We pulled up to the window. "Hello, welcome to Hardees," came the garbled sound through the box.

"Heeeellllooo," my dad said, using the slow and loud voice he reserved solely for the Hardees drive-thru speaker.

He turned to me. "Watch this. They're going to fuck this order up. These idiots can never get a damn order right." Then he turned to the speaker box and said, "I would like a kids' meal with chicken fingers and a small coffee."

"Will that be all?" the voice asked.

"Yes, can you repeat that back to me?" my dad asked.

"A chicken fingers kids' meal and a coffee," the voice said. "Please pull up."

My dad looked at me and said, "No fucking way they get this order right."

We pulled up. The guy working the cash register opened the window and held out the bag.

"That's two cheeseburgers and a small fries," he said.

My dad handed me the bag and gave me an I-told-you-so look.

As we pulled out of the lot, he turned to me, "Ronnie, just remember that. Be grateful you're a sleeper and not fucking stupid."

I unwrapped a cheeseburger and nodded.

LOSING IS ONE OF THE MOST DEVASTATING EXPERIENCES IN LIFE

I don't lean on the old wins. I always need a new one, which is why every fight means the world to me.

I forget wins all the time. I forget entire tournaments and countries, but the losses stay with me forever. Every single loss feels like a piece of my soul has died. I'm never the same after a loss.

For me, losing is second only to having a loved one die. When I lose, I mourn a piece of me dying. The only thing worse than that is mourning the death of somebody else.

Dad's spine was disintegrating. The doctor slid the X-ray onto the screen and told my parents that the deterioration was getting worse and that it would keep getting worse. Soon, he wouldn't be able to walk. Then he'd be quadriplegic. Then he would waste away until he died. There was no miracle cure. No cutting-edge operation. Just a couple more years—maybe less—of excruciating pain and paralysis.

Though he hid his pain from us, my dad had been suffering since the accident; his back was deteriorating and the chronic pain was getting worse. My mom got a new job at a small college on the other side of the state, in Jamestown, North Dakota. We all moved back in together—Mom, Dad, Maria, Jennifer, and me.

My dad quit his job, saying the ninety-mile commute each way was too much, but that was only partially true. The reality was that the pain was becoming unbearable and sitting all that time only made it worse. The doctor had prescribed painkillers, which my dad refused to take and that he couldn't have taken while driving anyway. I was just a kid; I didn't question why he was home. I was just happy to have my dad around.

The summer before I started third grade Dad was always there. He sat on the front stoop as we rode our bikes up and down the block, made us snacks, and turned on the sprinkler for us to run through on hot days. While my mom worked, he piled us into the car, trekking us to our various activities and friends' houses. When he was feeling up to it, he headed down to the basement where he had his woodworking tools set up. When I got bored of watching cartoons, I sat on the steps, peering down as the power saw buzzed, sending sawdust floating into beams of sunlight. Some days, when it was just the two of us, he and I would drive to our "special" spot, an out-of-the-way pond where we would skip rocks.

On August 11, 1995, Jennifer and I were home with Dad, watching cartoons on Nickelodeon. It was a summer day that blended into all the others.

Dad called Mom and told her to come home. Then he left.

I like to think he hugged Jennifer and me for longer than normal and told us he loved us and that he was going out, but honestly, I don't remember. For years, I hated myself for having been such a self-absorbed eight-year-old that I had no clue what was happening. I've tried to remember something from the *before* part of that day—what my dad was wearing, what he looked like, what he sounded like. Whether he hugged us that day. I wish I could remember the words he said to me before he walked out our front door. I can't. I just remember what came after.

My mom rushed in the front door.

"Where's your dad?" she asked.

Jennifer and I shrugged. We had no idea how radically our life was about to change. My mom, overcome, sat down at the dining room table.

My dad had walked down the four steps that led to the driveway. He got into the Bronco. He drove to the spot next to the pond where we skipped rocks. It was peaceful there. He parked the car, then took out a hose and put one end in the tailpipe, then brought the other end around to the driver's side window. He got in the car. He rolled up the window. He sat back in his seat. He closed his eyes. He went to sleep.

A few hours later, a policeman showed up at our door. My mom and the officer spoke in hushed voices in the entryway for a few minutes. When my mom came back into the living room, she sat us down on the living room couch. From the look on her face I knew it was something serious. Jen and I glanced at each other, making that silent sibling eye contact that says, "Do you know what this is all about? No, me neither."

"Dad went to heaven," my mom said. For the first time in my life, my mother started to cry. I don't know what she said next. The room was spinning too fast.

Everything in my life from those words on is part of the *after*.

I tried to stand up. I wanted to get away. I needed to leave the room, to leave the moment, but I felt my legs collapsing under me. It was as if they couldn't bear my weight. Everything that followed is a haze.

Maria had been out of town visiting family and was rushed home.

In the hours and days that followed, our house was filled with people. Some stayed the night, helping my mom and us. Some just dropped off food. There were so many casseroles and every-one whispered, they seemed to think that was the appropriate thing to do. In a hushed voice, I heard one woman question whether Dad could have a Catholic service even though he com-mitted suicide. The priest never hesitated. "Funerals are about the living," he said. "The dead are at peace with God."

The funeral home director was married to my second-grade teacher, Mrs. Lisko. She was with her husband when he came to discuss service and burial details. It was weird seeing her in my house.

I remember sitting with Jennifer and Maria on the stairs and overhearing as he asked my mom what kind of coffin Dad wanted.

"I don't think he cares," my mom said. "He's dead."

Mom tried not to cry in front of us kids. She would come out of her bedroom, her eyes red and puffy. Maria and I cried a lot. I cried so hard I felt like I was going to run out of tears. But Jennifer refused to cry. I looked at her and wished that I could stop. I told myself to pretend he was on a long business trip.

The night before the funeral, we sat in the funeral home parlor. The place was nearly empty; most visitors had left for the evening and it was quiet.

A woman I didn't know told my sisters and me that he looked peaceful and walked out.

I looked into the coffin. My dad was lying there, looking like my dad. His eyes were closed, but he didn't look like he was sleeping. His mouth, under his mustache, had been set in such a smile that it looked like he were about to laugh, as though he were playing a trick and the anticipation had become too much and he was about to spring up from the coffin and burst into laughter. I waited. I watched the coffin. I prayed for that moment even after my mom took me by the hand and led me away.

The service was a Catholic mass. The un-air-conditioned church was hot in mid-August. We sat in the front pew. I heard the priest talking at the altar, but was unable to focus on his words. A fly buzzed over the casket. It landed on my dad's nose. I wanted to jump up and shoo it away, but my mom was holding my hand too tightly. I hated that fly.

We rode to the cemetery in a white limousine. Stepping out of the car with its tinted windows, I shielded my eyes in the sunlight. I had never been to a funeral before, but always imagined them occurring on dark rainy days. Instead, it was muggy and the sun was beating down. I stood, sweating, in the black dress that had been bought for his funeral. I tried to fan myself with my hand, as if it would make any difference. It was the kind of day where my dad would have turned on the sprinkler for us to run through. But he was dead.

My dad received a military burial because of his service in the Army. A soldier played taps on a trumpet and guns were fired in the traditional salute. I covered my ears at the noise. As I watched my dad's coffin lowered slowly into the ground and out of sight, I felt empty inside. That feeling would never fully go away. The men folded the American flag that had been draped over my dad's coffin into a perfect triangle and handed it to my mother.

The flag stayed folded for the next thirteen years.

TRAGEDY PRECEDES SUCCESS

My great-grandmother always said, "God knows what he's doing, even when you don't." I agree with her. There is nothing in my life that I would go back and change, even the darkest moments. All the successes and greatest joys in my life are a result of the absolute worst things. Every missed opportunity is a blessing in disguise.

A loss leads to a victory. Being fired leads to a dream job. Death leads to a birth. I find comfort in believing that good things can grow out of tragedy.

The first few months after my dad died, I'd wake up and be surprised that the sun was still rising in the east; that people were still playing and going to school. Nothing seemed to have changed.

I did the best I could just to keep going. Sometimes, it felt like Dad wasn't home from work yet. Like he would walk through the door any minute, snowflakes on his mustache, and bellow, "It is colder than a witch's titty out there."

Other times, his absence was overwhelming. The sucker punch of stumbling across a half-chewed pack of his Wrigley's spearmint gum lodged in the couch cushions or a receipt with his signature buried in a pile of papers.

But after a while, him not being there started to seem normal. I still missed my dad. I still thought about him every day—I still think about him every day—but I knew not to expect him to walk through the door.

The second winter after my dad died, my mom started dating again. She met Dennis online. Dennis was a rocket scientist. (If you bring that up to him, he will say he wasn't actually a rocket scientist, but that he worked on the radar that was used with rockets—because clearly that's a big difference.) Dennis sent my mom a pink fractal for Valentine's Day. My mom was flattered. I didn't even know what a fractal was.

A few months later, Dennis asked my mom to marry him. My mom was really happy, and it made me happy. We moved back to California and in March 1998, just after my eleventh birthday, my sister Julia was born.

When we moved to Santa Monica, my mom reconnected with some of her old judo buddies in the Los Angeles area. They were guys she had trained with back in the day when she was on the world team. She was the first American to win the world judo championships, but that had been before I was born. Now, one of those friends had started his own club and invited my mom to work out there. One day, I just asked if I could go try it out.

The next Wednesday afternoon, I hopped in the car to head to judo. I didn't expect it to be a life-changing moment.

My dad's death set off a series of events that would not have occurred had he lived. We wouldn't have moved back to California. I wouldn't have a younger sister. I wouldn't have taken up judo. Who knows what I would be doing or how my life would have ended up.

But I wouldn't have ended up here.

DO NOT ACCEPT LESS THAN WHAT YOU'RE CAPABLE OF

My sister Jennifer says we grew up in a family where exceptional was considered average. If you got a report card with all A's and an A-minus, my mom would ask why you didn't get all A's. If I won a tournament, my mom would ask why I didn't win it by all *ippons*, judo's version of a knockout. She never expected more from us than we were capable of, but she never accepted less.

The very first time I stepped on the judo mat I fell in love with the sport. I was amazed by how complex judo was. How creative you had to be. There are so many little parts and so much thought that goes into every move and technique. I love the problem-solving aspect of fighting. It's about feeling and understanding and breaking down an opponent. It's not just "go faster."

I had been on a swim team for a couple of years. But after my dad died, I didn't want to swim anymore. Swimming is very introspective. It makes you think about things, and I didn't want to be thinking about my life. Judo was the opposite of swimming. One hundred percent of my focus had to be in the present moment. There was no time for introspection.

We hadn't even pulled out of the parking lot after that first judo practice before I asked my mom when I could go back.

My first judo tournament fell on my eleventh birthday. I had been in judo for about a month at this point. I really only knew one throw and one pin, but it was just a little local tournament.

We walked into the building where the tournament was being held. I followed my mom up to the registration table. The mats set up around the gymnasium seemed so much bigger than they did in practice. My eyes widened. I tugged nervously on the white belt that held my white gi top closed.

My mom sensed my hesitation. After she finished checking me in, she pulled me aside. I expected a pep talk about how it wasn't a big deal, about how it was just about doing my best, about how I should just go out and have fun. Instead she looked me straight in the eye and said three life-changing words: "You can win."

I won the entire tournament by all ippons (an instant win). I was euphoric. I had never really won anything before. I liked the way winning felt.

Two weeks later, I lost my second judo tournament. I finished second, losing to a girl named Anastasia. Afterward, her coach congratulated me.

"You did a great job. Don't feel bad, Anastasia is a junior national champion."

I felt consoled for about a second, until I noticed the look of disgust on Mom's face. I nodded at the coach and walked away.

Once we were out of earshot she lit into me: "I hope you know better than to believe what he said. You could have won that match. You had every chance to beat that girl. The fact that she is a junior national champion doesn't mean anything. That's why they have tournaments, so you can see who is better. They don't award medals based on what you won before. If you did your absolute best, if you were capable of doing nothing more, then that's enough. Then you can be content with the outcome. But if you could have done better, if you could have done more, then you should be disappointed. You should be upset you didn't win. You should go home and think about what you could have done differently and then next time do it differently. Don't you ever let anyone tell you that not doing your absolute best is good enough. You are a skinny blonde girl who lives by the beach, and unless you absolutely force them to, no one is ever going to expect anything from you in this sport. You prove them wrong."

I was ashamed that I had been so ready to accept losing, to accept as fact that someone else was simply better than me. The remorse lasted only a second before it was replaced by a more intense emotion. What I felt then was a deep desire to win, a motivation to show everyone on the planet that no one should ever doubt my ability to win again.

From that moment on, I wanted to win every time I stepped onto the mat. I expected to win. I would never accept losing again.

JUST BECAUSE IT'S A RULE DOESN'T MEAN IT'S RIGHT

In sports, there are rules that keep you safe. In life, there are rules that keep the world from descending into total chaos. In both, there are rules that people make up to hide behind or for their own benefit. You have to be smart enough to know the difference.

There were four major rules in my house growing up.

Rule No. 1: No taking things out of people's hands.

Rule No. 2: You are only allowed to hit someone if that person hits you first.

Rule No. 3: No being naked at the dining room table.

Rule No. 4: You are not allowed to eat anything bigger than your head.

Rule No. 4 was initiated because I always wanted those super-sized lollipops at Chuck E. Cheese's that were about four times the size of my head.

Rules No. 1 and 2 were instituted to combat the fighting that tends to occur when you have three children within four years. Rule No. 1 was meant to prevent the hitting that would engage

Rule No. 2. Moreover, because Rule No. 2 was structured so that you could only hit someone if she hit you first, you would think it would be a catch-22. It did not work out that way.

People talk about brothers roughhousing and fighting, but the three of us girls would throw punches, kicks, and elbows and inflict chokeholds that would put the neighbor boys to shame. In addition to our bodies, we often utilized everything in reach. We would launch ourselves off the stairs or furniture in order to gain leverage, taking advantage of the laws of physics when possible.

There was the time during a fight when—at about four years old—I threw a full can of Coke at Jennifer's eye, leaving a large gash.

"What do you have to say for yourself?" our mom asked me.

"Yes," I said, pumping my fist in victory.

And though I hate to admit it, I did not always emerge victorious. I was the youngest, so I did not have size on my side. (Ironically, I am now the tallest of the bunch. My older sisters like to joke they are among the only women on the planet who can claim to have beaten me in a fight. They also say we are now too old and mature for me to demand a rematch.)

There was the three-way fight between Maria, Jennifer, and I, where each of the thirty-two books of the *Encyclopaedia Britannica* (A through Z) was either used as a projectile or to whack another person over the head. If any one of us emerged victorious on that one, the joy of victory was quickly tempered by the rage my mom unleashed on all of us upon seeing the aftermath in the living room. After a serious yelling at, we were all grounded and assigned extensive amounts of household labor for the next several weeks.

One of the last fights was perhaps the most memorable. It was between Jennifer and me. I can't remember what it was over, but I am sure it was all Jennifer's fault. I had started judo, but knew better than to use the moves I had learned on my sister. I was more scared of the wrath of Mom than I was Jennifer. We were in the narrow front hallway, which had bookshelves against one of the walls. I was on Jennifer's back and had her in a headlock. I had the unquestionable advantage and was clearly winning.

"I don't want to hurt you, Jennifer," I said, cautiously. I knew my mom would be furious if I sent my sister to the emergency room.

"Fuck you," Jen said, my forearm still around her neck.

"I'm going to let you go," I informed her.

I slid off her back, peeling my arm away from her windpipe.

Jen turned on me. With incredible speed and a strength I didn't even know she possessed, she grabbed my head by the hair. Before I could fully process what was happening, she pounded my head several times into the nearest bookshelf.

The rule about hitting someone only if they hit you first was also in play outside of the house. We were in no way obligated to walk away if some bully smacked us on the playground, but we could not just pop a jerk who was teasing us.

I was a scrawny kid. One of my mom's nicknames for me is "Bean," because I was as skinny as a string bean—even after I started doing judo I didn't look like much of a fighter.

When I was in sixth grade, a boy named Adrian bullied me relentlessly all year. One day, he crept up behind me and reached around and grabbed my throat, squeezing me until it was hard to breathe. I didn't bother to push his hand away; I threw him over my hip, right onto the cement. The skin on the back of his head split open.

The kid was so embarrassed he just went to his next class

without saying anything to anyone, until his teacher realized he was bleeding. He ended up having to get several stitches.

I was sent to the office. My mom was called. I cried hysterically.

"We're not exactly sure what happened," the principal told my mom when she arrived. "It seems there was some sort of altercation between the two of them. He says he tripped, but other people said she pushed him."

"Well, it sounds like it was an accident," my mom said quickly.

"It was n—" I started to protest, but Mom thrust her hand over my mouth.

"Ronda is *very* sorry," she pressed on.

The principal seemed uncertain where to take the conversation next. Instead, he stared at his hands, then dismissed us. We walked to the car without saying a word.

I would like to say that word spread of my kick-ass skills, and no one messed with me again, but a few weeks later, I was waiting for Mom to pick me up when an eighth-grade girl shoved me. This girl must have weighed twice as much as me and she had been taunting me constantly. She would make fun of me carrying my bassoon through the hallways. She would throw leaves or crumpled-up pieces of paper at me. She threatened to beat me up. "Bring it," I told her.

I guess she decided that today was the day. I had been looking at the line of cars for my mom's minivan when I felt a shove. I turned, and was face-to-face with bully-girl. She shoved me again.

I dropped my backpack and a few seconds later I dropped the girl as well.

The school staff ran out to separate us, but that wasn't necessary—I was standing; she was down on the ground. We were led to the office and told suspensions would be handed down to both of us. The school secretary was picking up the phone to call our parents when my mom burst in.

I was already crying uncontrollably because my mom had made clear that there would be serious consequences if I got into another fight at school. I started to open my mouth to explain, but Mom shot me a silencing look. The sobs heaved out of my throat. Mom demanded to know who was in charge. The counselor came out of her office and started to explain that I and the big girl had gotten into a fight, but she did not know who she was dealing with.

"Did you see what happened?" my mom demanded.

The counselor opened her mouth to speak, but there was no need. It had been a rhetorical question.

"Because I did," my mom continued. "I was sitting in the car waiting for Ronda and saw the entire thing. Ronda was standing there when this girl"—my mom pointed at her—"walked up and started pushing Ronda."

"She will also be suspended," the counselor said.

"Also?" My mom was incredulous. "No, Ronda is not getting suspended."

"We have a very strict 'no physical violence' policy," the counselor said.

"And I have a very strict 'no being an asshole to my kids' policy," my mom said. "Ronda is not getting suspended. She was protecting herself against someone who resorted to 'physical violence' as you called it. She will be here bright and early tomorrow morning, and she will be going to class. If anyone tries to stop her, you will have me back in here again and will have to deal with me. And what you do not understand right now is *this* is me being nice and polite."

The counselor was tongue-tied.

"Come on," my mom said in my general direction. "We're out of here."

I grabbed my stuff and hustled out of the office.

The next day, my mom dropped me off at school and I went to class.

PAIN IS JUST ONE PIECE
OF INFORMATION

I have an ability to ignore all of the information coming from my body, even pain in general. I dissociate from pain, because I am not the pain that I am feeling. That's not me. That's not who I am. I refuse to allow pain to dictate my decision making. Pain is just one piece of information that I'm receiving. My nerves are communicating to my brain that there is something going on physically that I should be aware of. I can choose to acknowledge that information or I can choose to ignore it.

Let the following story serve as a cautionary tale if you are considering cutting class.

My sophomore year in high school I decided I was going to skip class. I had never ditched school before and I just wanted to try it.

My high school had a big gate and a chain-link fence surrounding the campus, both to keep unwanted visitors out and aspiring delinquents in. The fence was scalable, but there was a drop on the other side.

As I climbed the fence with my heavy backpack on I felt a twinge in my right toe, which I'd hurt at judo. When I jumped off the fence I realized I had underestimated the distance to the concrete sidewalk below. I landed, with all of my weight plus the weight of my backpack, on my good foot. As soon as I hit the ground I knew my left foot was broken.

I refused to accept defeat. I had skipped school to skip school, and I was going to do something during that period to make it worthwhile. I limped the quarter mile to Third Street Promenade, which is an outdoor shopping mall. I sat on a bench watching the stream of midday shoppers and tourists, my foot killing me.

This is bullshit, I thought. I felt my foot swelling up in my shoe. I angrily got up and shuffled the nearly mile-long walk home and climbed into bed. I knew there was no way I would be able to train that night. Fortunately, my mom was in Texas for work. That evening, I told my stepfather Dennis that I wasn't feeling well. More than happy not to have to drive me through two hours of traffic to practice, he didn't press the subject.

But I had a tournament the next day against a rival club from Northern California. The Anthonys, another family from my club, picked me up to take me to the tournament. I tried to walk normally to their car, but every step was like stepping on a shard of glass.

I have never been less excited to compete. We walked up to the table to register and Nadine Anthony started filling out the forms for her children and me. The guy working the table looked up. He looked at Nadine, then at me. Nadine is black.

"She needs a parent or guardian to register her for the tournament," he said, gesturing to me.

Joy surged through my body, but Nadine's expression hardened.

"What are you talking about *parent*?" Nadine spat. "I'm her mother. You got a problem with that?"

The guy's eyes widened. He looked around the registration table as if hoping to find an escape route.

"OK, then, of course," he said, taking the registration forms.

My heart sank.

When I was twelve years old we were at practice when one of my teammates twisted her ankle. She limped off the mat, and both of her parents descended upon her in concern. Her dad rushed out to their car, returning with a pillow. With her mom massaging her shoulders, my teammate sat with her foot propped up. Less than twenty minutes later, I jammed my foot doing *randori*, the judo version of sparring. I limped over to my mom, who was running the practice.

"I hurt my toe," I said. "I think it's broken."

"It's a toe," she said dismissively.

"But it hurts," I said crying. "Do you have a pillow for me?"

My mom looked at me like I had lost my mind.

"What the fuck do you mean a pillow?" she asked.

"She got a pillow," I said, pointing to my teammate.

"You're not getting a goddamned pillow," she said. "Go run laps."

My eyes widened.

"I'm serious," my mom said. "Go run."

I hobbled away, more hopping than running.

"I said 'run laps,' not hop laps," my mom said.

"Run." I shuffled around the mat, my toe throbbing.

In the car on the way home, I stared out the window pouting, because I had such a cruel mother.

"You know why I did that?" my mom asked.

"Because you hate me."

"No, it was to show you that you could do it," my mom said. "If you want to win the way you say you do, you need to be able to compete, even when you're in pain. You need to be able to push through. Now you know you can."

In the years since then, I have competed with broken toes and sprained ankles—not to mention with the flu and bronchitis—but a broken foot was my biggest challenge to date. It took all of my focus to simply block out the pain, leaving me little ability to concentrate on each match. I was competing solely on instinct to carry me through. The day went on and the pain grew worse. Beads of sweat started forming on my forehead every time tournament office called me "on deck." By pure determination, I won the double-elimination tournament, but en route, I lost a match. My lone loss came to Marti Malloy. Marti would win a bronze medal in the 2012 Olympics.

My mom called that evening to see how I did. Hearing I lost to Marti, my mom was shocked. I never lost, especially not at some local tournament.

"What happened?" she asked.

Considering my capacity for lying is pretty terrible, I had no choice but to explain.

"Mom, I jumped over a fence while ditching school and broke my foot," I said.

"Instead of telling someone, you competed on it?" I couldn't tell if my mom's tone was incredulous or angry.

"I didn't want to get in trouble," I said quietly.

"Well, that's the stupidest thing I have ever heard," my mom said. "But competing on a broken foot is a pretty good punishment."

"So I'm not in trouble?" I asked.

"Oh no, you're totally grounded," she said.

My punishment lasted a month. Knowing I could push through pain and succeed has lasted a lifetime. Pain was just something I became accustomed to as part of life. If you're an athlete and want to win, something always hurts. You are always dealing with bruises and injuries. You're testing how far you can push the human body, and whoever pushes it the furthest wins. Since the very first time I stepped on the mat, I was determined to be the one who wins.

TURN LIMITATIONS INTO OPPORTUNITIES

I've seen a positive benefit from every negative thing that has happened in my life, including every injury. My career has been filled with injuries, but not derailed by them. Too many people see an injury as something that prevents them from progressing. I've used every physical setback to develop in another area I wouldn't have otherwise addressed. When I broke my right hand, I said, "I'm going to have a badass left hook when this is all said and done." When I ended up with stitches in my foot days before a fight, I was driven to make sure I ended that fight definitively and fast.

Don't focus on what you can't do. Focus on what you can.

I was sparring at my club, Venice Judo, which despite its name is actually located in Culver City, California. One day this kid, who would randomly come to practice, showed up. He was my age, but way bigger. We had been going to the same club for years, and I had always wiped the mat with him. Then he hit that high-school growth spurt, which gave him about five inches and sixty pounds more than me. I still wiped the mat with him, but whenever we trained it turned into a battle for teenage pride.

I was still favoring my left foot. The break was largely healed, but my foot was still sore. We approached the edge of the mat. (In an actual match, you don't let approaching the edge of the mat stop you. But in practice, you stop at the edge of the mat because you don't want anyone getting hurt on the ground.) This was practice. I stopped. He did not.

He came in for a throw, but because I had stopped at the edge of the mat, instead of coming in for my leg straight on, he came in sideways. He went in to sweep my foot, but caught my knee. All of his momentum crashed into my stationary right knee. The joint immediately buckled. I knew it was bad right away.

I tried to stand up, but collapsed. My knee felt like Jell-O. I sat on the mat, uncertain what else to do as my mom and coach rushed over.

I started to cry. "It hurts," I said.

"You're always crying about something that hurts," my mom said unsympathetically. "Ice it when we get home."

I finished practice, favoring my left leg.

My knee was still bothering me when my mom brought me to practice the next morning. It was worse than it had been the day before. I couldn't train on it. I asked another of my coaches, Hayward Nishioka, to look at it. I pulled up the leg of my gi pants.

"AnnMaria, you better take her to the doctor," he told my mom.

The next afternoon, I sat on the white crinkly paper they pull over the doctor's table waiting for the results of my MRI.

It was the first of many appointments I would have with Dr. Thomas Knapp, knee-repair surgeon extraordinaire.

He pulled out the black-and-white image and put it up on the backlit board.

"Well, your ACL is definitely torn," Dr. Knapp said.

My stomach surged into my heart, my eyes started to burn, and suddenly I was sobbing. Standing next to me, my mom patted me on the shoulder. I had expected this news, but hearing it said aloud felt like a punch to the stomach.

"The good news is it is relatively straightforward to repair," he said. "I see these all the time. We'll get you all fixed up and back out there before you know it."

"How long?" I asked.

"Depends on how quickly you recover, but as a general rule, I would say no competition for six months."

I started doing the math in my head. It was April. The senior nationals scheduled for later that month were out. The Junior US Open—the most competitive youth tournament in the nation— this summer was a warm-up for my senior international level debut at the US Open in October.

"What if I recover really quickly? The Junior US Open is in August..." My voice was hopeful.

"August, huh?" Dr. Knapp said. "You know what that means right?"

I looked up. I had been staring at my knee as if I could will it healed.

"You won't be going."

This was supposed to be my breakout year. I was supposed to go to the high school nationals and senior nationals. I was already dreaming of the 2008 Olympics. An unbearable feeling of uncertainty overwhelmed me. Was my judo career over? Would I ever be one hundred percent? If not, would I still be good enough to succeed? I worried about how long I'd be out and how much momentum I would lose and how much skill my competitors would gain while I was stuck in bed. I grappled with the realization that I was not invincible.

Four days later, I was lying on a gurney, hooked up to an IV, and ready to be wheeled into surgery. The anesthesiologist came into the room in his blue scrubs. He started the drip into my IV.

"Now, count backwards from ten," he told me.

I lay my head back on the pillow and closed my eyes. I said a silent prayer that the surgery would go well and that my entire life would not be changed when I opened them back up again.

"Ten, nine, eight, seven..." I drifted off into a deep, dreamless sleep.

I awoke in a nauseous anesthesia-induced haze. My knee hurt. My mouth felt dry. There was the whir of the cooling machine, pumping ice-cold water through a brace wrapped around my knee. The beeping of the monitors. I looked down at my leg in the large black brace, and once again, tears started to pour down my cheeks.

"It only gets better from here," the nurse said.

After the surgery, my doctor told me the most important thing I could do for my recovery was to do all of the physical therapy and not to do anything stupid as far as trying to get back out on the mat sooner.

I started physical therapy later that week, and my physical therapist assured me he would do everything he could to get me back out competing and as good as new. "Everything" involved a lot of range-of-motion exercises and minor stretches. The "workouts" were a far cry from the training sessions I was used to, but at the beginning left me tired and sore. My coach, Trace, told me it wasn't the end of the world, even if it felt that way.

And I told myself I'd be back, that this was just a temporary setback. But it was my mom who saved me.

For the first few days after I came home from the hospital, I sat on the couch and iced my leg, kept it elevated, and generally wallowed— watching Animal Planet and playing Pokémon games. Then a week after the surgery my mom came into the living room and told me, "That's enough."

"I just had knee surgery," I said defensively.

"It's been a week," she said. "Time to get over feeling sorry for yourself."

"Didn't you hear the doctor?" I snapped. "I'm not supposed to overdo it with my knee."

"Yeah, well, what about your other leg?" she asked, rhetorically. "Do some leg lifts. What about your abs? Last time I checked sit-ups didn't involve knees. Do some curls. Those involve arms, which last time I checked are not knees."

Two weeks later, she took me to Hayastan, a club in Hollywood where I regularly trained, to workout. My friend Manny Gamburyan unlocked the club for us. The dojo smelled like sweaty Armenians and Axe body spray. As I lowered myself to the blue and seafoam green mats, they felt firm and familiar. All of the anxiety that had been plaguing me since the day I hurt my knee faded.

I'm back, bitches, I thought to myself.

Every day I would limp to the car and into the club. Mom would have me practice pins, chokes, and armbars (a submission move where you dislocate your opponent's elbow) with Manny. Gradually my limp improved, as did my matwork.

The pain started to fade as well, but there were many nights where I woke up to a throbbing pain in my knee. I took two aspirin, limped downstairs to the kitchen to get a bag of ice, limped back upstairs, and climbed into bed, trying to push the pain out of my head long enough to fall back to sleep. A few hours later, I woke up again, the pain back and a puddle in my bed where ice had melted and leaked out of the bag.

Before my injury, I had built up a reputation as a standup fighter. It wasn't that I couldn't do matwork, but if you're really good at throwing people you can win right away, so you don't end up grappling. I spent the whole year doing matwork. I did thousands of armbars.

Six months after having my ACL repaired, I made my senior international level debut and finished second at the US Open. I was seconds away from winning the match, having gotten Sarah Clark in a pin, but Clark escaped and ultimately beat me on points. However, I was the top American finisher in my division. I had beat Grace Jividen, the No. 1 woman in my division, by ippon. The next weekend I won the Rendez-Vous (the Canadian Open). The pair of performances catapulted me to the No. 1 spot in the country in the women's sixty-three-kilo division.

That entire year changed me. Even more significant than the perfection of my armbar was the shift in how I thought about my skills, my body, and myself. I knew that I could emerge from adversity stronger than before. I also knew I was a true fighter; I came out of that year believing in myself.

TRUST IN KNOWLEDGE,
NOT IN STRENGTH

When it comes to fighting, physical strength really has very little to do with it. One of the tenets that judo is founded upon is "Maximum efficiency, minimum effort." That has really defined my career. It is the foundation of all the techniques and everything I do. It's one reason why I don't get tired. It's one reason why I am able to fight girls who are a head taller than me, or chicks who are on steroids. People who cheat or dope lack the one thing every true champion must have: belief. No drug or amount of money or favoritism can ever give you belief in yourself.

After the US Open, I became the youngest judo competitor on the US national team. I was sixteen. The national team is composed of the top athletes in the sport and represents the country in international competition. (The Olympic and world teams are the versions of the national team that compete in the Olympics and world championships, respectively.) Competing at that level meant the stakes were higher and there were a number of mandatory events I had to attend, including meetings and training

62

camps. The first of those sessions was part of a training camp in Colorado Springs, Colorado.

During the session on banned substances, a representative from the US Olympic Committee spent several hours educating us on the lengthy list of substances considered performance enhancers. The woman handed us a ten-page document containing dozens of words I had never seen before. Lots of -ines, -ides, -oids, -ates, and -anes. In fact, some of the items weren't even words. They were chemical compounds. (I was still taking high school biology. I hadn't gotten to chemistry yet.)

"It is not just about avoiding steroids," the woman said. "It is your responsibility as an athlete to be fully accountable for any substance you put in your body. This applies to vitamins, supplements, creams, shots, prescriptions. If you are not absolutely certain about what you might be taking, you need to find out. 'I didn't know' is not an acceptable defense in the case of a failed drug test."

I raised my hand. All of the eyeballs in the room were on me. The woman gave me a nod.

"What about Flintstones vitamins?" I asked.

She laughed. The room laughed. Two of the women who were my national "teammates" rolled their eyes at me. Then the anti-doping lady continued on with her speech.

I raised my hand again. Again, the head nod.

"No, I'm serious," I said. "I take those. Are those OK?"

The woman, caught off guard, paused. "Yes," she said. "There are no steroids in Flintstones vitamins."

I had a follow-up.

"Anything besides steroids that might be in them that you're not allowed to have?" I asked.

One of the women who had rolled their eyes sighed loudly. I

was already performing better than all of them in competition, and this conversation was a reminder that I was considerably younger than them as well.

The woman giving the lecture didn't even pause to think about my question.

"Nope, I feel very confident telling you that there are no banned substances in Flintstones vitamins," she said.

Flintstones chewable vitamins with iron is the closest I have ever come to taking an unknown substance.

Doping is one of the most selfish things you can do in sports, but the reality is that performance-enhancing drugs are very much a part of the combat sports world. In judo, doping ruins the sport by stealing success from athletes who are competing with honor. In MMA, doping is almost negligent homicide. The premise of MMA is to get into an enclosed cage with another person and try to beat them into submission or unconsciousness. A person who is taking a substance that makes him or her stronger than normal could really kill someone.

Athletes who dope don't believe in themselves.

I train to beat anyone. I hold myself to the standard that I need to be good enough to beat people whether or not they're doping. I would never publicly name an opponent who hasn't tested positive, but there are opponents who I definitely knew were doping. There are opponents whom I have strongly suspected of doping. There are opponents who have later been popped for doping. Just looking at the prevalence of doping in sports, fighting someone using performance-enhancing drugs is inevitable. It pisses me off. But I have beaten those girls all the same.

The one thing they couldn't inject into their asses is belief.

KNOW WHEN TO MOVE ON

Taking the next step isn't always easy. People stay in jobs they've outgrown because they're afraid of having to prove themselves anew. People stay in unhappy relationships because they're afraid of being alone. Athletes stick with a coach who can't help them develop further because they are afraid of being tested, of not measuring up to someone else's standards, because they're afraid to upset someone they care about. They let fear hold them back.

If you're unwilling to leave someplace you've outgrown, you will never reach your full potential. To be the best, you have to constantly be challenging yourself, raising the bar, pushing the limits of what you can do. Don't stand still, leap forward.

The first time I met Jim Pedro, aka Big Jim, was at the 2003 senior nationals. I was less than a month out from having my ACL repaired and still on crutches. I couldn't compete, but the tournament was in Las Vegas, a four-hour drive from L.A. We already had a room reservation, and at the very least, I could scope out the women I would be competing against when I returned from my injury.

But, as I sat on a metal folding chair at the Riviera Hotel, attending the tournament seemed like the worst idea ever. My mom had hoped I would be motivated to get back. But watching girls I knew I could beat battle it out for what should have been my medal was unbearable.

Tears of anger welled up in my eyes.

"What the hell is the matter with you?" a gravelly voice asked me.

I looked up. The man standing next to me looked like a cross between Santa Claus and a guy you'd meet at the Jersey shore. He had curly white hair and a bushy mustache. He was wearing a polo shirt, and a large tuft of chest hair was visible at the neck.

"I'm supposed to be out there," I said between sniffles. "I could have won."

He looked down at my leg extended in the large black brace.

"Kinda hard to compete with that thing on ya leg." He had a thick New England accent.

I nodded. Then I told him how this was supposed to be my year, how this tournament was supposed to have been my senior-level debut, and how my entire plan had been derailed. Tears were running down my face by the time I finished.

"Well, the way I see it, you have two choices," the guy said. "You can sit here and cry about it. That's one. But if I was you, I'd go to the gym and train and get stronger than a couple of ox. Make it even easier to beat all these girls when you come back. Then when you get better, you can come train with me."

I straightened up a bit in my chair. He was right.

"What's your name?" he asked.

"Ronda Rousey," I said.

He stuck out his hand. "Nice to meet ya, Ronda. I'm Jim Pedro, but you can just call me Big Jim."

Everyone in judo had heard of his son—Jimmy Pedro, aka Little Jimmy—who had won the world championships in 1999. Big Jim was his coach.

When I returned from Vegas, I was more driven than ever to get back on the mat. I was going to come back stronger than anyone expected. In my US Open debut, I shocked pretty much everyone except for my mom and myself. I always knew I was going to be the top American athlete in my division. It was simply a matter of time. Now, my time had come.

Trace Nishiyama, who I'd been training with since I was eleven, is an amazing coach. He was never possessive. Most judo clubs only have practice twice a week. But I needed—and wanted—to practice more, so my mom mapped out what clubs were good and who had practice what nights. Then the two of us would hop in the car, often just as rush hour was beginning, and move through traffic at a crawl so I could train daily. We spent the weekday evenings crisscrossing the L.A. area to practice at various dojos and weekends at tournaments.

My mom and I spent upwards of thirty hours a week in the car on the way to and from practice. Our conversations often centered on judo, but ranged from insights she saw in watching me train to mental strategy. My favorite stories, however, were the ones from when she was competing, many of which involved much younger and more colorful versions of the coaches I knew.

Where some coaches feel threatened seeing their athletes train at other clubs, Trace didn't mind. Trace knew how to do a killer drop shoulder throw and he taught me how to do one, but he also knew there were coaches who knew how to do other moves better than him. He encouraged me to learn from them as well. And I did. But, by the time I was fifteen, it was clear that I needed more than Trace or any other coach in L.A. had to offer. This was a moment my mom had been preparing me for since I began showing an extraordinary combination of promise and drive as a thirteen-year-old kid.

"At some point, you'll have to move on," my mom told me. "That's a mistake people make. They get comfortable and stay at the same place a long time. But after a while, people run out of what they can teach you. Eventually, you'll know ninety percent of what a coach can teach you. When that happens, you're best served going somewhere else. The new coach might not be any better than the one you have, but will be able to teach you something you don't already know. That's what it takes to improve. You've always got to be looking ahead to that next step."

By the time I was sixteen, I was ready to take that next step.

Just after Thanksgiving in 2003, I walked into the community center where the club was located. As always, the place smelled of delicious Japanese food, coming from the cooking classes happening in one of the rooms adjacent to the gym. I had arrived a little early and the room was still largely empty.

Trace was setting up the mats. He looked up, surprised to see me. I was never early.

"Hey, Ronda," he said.

I smiled, weakly. "Hey, Trace."

"What's up?" he asked. "Everything OK?"

I helped him position the blue crash pads.

My voice choked up, and it all came pouring out. I explained to him that, since the US Open, the whole trajectory of my life felt as if it had accelerated. Things were moving so much faster than I had expected. I told him it had been an honor to be a part of his club for so many years and that I wouldn't be where I was without him, but that I had reached a point where I needed more. I told him I was going out to Boston in a couple of weeks and that I might end up training at the Pedros' club. I told Trace I didn't want him to be upset with me for leaving. By the end of the conversation, I was crying.

Trace wrapped an arm around me. "You got to go to grow, kid."

I felt like a weight had been lifted, like I was a little dove whose cage had been opened to be set free.

I will always love and appreciate Trace, not just for what he taught me, but also for recognizing when the day came that he couldn't teach me any more.

The practice that followed was an emotional one. As I helped put up the mats, I looked around the room at my coaches, my teammates, their parents, their siblings. I was struck by the realization that soon I would walk out of the club doors for the final time and probably never see many of them ever again. I started to cry. The fact that no one asked me why I was crying made it even worse, not because I wanted someone to ask, but because it showed that these people really knew me. I cried all the time— when I got thrown, when I got frustrated at practice, when I opened my judo bag and realized I'd forgotten my belt, when I got cut in front of while in line for the water fountain. Now I was off to a new place where they wouldn't know that I cried all the time and would ask me why I was crying. I would feel pressured to stop crying, which only makes me cry more.

On the way out to the car, I paused in front of our club trophy case. Several of my medals and trophies were on display. I looked at the Player of the Year trophy awarded to the top athlete from the club. I had won it four years straight. Suddenly, the idea that I would never win it again seemed overwhelming. Everything was going to change. While I knew it was the right decision, while I had my coach's blessing, while it was the inevitable next step I had been preparing for, it was still hard.

The next morning, my mom showed me an email that Trace had written to the Pedros. He told them he was entrusting me to their care, that I had tremendous potential, and that they should let him know if I ever needed anything.

That's a person who actually cares about you.

My mom knew about what it took to become a world-class athlete; she knew I needed a new coach who could take me to the next level as an elite international competitor; and she knew that meant I had to leave home, but she left the choice up to me.

"There isn't a best coach; there's a best coach for you," my mom told me. "You're not picking your coach to suit your mom or your friends or the people who run USA Judo, you need to pick the coach who is going to be the best person to coach you." (USA Judo is the sport's national governing body.)

She had started sending me to the top clubs around the country for camps and clinics when I was thirteen, so I could check clubs and coaches out with an eye toward the future.

I ended up with new friends around the country, but none of the clubs I had visited had felt right. I didn't get that inexplicable, you-know-it-when-you-feel-it feeling.

In January 2004, I boarded a plane to Boston.

Beyond our brief meeting at the senior nationals, I didn't know much about Big Jim. He was known for his expertise when it came to groundwork. In addition to coaching Little Jimmy to a world championship, he had trained half a dozen Olympians and close to one hundred junior and senior national champions. Moreover, my mom approved of him, and my mom's seal of approval is harder to earn than a Nobel Prize.

Big Jim is tough. He might be as hairy as a teddy bear, but that's where any comparisons between him and something cuddly end. He has a booming voice and a furious intensity. He will tell you in no uncertain terms when he thinks you're doing a shit job. He openly admitted to having slapped a referee. His personality made him a polarizing figure within judo, but no one ever questioned his knowledge and ability as a coach.

I went out to the Pedros' club on a trial basis. Walking off the airplane at Logan Airport, I felt a wave of nervous excitement. Big Jim had left an impression on me.

I was also going to be training with Jimmy Pedro. A month or so after I had met Big Jim, Jimmy came to L.A. to do a clinic. I was coming off my knee surgery, but determined to attend. Jimmy Pedro was one of the most decorated American athletes in judo history and the guy I looked up to as a kid in the sport. I could not wait to meet Jimmy, but was disappointed that my injury limited my ability to participate.

I spent the day relegated to what I referred to as "Ronda's Happy Corner of Matwork," where I grappled the entire time. I couldn't use my leg at all. As the afternoon session wrapped up, the event organizer made an announcement.

"Following this session, we ask you all to stay as Jimmy Pedro will be presenting awards," he said. "These are awards that Jimmy has determined himself. Afterward, Jimmy will be signing autographs."

The disappointment I had felt on the way to the clinic returned, only worse.

"Can we leave?" I asked my mom.

"I thought you wanted him to sign your belt," my mom said. "I just want to go," I said.

"OK," she shrugged.

I was hobbling over to get my bag, when Jimmy walked to the front of the room.

"First of all, thank you so much for coming out here today," Jimmy said. The room cheered.

"I was really impressed by everyone," he continued. "I see a lot of potential when I look around this room."

Dozens of kids sitting cross-legged on the mats suddenly straightened up. I felt my eyes start to burn. There were more than one hundred kids from around the L.A. area at the clinic, and I knew I was better at judo than every single one of them. I also knew there was no way I was getting an award.

"The first award, is one that I hope will soon be near and dear to my heart," Jimmy said with a smile. "This is the 'Future Olympic Champion' award."

The room laughed as if Jimmy had told a hilarious joke. A three-time Olympian who had won bronze in 1996, Jimmy was making one final push at an Olympic gold.

Jimmy called the name of a boy who jumped up, cheering as if he had actually won the Olympics.

I shoved everything into my bag as fast as I could.

"The next award I want to give out today is one that is certainly near and dear to my heart—'Future World Champion,'" Jimmy said.

At the mention of world champion, the room burst into applause. "And the winner is…"—Jimmy paused for dramatic effect—"Ronda Rousey."

I froze, then dropped my bag. I felt my cheeks flush as every head in the place turned to look at me.

"Go up there," my mom urged as the room applauded.

I limped up to the front of the room to shake Jimmy's hand. *He picked me as future world champion,* I thought. *Me.* I was thrilled and flattered and in disbelief.

I waited in line to get his autograph after the impromptu ceremony.

"Ronda Rousey," he said, grinning when it was my turn to approach the table.

I still couldn't believe he knew my name.

He grabbed one of the photographs provided by the event organizers for him to sign.

He scribbled out a message with a Sharpie and handed the paper to me. I looked down at the photo in my hands.

To Ronda, Keep training hard and see you at the top. Jimmy Pedro.

I read and re-read the words "see you at the top" the entire way home. I was overwhelmed by the idea that he had faith that I had so much potential that someday I would be at the pinnacle of the sport like he was.

When we got home, I taped the photo on my wall, where I looked at it through the rest of my recovery.

Now a blast of cold air hit me as I stepped onto the Jetway, pulling me back into the present. But reality seemed surreal. If this worked out, Big Jim was going to be my coach. I would be training with Little Jimmy.

After two weeks, I called my mom.

"This is the place," I said. "Big Jim is the coach."

"OK," my mom said. "We'll figure something out."

FIND FULFILLMENT
IN THE SACRIFICES

People love the idea of winning an Olympic medal or a world title. But what few people realize is that pretty much every second leading up to the actual win is uncomfortable, painful, and impossibly daunting— physically and mentally. Most people focus on the wrong thing: They focus on the result, not the process. The process is the sacrifice; it is all the hard parts—the sweat, the pain, the tears, the losses. You make the sacrifices anyway. You learn to enjoy them, or at least embrace them. In the end, it is the sacrifices that must fulfill you.

I didn't want to move away from my family at sixteen. And I certainly didn't want to move away to some little town along the Massachusetts–New Hampshire border to live with people I didn't know. But I wanted to win the Olympics one day. I wanted to be the world champion. I wanted to be the best judoka in the world. And I was willing to do whatever it took.

My mom, Big Jim, and Jimmy decided it would be best if I stayed with Little Jimmy and his family.

"Ronda's going to be like your new big sister," Jimmy's wife,

Marie, said to their three young kids the day I arrived at their house.

I slept on a futon in their home office, which should have been a warning that the arrangement wouldn't last. At first I ate too much food. So my mom paid Jimmy more money for more food, but the situation got worse, not better. The closet where I was keeping all of my things was deemed too disorganized. I left too much water on the floor after I showered. I forgot to put dishes in the sink. I tried my absolute hardest, but it felt like the harder I tried, the more I messed up. I called my mom crying every day.

The final straw came three weeks later when the son of a family friend of the Pedros asked Jimmy if he could stay at their house for a week while he came to train at the club. The guy, Dick IttyBitty (possibly not his real name), was in his early twenties, and we had met at a camp in Chicago just before I moved to Massachusetts. My mom didn't like the idea of a twenty-something guy staying at the same house as me. Big Jim also thought it was a bad idea. Still Little Jimmy and Marie were debating whether to let him stay when Marie sent my mom an email asking what she would do.

My mom typed up her reply: *You asked me what I would do. I would never allow it in a million years. It's a terrible fucking idea.* Then my mom hit Send.

The next night Jimmy, with Marie standing beside him, told me, "It's just not working out."

I stared at them both, speechless and embarrassed. I was a sixteen-year-old kid who just wanted to do judo. I was heartbroken. I had finally found my place, my coach, and now, it was being ripped away from me. I made another tearful phone call to my mom.

"Don't worry about it," my mom said. "We'll figure something out."

Big Jim ended up taking me in. Mom offered to pay for my living expenses, just like she had paid Jimmy, but he refused to accept any money. Big Jim lived in a small house on a lake in the middle of nowhere New Hampshire, right outside the greater Boston area. Living at Big Jim's was boring as hell. But more than that, it was lonely.

Big Jim knows more about coaching judo than possibly anyone else in the country, but he's not exactly the social type and we didn't have much to say to one another anyway. He was a several-times divorced New England fireman who liked to smoke cigars (or cig-ahs as he called them). He had a permanent tobacco stain in his white mustache. I was a girl who read science fiction and drew pictures in a sketchpad.

The days at Big Jim's blurred into one another. The eight months I spent there in 2004 were marked by boredom, soreness, silence, and hunger.

To compete in the sixty-three-kilogram weight division I had to weigh no more than sixty-three kilos before each tournament.

Virtually no athlete competes in a division that is actually their weight. Most athletes walk around considerably heavier than competition weight in daily life. In the UFC, I fight at 135 pounds—and for about four hours a year, I weigh 135 pounds. My actual weight is closer to 150. I can make 135 pounds because the weigh-in process is very different in MMA. I only fight every few months and weigh in the night before and then have a chance to recover from the physical strain of cutting weight before I fight again. When I was doing judo, I was constantly competing. I had to make weight as many as four weekends in a row and I might only have an hour from weigh-in to fight time.

Because I was always struggling to make weight, Big Jim limited the food we had in the house, which made it even worse. When the weather was warm, Big Jim's family and members of the club would come to the lake house for a barbecue and to swim in the lake. I wasn't supposed to eat, but I would sneak graham crackers and eat them in the basement. In the morning, Big Jim would see the crumbs.

"You have no discipline," he would say.

I started making deals with myself when it came to food. I would figure out exactly how many calories I ate, then determine what I needed to do to burn them off. But it got to the point where I would binge eat and not go run; it was just too much on my body to run off all that I put in it. Once it got to a point where I ate so much and I felt like I couldn't compensate for it through exercising, I would just throw it up.

The first time I tried, I failed. While Big Jim was at work, I ate a bagel, some chicken, a huge bowl of oatmeal, and an apple, but instead of being glad to be free of my constant hunger, I was overcome by guilt. I went to the bathroom and stuck my hand down my throat. I heaved, but nothing happened. I tried again, and again, nothing.

I guess I'm not doing it right, I thought.

The next few times I overate, I tried to make myself throw up again but with no luck. Then a week later, there was a barbecue at Big Jim's house. I ate until I was full. Two hamburgers, watermelon, a bunch of little carrots, chips, a couple of cookies.

I went into the downstairs bathroom, determined to undo the damage I had just done. That particular day I ate so much that I felt incredibly guilty and terrible that I wouldn't give up.

I stood, doubled over the toilet, shoving my hand down my throat. Sweat broke out on my forehead as my body tensed. My stomach strained, trying to maintain its contents. I tried, and tried, shoving my hand farther down. My eyes were tearing up, snot was coming out of my nose. Then it happened. It finally worked. The contents of my stomach came hurling back up. Relief.

The next time I forced myself to throw up, it was easier.

I was still mindful of limiting what I was eating, but my weight refused to budge. Every time I looked in the mirror, I saw huge shoulders, giant arms, this hulking body reflected back at me. I started forcing myself to throw up more often. A couple times a week, sometimes every other day.

I was scared of being caught. Once when Big Jim had a couple of visiting athletes staying in his downstairs apartment, I heard a sound outside the bathroom door and froze. I turned on the water in the sink to try to muffle the unavoidable retching sound.

My constant hunger was the result of trying to maintain an unrealistic weight while executing a grueling training schedule. I woke up between eight and nine in the morning. My muscles were sore from the day before. My body always ached. I reached my arms above my head and heaved myself out of bed. Big Jim always got up before me and when I emerged from my room, a hot pot of coffee was brewing and my mug was set out next to it.

Mornings were reserved for conditioning. Everything I owned fit in two duffle bags, the contents of which were usually strewn around my room. I dug through the piles looking for something clean enough to work out in.

In his basement, Big Jim had set up the world's smallest workout room. It was probably no more than ten feet by ten feet, in which he had managed to cram in a set of free weights, a bench press, a treadmill, an elliptical machine, and a few other workout machines that looked older than I was. He had created a circuit for me that incorporated cardio, weight training, and judo drills.

The elliptical and treadmill were so old that they didn't have any digital readout. For those parts of the circuit, I had to count four hundred to eight hundred steps, then move on to the next area. The ceiling was so low that when I did the elliptical, I had to duck my head. When I did cleans, I had about three inches of clearance on either side. Anything but perfect form and I was hitting the wall or nicking a cardio machine. The only thing not in that tiny room was the bungee cord for doing *uchikomis* (a judo throw drill). That station was set up right outside the workout room, next to the washer and dryer. The whole time Big Jim would be upstairs with his stopwatch.

There was no clock anywhere in the workout room, which was part of Big Jim's strategy. Every day, I was supposed to complete the circuit faster than the day before. If I didn't beat my time, then the next day Big Jim would add another set on to the end of the circuit and my time would start all over. Without a way to time myself, I had to try to keep pace in my head. The first day of a new circuit, I would go as slow as humanly possible. But as the days passed, I had no choice but to go faster. After I was done, I would head back upstairs, where Big Jim never told me my time, just how much I beat or missed my time by.

The time it took me to do the circuit crept upward from around half an hour to nearly an hour as Big Jim added more repetitions. I felt myself growing stronger and faster. My shoulders got broader; my calves firmer. As a kid, I used to stare at the veins on my mom's forearms, still muscular from her judo days. Now my arms looked just like hers. I had been self-conscious of my arms since middle school when kids had teased me, calling me "Miss Man" because of the size of my biceps and shoulders. But whenever I looked in the mirror at my changing shape, I reminded myself I was training to win the Olympics, not a beauty pageant.

In the kitchen, Big Jim would give me instructions for my run. I always ran the almost three-mile loop around the lake behind the house, but he mixed up the routine. Some mornings, I could just jog the entire way. Other mornings, he gave me intervals: jog to one lamppost, sprint to the next; or jog to one lamppost, sprint the next two; or jog two, sprint four.

Most days, Big Jim sat on the porch, with a piece of rope he used to practice tying various knots, and watched as I ran around the lake. Other days, once I hit the halfway point, he would jump into his car and drive along the road to make sure that I wasn't dragging ass. I rolled my eyes when I looked back and saw his SUV coming up the road, but it meant something to me that he would go out of his way to try to find me and make sure I was running.

After I got back from my run, it was time to go offer estimates for trees. Big Jim was a fireman, but during the week, he worked for a local tree removal business and drove around the area giving people quotes. The two of us loaded into the car and drove around for hours, stopping in little towns around New Hampshire and Massachusetts. Big Jim puffed away on his cigar, and I sat in the car inhaling secondhand smoke. We didn't talk, just listened to the oldies station Big Jim always had playing. When we pulled up to a house, Big Jim would size up the tree in question, looking it up and down, occasionally walking around it, then he'd jot some notes on a clipboard and hand the paperwork to the homeowner.

"That'll be two hundred dollars, ma'am," he'd say.

Then we'd drive to the next house.

Around three p.m. we'd cross over into Massachusetts. Before heading to the Pedros' judo club in Wakefield, we'd stop at Daddy's Donuts, where Big Jim met up with his friend Bobby, a burly bald guy from the judo club. Big Jim ordered a cup of coffee and a bran muffin. We always sat at the same table by the window. Big Jim would pull off the top of his muffin, sliding the bottom over to me. I was always hungry from cutting weight, and this small muffin butt was the greatest pleasure of my day.

Then we opened up the dojo at four p.m. There were a few hours before the senior practice, and I sat there with a textbook open pretending I was studying while Big Jim ran the younger kids classes.

At the club, there were about ten of us who were considered part of the club's senior-level group of athletes. It was good to be outside of what I lovingly referred to as the Unabomber's cabin, but it wasn't like my social life blossomed within the club. Judo is a sport where athletes peak in their mid-to late twenties, making me at least a decade younger than my teammates. Besides, there wasn't a lot of time for chitchat at practice. The minute the clock hit seven p.m., Big Jim started barking out commands and criticisms.

"Why the hell are you doing it like that?" Big Jim shouted whenever he saw me doing a drill imperfectly.

"I just..." I started to respond.

"I just, I just," he said in a high mocking tone.

I hated him in those moments.

Other times, he would walk by me on the mat and simply sigh loudly and shake his head, as if resigned to accept the fact that I was a lost cause. But I knew that it was better to be criticized by Big Jim than ignored altogether. If he didn't think you had potential, he wouldn't acknowledge you at all.

We practiced for two hours a day, doing throws, drills, and

randori (sparring) until I felt like I was going to collapse. Then Big Jim had us do more.

When we got home, Big Jim cooked us chicken and rice. He'd mix barbecue sauce in with my rice, which I thought was a weird combination, but I never said anything. I was just so happy to be able to eat at the end of the day. We didn't talk over dinner. I shoveled the food into my mouth, dwelling on my unhappiness.

Exhausted and sore from training, I threw my sweaty judo gi on the floor, took a shower, and fell into bed, my hair still soaking wet. The next day was the exact same thing.

On the weekends, Big Jim went to work at the fire station. I had no car and wasn't allowed to so much as leave his little cabin. I would go all weekend without seeing another person. I might not speak out loud once between Friday night and Monday morning. I would play the movie *50 First Dates* over and over just to hear the sound of human voices in the cabin. Every few hours, I foraged in the kitchen for food.

I would eat Bran Buds out of a coffee cup without any milk. The dry bits in my cup looked just like guinea pig food. As I chewed, I would imagine being abducted by aliens, kept as their pet, and fed Bran Buds.

That was my entire life for the better part of the year leading up to the 2004 Olympics. My existence was miserable, but my judo had never been better.

"If winning the Olympics was easy, everybody would do it," I reminded myself.

Back then I still believed that the more miserable I was the more productive I was being. I hated every day, but I promised myself that it would be worth it. I didn't think it was possible to be happy every day and succeed. It took me years to embrace the sacrifices and the pain as a satisfying part of my process.

Everyone wants to win. But to truly succeed—whether it is at a sport or at your job or in your life—you have to be willing to do the hard work, overcome the challenges, and make the sacrifices it takes to be the best at what you do.

YOU HAVE TO BE THE BEST
ON YOUR WORST DAY

My mom always says that to be the best in the world, you have to be good enough to win on a bad day because you never know if the Olympics are going to fall on a bad day.

She taught me that it is not enough to just be better than everyone else. You have to be so much better that no one can deny your superiority. You have to realize that the judges are not always going to give the win to you. You have to win so clearly that they have no choice but to declare you the winner. You have to be able to win every match twice on your worst day.

From the time I was six years old, I dreamed of winning the Olympics. Back then I was on the local swim team, so I imagined winning in the fifty-meter backstroke. I dreamed of standing on that podium with my gold medal hanging around my neck. Dad had told me I would shine on the world stage. I dreamed of the crowd's roar and the way the national anthem would fill the natatorium. When I started judo, I took my dream of winning the Olympics with me.

My mom agreed to let me get a cat. I named her Beijing, after the host city of the 2008 Olympics. I'd never imagined that I'd compete in Athens in the 2004 Olympics. Though I'd been dominant at the junior level, I was unranked at the senior level and was still recovering from the ACL surgery. But, after I returned from my injury and catapulted myself atop the national rankings, I realized that I could make the 2004 Olympic team. There was nothing that I wanted more. After I won the 2004 senior nationals that spring, again beating Grace Jividen, who previously held the No. 1 spot at sixty-three kilograms, I went from dark horse to favorite. Suddenly, the spot on the Olympic roster was mine to lose and I was not going to give it up.

Not everyone was thrilled with my rapid rise. At thirty-nine, Grace was more than twice my age and had actually been a teammate of my mom's six years before I was born. Grace wasn't happy to lose her top ranking to a teenager, but she was always nice to me. The same couldn't be said for some of my new US teammates.

Several Olympic team hopefuls trained at the US Olympic Training Center in Colorado Springs. The OTC judo clique was largely a bunch of partying mid-to late twenty-somethings who were pursuing the Olympic dream without a prayer in hell of achieving any level of international success. I was a seventeen-year-old kid already making a name for myself. When they looked at me, they saw what they would never accomplish. When I beat Grace for the top spot in the division, they had an excuse to be openly cold toward me.

At the Olympic Trials in San Jose, I breezed through the opening rounds with ease. During the break between the semifinals and finals, I sat playing my Game Boy on the cool linoleum in a hallway dotted with athletes—some disappointed to have been eliminated, others jogging up and down the hallway.

Coaches and officials milled around waiting for the championship round. My mom and her friend Lanny stood next to me, recounting their judo war stories.

Two chicks from the USOTC team whispered as they walked past me. I heard my name, but couldn't make out anything else. A few minutes later, they passed by again, this time shooting dirty looks my way.

"Look at them," Lanny said to my mom. "Trying to psych Ronda out before she goes out to fight Grace. You better tell her to be mentally ready."

My mom laughed and gestured at me. "I'm not telling her anything. Ronda never thinks about those women walking by her trying to stare her down, and she isn't going to be psyched out by Grace or anyone else. If anything, she's thinking about if Big Jim will let her have a chocolate donut if she wins."

I looked up. "Big Jim would never let me have a donut."

I went back to playing my Game Boy. Then I beat Grace by ippon, locking up my spot on the Olympic team.

Less than two months later, I was on the plane bound for Greece.

We arrived two weeks before competition to train and acclimate to the time difference. From the moment we landed in Athens, my teammates were eager to soak up the Olympic experience. They made plans to visit the Acropolis. They buzzed with excitement over the Opening Ceremony. They sorted through the bags of sponsor swag distributed to each member of Team USA.

For me, competition was the only thing I was thinking about. I would wake up in the middle of the night and sneak out the window to go running around the Olympic Village. As I slipped through the window, I had the biggest smile on my face. My story, my adventure, was just beginning. It was quiet as I ran around the village, past the dorms filled with sleeping athletes. *Everyone is sleeping but me,* I thought. *I'm the only one out here training right now, and it's because I want it more than anyone.*

With the competition coming up, I had to cut weight. My Athens roommate and teammate, Nikki Kubes, had the opposite problem. A heavyweight, she was having trouble keeping her weight up. I usually made weight by a fraction of an ounce, so I wasn't really eating, but I went with Nikki to the Olympic cafeteria anyway.

It was the most magical place in the whole village. The very first time I walked in I was filled with such wonderment at all the different people and all the food that I wasn't even angry I was cutting weight and couldn't eat. The cafeteria was this huge, almost warehouse with tent doors. The middle was filled with enough tables and chairs for at least one thousand athletes. Olympians from around the world were chatting away in languages I could not understand. There was food station after food station, any kind of food you could think of: Chinese, Italian, Mexican, Halal, Japanese. There were fruit stations, salad stations, bread stations, dessert stations, even McDonald's had stations. The food was unlimited and free.

Nikki and I filled our trays and sat down. I passed Nikki my tray. "Here you go," I said. "Enjoy."

Her face twisted in an odd mixture of guilt and awe.

"Eat up," I said trying not to hate her. "Start with the pizza. Then that..."

"What is that?" Nikki asked.

"I have no idea," I said. "I got it from the Asian food area. It looks delicious. Make sure you put kimchi on it."

Nikki picked up her fork. I looked longingly at the food. My stomach grumbled. I took a swig of water.

When Nikki was ready for her next course, I slid over a plate topped with pastries.

"But I really just want a salad," Nikki said. Her thick Texas drawl was even more pronounced when she whined.

"Fuck your salad, eat the pastries," I snapped. Nikki looked at my face to see if I was joking, but even I was unsure whether I was being sarcastic.

A few days before the Games started, we visited the Olympic competition venue. It was the biggest arena I had ever seen. The competition floor was set a level below, with the seats looking down into the bowl. Rows and rows of seats surrounded the rim, reaching up higher than I could see. My teammates stood around me; we marveled at the vastness of the space. I looked up toward the rafters where the winners' flags would be raised.

This is the place, I thought. *This is where I am going to shock the world.* I was not just the youngest judo competitor on the US team. I was the youngest judo competitor in the entire Athens Olympic field. No one expected anything of me. I was going to prove them all wrong.

Like always, I went to bed the night before I fought, thirsty and starving.

A few hours later, I bolted upright. The dream had felt so real. I had been standing in a room, not the dorm room, but an unknown room. I was lying on my back and balancing a bottle of Pepsi in my mouth. It was opened and the contents were pouring down my throat as I drank it thirstily with no hands.

I woke up feeling that I had done something I should not have. Then it hit me, it was just a dream and I drifted back into a restless sleep, hungry and dehydrated.

In the morning the shadow of the dream was gone. I felt ready. It was "showtime." I was going to win.

I headed straight to the bathroom to force myself to pee. I was dehydrated so I didn't have much, but I needed every possible ounce out of my body. I stepped on the scale and held my breath. Its digital readout registered sixty-three kilograms exactly. I exhaled.

I wasn't going to risk showering and having wet hair put me over weight. I threw on some sweats, tossed a couple bottles of water and a banana in my bag, then grabbed a few more bottles of water. I checked twice to make sure I had my ID, both times realizing it was on a lanyard dangling around my neck. I looked at the clock: 7:43.

I walked across a dirt patch that probably should have been a courtyard garden, but had been unfinished in the rush to get all the essential buildings done for the Games. The air was warm and the sun was beating down, but I was so dehydrated that, even though I was walking briskly, I didn't break a sweat. I checked in. There were only a few other girls from my division there. We ignored each other as we waited. I slipped off my Team USA sweats, my bra and underwear, walked up to the scale, and stepped on the scale completely naked. Sixty-three kilograms exactly. A female official with a clipboard recorded the weight, then gave me a nod.

I jumped off the scale, pulled on my underwear and grabbed a bottle of water and chugged the entire thing. I downed another bottle as I pulled my sweats back on. I devoured my banana in two bites, then headed back into the village courtyard drinking another bottle of water. My all-you-can-eat cafeteria extravaganza would have to wait until after I competed, but oatmeal had never tasted so amazing.

On the shuttle bus to the arena, I listened to Green Day's "Waiting" on repeat and thought about how my wait was almost over.

Officials led us from the underground garage through a concrete tunnel lit by fluorescent lighting. The warm-up room was large and open and filled with mats.

Usually the coaching staff brings in the person on the team who fought the day before to help you warm up, but that person was Ellen Wilson, and as one of the Olympic Training Center crew, she wasn't going to show up to help me out. Instead, I warmed up with Marisa Pedulla, one of our coaches. It was a quick warm-up, then I went and took a nap. It was a restful sleep, but not a deep one.

I was ready.

"Ronda Rousey," a man with a clipboard was calling my name. My match was up next. I walked over with Marisa to the volunteer assigned to carry the basket where I would put my sweats and shoes while I fought.

"Nice to meet you," I said, handing my basket carrier my stuff. "Thanks so much."

We stood waiting in line. My opponent, Claudia Heill of Austria, was right next to me. We did not acknowledge each other.

And so it begins, I thought.

The official led us into the arena. It was early in the day, so the place was only about a quarter filled, but the crowd was already loud.

"Go Ronda! Yeah, Ronda!" I did not look around, but I could hear my mom and sister Maria from the stands. No matter how large the venue, my family is so loud they can be heard from anywhere.

I stepped onto the mat and bowed. I stomped my left foot twice. Then my right. I jumped. I took a few steps, shaking my arms. I slapped my right shoulder, then my left, then my thighs. I touched the ground. It was time.

I lost in the first round. It was a bullshit call. I threw her and the officials acted like nothing had happened.

As if watching from an extreme distance, I saw the referee right next to me raise a hand in my opponent's direction. I felt disoriented. I didn't know what to do or where to go or how to process what was happening. *This is not how it was supposed to go,* I thought. It was as if the world had been turned upside down. I was in shock. I walked off the mat fighting back tears.

She knew it was a bullshit call, but she took the win over me and went on to take the silver medal. I was not yet good enough to win twice on a bad day.

Then I had to wait. In international judo competition, if you lose to someone who makes the semifinal, you are entered into repechage, a consolation bracket with a chance to fight for the bronze medal. Because Heill made it to the semifinals, I was entered into the repechage bracket. I tried to refocus and pull myself together. *You still have to fight,* I reminded myself. *Your day is not over*. But my heart felt broken.

I won my first repechage match against Great Britain's Sarah Clark, the same girl who beat me at the US Open. I was one step closer to an Olympic medal. It wouldn't be gold, but a bronze would still be a pretty impressive finish for a seventeen-year-old kid. *You'll be OK with that,* I tried to convince myself. Then I lost to Hong Ok-song of Korea the next round. It wasn't a dramatic defeat. She didn't even do anything. She won by a minor score against me on a penalty. I kept attacking until the very end, but time ran out. I was out of the tournament.

I felt numb at the sound of the buzzer. I waited for the emotion to wash over me, for the tears to fall, for my knees to give out. But I realized that I couldn't feel any more pain. I had lost the Olympics, but it wasn't in that match. I had lost them when the officials called my win for Claudia Heill. I had fought two more matches since that one, but I never came back.

Overall, I finished ninth, the best finish of any woman on the US judo team. But it wasn't good enough for me.

After I was eliminated, I gathered my things. The team's media relations manager led me back through the maze of hallways. We passed athletes, coaches, cameramen, security guards, event volunteers in electric blue polo shirts, and various Olympic officials. We headed up two flights of concrete stairs, our footsteps echoing as we ascended the empty, dimly lit stairwell. We reached the second landing and a security guard pushed open the door. The light of the arena made me squint. My mom and Maria were standing on the other side of the door.

My mom had the look of genuine concern she only reserves for when you're really sick. Her sympathy was unbearable. I wanted disappointment. I wanted anger. I wanted her to tell me I could have done more. Sympathy meant she believed I had lost despite giving it everything I had. I lowered my eyes.

"I'm so sorry," I said. As the words tumbled out, the reality set in. I had lost.

Huge sobs racked my body. I fell into my mom's arms and cried harder than I've ever cried. My mom held me tight, and I buried my face in her shoulder.

"You don't have to apologize," my mom said, stroking my hair.

"But I let everyone down," I choked out between sobs. "I let you down."

"You didn't let me down," my mom said. "You just had a bad day."

As an athlete, you go through your career thinking the Olympics are going to be the pinnacle of your entire life.

Olympian is a title that you have forever. Even when you die, you are an Olympian. But sometimes the moments you are led to expect will be the most life changing aren't.

The Olympic coach told me I should be proud of myself. My teammates congratulated me. Big Jim told me he saw some things we had to work on. I surpassed everyone's expectations, but fell short of my own. People had expected me to take part, but I had expected to take over.

I just wanted to get the hell out of Athens, away from my failure.

I caught the first flight home, leaving a week before the Games ended. I had wanted to fly with Mom but everything out of Athens was completely booked. Instead, I flew back to the States alone, staring at the seatback in front of me and replaying my losses in my head over and over, breaking them down, rewinding the missed opportunities. Each time I cycled through a match, the pain of the loss felt fresh. I had lost tournaments before, but I had never felt this level of crushing devastation. To be a competitor on the world's biggest stage was not enough. I was there for one reason: I was there to win.

NO ONE HAS THE RIGHT
TO BEAT YOU

I am determined to prove that there is no advantage anyone can have over me that will ever make a difference. At the beginning of a match, you and your opponent both start from zero. Where you take it from there is up to you.

Other people's advantages are not an excuse for you to lose; they should motivate you to beat them. Just because a person has all the development resources—all the coaches, all the scouting, all the tools to train at the highest level—just because a person won the last Olympics or beat you the last time you met or is pumped full of steroids, they don't get an extra score on the board when the fight starts.

The fight is yours to win.

My first major tournament after the Olympics was in Budapest, the 2004 Junior World Judo Championships that fall. I went into the tournament unaware of what a big deal it actually was. The junior worlds bring together the world's best competitors who are under the age of twenty-one. Competing at both the junior and senior levels internationally is rare, which meant I went from facing Olympians to facing future Olympians.

I took two weeks off after Athens, during which time I wallowed in self-pity. Then one day, my mom came into my room.

"That's enough of feeling sorry for yourself. Get up, you're going to practice," she said. "Lying around saying 'Poor me, I lost the Olympics' isn't going to change anything. You shouldn't be sad you lost, you should be angry."

She was right. I went to practice that evening and slammed everyone. I was pissed off and embarrassed about how I did in Athens. I was still angry when I went back to Big Jim three weeks later. And I carried that with me when I headed to the 2004 junior worlds two months later.

Big Jim never addressed the 2004 Olympics with me, but he let Lillie McNulty, a friend I had made at a camp, come out for a week to train with me. That was his way of acknowledging how hard the loss must have been for me.

Matchups in judo tournaments are determined by a draw, where competitors are placed in two sides of a bracket and then paired up semi-randomly from there. (The overwhelming number of matchups between US and Japanese fighters in the first round of international competition makes me skeptical of just how "random" many draws actually are.) Some routes to the final can seem much easier than others.

Many competitors hope for the easy draw. People don't want to face the No. 1 in the first round. They want to get as far as they can without having to put out the effort. They hope someone else beats the person they're afraid of facing. They don't want to go through the best to be the best.

"Don't hope for the easy draw," my mom used to tell me. "You are the bad draw. You be the person other girls hope they don't have to face."

You don't look at the matchups and hope to have a good draw, making it easier for you to win. It doesn't matter who you have to fight and what order you have to fight them because to be the best in the world, you have to beat them all anyway.

I came out of the worst possible draw at the junior worlds, but it did not matter. I won my first three matches by ippon on the first day of the tournament, sending me to the semifinal. As we sat eating dinner that night, one of my teammates said that USA Judo officials were scrambling to find an American flag and a copy of the national anthem in Budapest. Each nation's delegation is tasked with bringing its own flag and copy of its anthem for the award ceremony. I laughed.

"No," he said. "They really don't have it."

They expected us all to lose, so no one thought to bring one.

It had never even crossed my mind that I would leave the tournament with anything but a gold medal. USA Judo hadn't even considered that a possibility.

As I prepared to face a girl from Russia, I had one question for the person appointed by USA Judo to coach me. He was not actually my coach. For major international competitions, the sport's governing body appoints a coaching team to travel with the athletes. For the most part, the coaching staff is purely symbolic. Success is not going to hinge on something a person you hardly know tells you as you're heading onto the mat. Success is born out of everything that leads up to you stepping on the mat. Before each of my matches, I asked members of the USA coaching staff whether my opponent was right-or left-handed so I could plan my first exchange. Each time, I was told, "I don't know. I wasn't paying attention to her last match, I was watching you."

This time, I didn't even bother asking, I launched right into warming up with Lillie.

"Wait a minute," my appointed coach said, watching us. "You're left-handed?"

My mouth dropped.

"Wait a minute, the only reason that you told me that you couldn't tell me whether these girls were left-or right-handed is because you were busy watching me and you don't even know that I'm left-handed?"

I walked away in total disgust. Across the mat, I saw my opponent's coach giving her instruction. I saw the coach go in toward her as if to demonstrate what I might do. He looked at her and tapped his left hand, indicating that I was a left-handed fighter. She nodded. All of the anger that I had been carrying with me rose to the surface. The Olympics. The missing American flag. The half-ass coaching. I had had enough, and this girl was going to pay.

I walked out onto the mat and bowed in. My faux coach shouted something to me from the chair, but without even processing what he said I determined it was nonessential information.

The Russian girl didn't stand a chance. I ran up the score against her by so much that she must have been embarrassed. We walked off the mat and the US coach tried to give me a hug. I held my arms by my side.

I slammed the girl from China to win the final. The entire match took four seconds. (That is not a typo—four seconds, which is less time than it takes to read this sentence.)

I became the first American to win the junior worlds in a generation. I stood on the podium and watched as the American flag was raised to the rafters. I couldn't put my finger on it, but something about it looked off, like it was a bootleg bought at a ninety-nine-cent store and noticeably smaller than the other flags. It might only have had forty-nine stars, but I couldn't tell. I was too distracted by the crunchy sound of the national anthem, it sounded like someone was playing it into a microphone off a Walkman.

A few months after the junior worlds, I flew to Spain for an annual training camp in Castelldefels, a coastal town right outside of Barcelona. Of all the training camps I attended, Castelldefels was my favorite. Not only was it in a beautiful setting, but it was one of the only major training camps not attached to a tournament, so no one was coming into it disappointed over having lost or worried about making weight. It was an opportunity to go up against the best in the world as I sought to establish myself as one of them.

It was also at this training camp, and the camps that would follow, that I saw the enormous disparity between the resources provided to athletes from other countries and what we had as members of the US judo team. At Castelldefels, USA Judo sent one coach, which was more than we usually had. Other teams had a 1:1 coaching ratio. I saw my competitors' coaches observing them intently, scribbling down notes not just about their own athletes but about their athletes' opponents.

It wasn't only about coaching. I would have traded our coach for some athletic tape and ice. The French team had a dedicated physiotherapist who had dozens of rolls of tape and a cooler full of ice. The Germans, Spanish, and the Canadians had physios as well. The Americans did not. I looked into my bag at the single, now depleted, roll of white athletic tape that I had brought and realized that I was going to need to ask someone from another country for tape.

"Look at this, it's so unfair," one of my teammates lamented as she watched the French physio wrap his athletes' ankles with professional precision.

"If we had this…" she trailed off, but her implication was clear: If we had this, we'd be better.

Fuck that, I thought. *They can have their tape and their coolers full of ice and their nine hundred coaches, and I'm still going to kick their asses.*

Training practices were the most grueling workouts of my life. We would do ten rounds or more of randori in the morning. I went all out every single round, every single day. Between sessions, I would lie on the mat, uncertain if I would ever have enough energy to move again. Then they would bring in lunch, and I would roll to my side and hoist myself up slowly to eat.

"Please let it be fish," I would whisper. On days when it was *jamón y melón*—or as I referred to it, raw bacon and cantaloupe melon meat—I would just eat bread and cheese.

In the afternoon, we would do another fifteen rounds of randori. The level of competition was so high you would see practice rounds the caliber of Olympic finals happening all around. After camp was over, we all headed out to a bar, drinking sangria and communicating in broken English and mangled Spanish or hand gestures.

As the week wore on, there was one notable difference from day to day: the worsening smell. Staying in a hotel where there was nowhere for anyone to wash their gis after training in them from morning to night, the scent of body odor became more and more overpowering. Everyone smelled of sweat and mildew, except for me. I smelled like sweat and mildew and the not-quite-overpowering scent of Febreze, which I packed for every camp and used to spray down my gi every night, before hanging the stiff cotton jacket out of the window to dry.

My relentlessness earned me respect. I was someone that other girls wanted to go up against because they knew I would challenge them. I used that to my advantage. I memorized all their tendencies, all the moves that worked especially well for them, all the techniques they relied on. I didn't have a coach to do that for me, so I had to do it for myself.

I watched as a member of the British coaching staff took out his little notebook where he jotted down observations and scribbled out strategies.

"You don't need to write up this one," I wanted to say. "After we're done out there, this bitch will remember me."

Most athletes at the training camps are just trying to get through the day's workouts. I was trying to leave an impression on every single person in my division. I used every training camp not only to learn about my opponents but to beat the living shit out of them. I wanted to intimidate my opponents. I wanted all the other competitors in my division to leave thinking, *Fuck, this chick's good. She threw me fifteen times today.* I wanted them to get used to the fact that I would beat them.

They could tell themselves, "It was just training camp." But, the next time they saw me, they would remember that I slammed them fifteen times.

I might not have had the tools at my disposal that my opponents had, but I created advantages of my own.

YOU WILL NEVER WIN A
FIGHT BY RUNNING AWAY

Judo grew out of Bushido, which is Japanese for the "way of the warrior." The original Bushido martial art was used in samurai warfare; it was a means to survive. To me, judo is about the fight, and the person who wins the fight ought to be the best fighter.

But there are many elite-level fighters who don't fight to lay it all on the line. They fight for points. They will get ahead by a minor score, then spend the rest of the match trying to make it look like they're fighting when they're really running away. It's like fighting a lawyer. It's not about who's right or wrong, it's not about justice, it's about who can find the loopholes in the rules, and eke out a win.

I cannot stand points fighters. Points fighting is cowardly. Points fighting is fighting without honor. If you are fighting for points, you're not fighting at all. Points fighters are just there to compete, even if that means running and hiding the entire match. You should give one hundred percent all of the time.

It's not just about winning, it is about how you win. It's not about winning pretty, it is about winning honorably. I'm not there for competition. I am there for a fight.

I met Dick IttyBitty at a camp in Chicago in 2002, but he didn't leave an impression on me. (Knowing this guy, he will still probably take satisfaction in being referenced. However, I can live with the fact that in order to do so, he will have to say, "You know that backstabbing boyfriend who constantly put Ronda down? That's me! I'm Dick IttyBitty.") A year later, something had changed. I had been successful at the US Open, but I was still recovering from my knee surgery. The biggest challenge wasn't actually the physical pain but the mental block. Deep in the back of my mind, I was worried about hurting my knee again. My injury had shown me that I wasn't as invincible as I thought. My signature throw before I got injured was a left *uchi mata*. It translates to inner-thigh throw because you plant your right leg, then sweep your left leg between your opponent's legs, up to their inner thigh, and while turning, throw her over your hip. It's one of the most effective throws in judo and a solid uchi mata is hard to defend against. My mom noticed that I was favoring my right leg. There were moments in practice where I wouldn't go in for the throw. Or I tried a less effective throw that didn't require putting full weight on my right leg. In competition, that hesitation means the difference between being on the podium and being eliminated. My mom called Nick, an acquaintance from her judo days who was running the camp, and told him what she had seen.

"I'm not going to say anything to her, but she's going to do one thousand uchi matas over the course of the week," Nick told my mom. "We're going to drill her on that with all types of people. Big, little, old, young, guys, girls, anyone who walks into our club. And by the end, she'll see that if her knee was going to go out again, it would have happened within the first one thousand times."

The first day, I took it slow, but my knee held up. By the third day, I started picking up speed, just wanting to get the throws over. By the end of the week, it sounded like a machine gun as I slammed person after person into the blue crash pads. *Bam. Bam. Bam. Bam. Bam.* When I left Chicago, I had a renewed level of confidence.

I was used to being around guys in judo, but they always seemed to see me as a sister. Dick was not interested in me in a sisterly way. At first, I didn't think it was anything, just some flirting at the camp. Then he tried to kiss me. I froze. He laughed off the awkwardness and we kept in touch.

Dick was persistent (of course, it's easier to be persistent when you're sleeping with several other people), and after I left Chicago, he would message me online and text me constantly. I was flattered.

Two weeks after I had returned from Chicago, my mom and I were headed to practice when she said, "I heard Dick IttyBitty and you hit it off." Her tone was casual, but I wasn't fooled; there was nothing casual about this conversation.

"He's cool," I said with a shrug.

"Really? I've heard he's a dirtbag," my mom said.

"That's not true," I said.

My mom gave me a skeptical look. "From what I hear, he sleeps with anything that has a vagina," my mom said. "Despite looking like he got hit by an ugly stick, it sounds like he gets more ass than a toilet seat. I guess he's not very selective."

"Those are just lies started by these girls who were jealous because he was not interested in them." I spouted out the explanation he had given me.

My mom stared at me with a look that said, *You can't be that fucking stupid.*

I slid down in the passenger seat and looked out the window, debating whether opening the door and hurling myself out of a moving vehicle on the freeway would be better than continuing this conversation. "Ronda, you know why a guy in his twenties goes after sixteen-year-old girls? Because they're dumb enough to believe his bullshit. I would like to believe you're smarter than that. Seriously, it's creepy."

"OK, enough with the lecture," I said exasperated. "It's not like anything happened or is going to. Let's just change the subject."

"Nothing better happen," my mom said.

Two weeks later, I moved east to train with Big Jim. I had limited my communications with Dick when I was at my mom's, but now we started texting more regularly. Then one day, in the middle of practice, he just walked into the club.

My jaw dropped. My stomach flipped. A little piece of me wanted to break into a happy dance, but the rest of me knew this was not going to go over well.

Mom was pissed. And the way Big Jim acted around Dick made me realize that he wasn't a friend of the *entire* Pedro family. Big Jim had little tolerance for people who said they were training to be elite athletes, but failed to put in the effort. Dick was one of those people. And, while Big Jim would never have admitted it, he had become protective of me. Big Jim wanted him gone as much as my mom did. He made it clear under no circumstance was I to be near Dick.

"Don't do anything stupid," Big Jim said.

But Big Jim couldn't watch us every second. While he was working at the firehouse for the weekend, his youngest son, Mikey, decided to have a barbecue.

While Mikey fired up the grill, Dick fired up one of the Jet-Skis. I jumped on the back and we sped off to the middle of the lake, out of clear sight from the shore, we slowed to a stop and Dick leaned over and kissed me again. I froze. A deer in headlights. It felt awkward, but it was also exciting and forbidden.

Two nights later, with Big Jim still at work, Dick made sure I was drunk and kissed me once more, and I don't remember much, but I didn't freeze. Then he went back to Chicago, and all of my focus shifted to the Olympics.

But we kept in touch, hooking up at various tournaments. We thought we were slick, but it was an open secret.

In February 2005, we were in Hamburg for the Otto World Cup, where we were both competing. I lost in the preliminaries. I got caught in an armbar and didn't tap. So the girl dislocated my elbow, and it swelled up the size of a grapefruit. I won that match, but I lost the next one in the first exchange. I entered into repechage, where I won one hard-fought and painful match, before I lost the next match and was eliminated from the tournament. I went back to the hotel, and Dick IttyBitty, who was knocked out of the tournament early, came with me. I knew it wasn't a good idea, but I was depressed over losing and hurting my arm and wanted the company. We were lying on the bed, on top of the white comforter, when I heard the whoosh of the door being unlocked by a keycard.

"What the f—" I didn't even have time to get the words out when the door flew open and Big Jim was standing in the doorway.

"What the fuck is your problem?" Big Jim screamed. "You just can't listen, can you?"

He had crazy eyes.

Dick jumped up and tried to explain, but only managed a stutter.

"You shut the fuck up," Big Jim said in Dick's direction, but without taking his eyes off me. Dick fell silent.

"That's it," Big Jim said. "I'm done with you. You're your mother's problem now."

My stomach lurched into my throat. Big Jim looked at me with disgust and disappointment, then walked away.

The tournament was over, but was followed by an elite training camp. I had to face Big Jim every day for the next week.

"What the hell is the problem?" he barked at me during one of the practices. I was having trouble keeping my opponents away when they came in to get a grip or do a throw because of my injured arm.

"I hurt my elbow," I said.

"Stop it," he said. "Your elbow's not hurt. You're too weak to hold them away. You're not strong enough."

Nothing I could say would change his mind, so I did what I always did when Big Jim got mad, I bit my tongue and pushed myself harder. I fought through the pain in silence.

The pain was nothing compared with what was yet to come. Big Jim told my mom. I spent the entire flight back to Los Angeles overwhelmed with dread. I had never wanted not to see someone so badly. I stood on the curb at LAX, simultaneously looking for my mom's car and praying she would forget to come. For the first time in my life, my mom was on time to pick me up.

"Get in," she said through the open passenger-side window. I braced myself.

Before we had pulled away from the curb Mom started, "What the fuck were you thinking?"

I opened my mouth.

"Don't even answer that," she said, cutting me off. "I don't even want to hear whatever you're going to say, because there's no answer that could justify such a complete lack of respect, not to mention stupidity."

Her voice was raised, but she wasn't yelling.

Silence was going to be my best tactic. I looked down at my hands, fighting back tears.

She turned right onto Sepulveda Boulevard. I was relieved to see traffic was light. The only thing that could make this moment worse would be having it extended by an L.A. traffic jam.

"Dick fucking IttyBitty?" my mom asked incredulous. "He's so amazing that you're willing to ruin your relationship with your coach, to go against what Big Jim and I explicitly told you? Give me a break. He'll sleep with anyone. He's a total sleazeball."

The back of my neck got hot. I felt like I couldn't breathe. I rolled down my window, but the fresh air didn't make any difference. I was jet-lagged. I was hungry. My elbow was throbbing. My coach had thrown me out. I leaned my head back on the beige fabric headrest.

"Things are going to change," my mom pressed on. "You don't know how good you had it, little girl. You're eighteen, which is technically an adult, even if you act like a spoiled brat. You need to get your act together. The Olympics are over. We made a lot of exceptions and let you get away with a lot of shit, but no more. You're going to take a year away from judo. You need to finish high school. You need to get a job. You need to start paying rent. It's time for you to live in the real world. And the real world is going to be a major wakeup call."

I stared straight at the windshield, wishing I was anywhere else. But I didn't have anywhere else to go and I didn't know what I was going to do. What I did know was that if I was going to pay rent, it sure as hell wasn't going to be to live in my mom's house.

Our house was less than a twenty-minute drive to the airport, and I had never been so glad to pull onto our street. As soon as my mom parked, I threw open the door and stormed in the house and up the stairs to the bedroom I shared with Julia. I slammed the door and threw myself onto the bottom bunk. The sea lion stared out at me from the under-the-sea mural I had painted on our bedroom wall.

I was devastated to be thrown out of Big Jim's house. I was humiliated to have him catch me with Dick in my room. I was sorry to have let my mom and Big Jim down. I was furious at them for interfering with my personal life and treating me like I couldn't make my own decisions.

Staring up at the slats of the top bunk, I cried hysterically.

I had spent the first several years of my life unable to communicate because of a speech disorder. Now, a decade and a half later, though I was able to speak, I found myself struggling to convey what I wanted to say. I did not know how to talk to my mom or Big Jim. I felt like when I tried they dismissed me. I didn't have the confidence to be able to hold my own in an argument. Part of me felt like they would not respect my opinion, but more than that, I wasn't sure that I had enough experience to make the right decisions for myself. It wasn't at all about Dick IttyBitty; he was just the catalyst for something that had been boiling within me for years. My life was out of my control. It had been a slow creep, but the feeling had become overwhelming, like standing in a room with no exit as it fills with water.

I needed to be in charge of my life. I wanted to prove that I did know a few things and that Mom and my coaches should listen to me. But it seemed much easier to move across the country in the middle of the night by myself than to walk into our living room and have a real conversation with my mom.

I began to plan my "great" escape. Because my dad had died, I was receiving Social Security benefits. The benefits would continue until I turned eighteen or graduated high school, whichever came second. Technically, because I was taking correspondence classes, I was still enrolled in high school. I had just turned eighteen two weeks earlier, so now the checks were coming in my name. I went to the bank, opened my own account, and had the checks directly deposited.

As soon as I had enough money I bought a plane ticket to upstate New York. I figured I could train at Jim Hrbek's club while staying with my friend Lillie and her family. Hrbek had been one of the top coaches in the nation dating back to when my mom had been competing. At least, I hoped they would all be OK with my being there once I showed up. I could not risk my mom finding out about my plan, so I told Lillie, but no one else.

My mom's anger faded over the next few weeks.

Then one morning—two weeks after I had returned and less than a week before I was set to leave—my mom woke up and she wasn't mad at me anymore.

"Let's go down to the Promenade," she suggested. "OK," I said, glad not to have her yelling at me.

We walked the six blocks to the same shopping area I'd gone to the day I ditched school and broke my foot. My mom suggested we check out Armani Exchange. There among the racks of clothes she zeroed in on a white leather jacket.

"This looks like something you'd like," my mom said. It was an awesome jacket.

"Try it on," she urged.

I slipped it on. It fit me perfectly. I felt amazing. "You need to have that," my mom said.

I checked the price tag. "Please, it's too much," I said. My mom gave me a hug.

"You deserve it," she said. "Besides you were at Big Jim's for your birthday. We owe you a gift."

She brought the jacket up to the cashier, where the sales clerk wrapped it in tissue paper and slipped it into a bag. My eyes stung, my chest ached, my resolve was crumbling. But then I thought about my mom's complete lack of understanding of me. I wanted to be in control of my life—and I wanted to prove to my mom and Big Jim that I could be in control of my life. I knew I had to go. But I wished she was still mad at me. It would have made leaving easier.

The night before I left, I waited until my family fell asleep. I packed my bags, jumping at every sound. Then I sat on my bed, waiting for the hours to pass. At 4:55 a.m., I crept out of my room and walked downstairs. I left a note for my mom, explaining that this was something I had to do and I hoped she would understand. Then I walked out the door.

The world outside was quiet. The sun wasn't up yet and the air was cool and humid from the ocean a few blocks away. I wanted to pull my new jacket out of my bag, but I was afraid to stop. I threw my navy blue 2004 Olympic team duffle bag over my shoulder and picked up my black duffle bag, carrying it by my side. As if a backward glance would wake my mom, I trained my eyes straight ahead and walked away.

I hauled my bags four blocks and sat down at a bus stop, but bus service didn't start until later in the morning so I called a cab and a few minutes later a yellow taxi stopped in front of me. As the cabbie drove toward the airport, I waited for the relief to set in, for the feeling of liberation that I was so certain would accompany my escape.

I didn't feel triumphant. I felt like a coward. I had run away. I may have won the match, but I had been competing for points, not fighting with honor.

DON'T RELY ON OTHERS
TO MAKE YOUR DECISIONS

I used to have a teammate who always needed the coach to tell her what to do. She could execute that instruction almost flawlessly. The problem was, she was only as good as the person coaching her and as good as the information that she was receiving.

My mom purposely sent me to tournaments without a coach all the time. When I was on the mat, I had to think for myself. If there was a bad score, there was no one to correct it. If a call went against me, there was no one to speak up for me. I would just have to do better and do it again. If I was in a bad situation, I had to problem-solve and figure it out.

I had carefully planned my escape from L.A., but hadn't put much thought into what would come next. Lillie's family was surprised when I basically showed up on their doorstep, but her parents agreed to let me stay. So I hauled my two duffle bags up to her room.

When I first got to New York, I talked a lot about the injustice of my situation, how my mom and Big Jim were so unfair, how every element of my life—from what I ate to how I trained—was regimented by someone else, how no one believed in my relationship, how no one ever asked for my input, how people treated me like I was a kid. The more I talked about it, the angrier I got. I wasn't a kid. I was an adult, as recognized by the US government. Hell, I was a goddamned Olympian. Lillie listened. Lots of nights, we would stay up late talking, sharing a bed. Other nights, it felt like we were just two kids having a sleepover as we stayed up watching romantic comedies and giggling over inside jokes.

Lillie went to Siena College, and I accompanied her to campus on the days she went to class. I bought a Siena College hoodie at the bookstore and wore it to the gym, where they let me in assuming I was a student. While Lillie was in class, I worked out. As I rode the elliptical, I tried to figure out how everything had spiraled so out of control, why I had run away, if I could ever go back, how I could prove to everyone it wasn't about Dick, what the future held for him and I, where I was going to go from here. I didn't have any answers.

The third Thursday I was there, Lillie and I were heading out to practice when Marina Shafir called and said she wasn't going to make it. Marina was one of the top girls in her division and, along with Lillie, was one of the few girls I really liked in judo. She was one of the few elite competitors who weren't concerned with the politics of the sport. We were about halfway to the club when Nina, another girl from the club, called and said she wasn't going to make it.

"It's going to be a slow practice if hardly anyone is there," Lillie said.

"Fuck it. Let's not go to practice."

"Well, what do you want to do?" Lillie asked.

Out the window I saw the familiar orange and pink sign.

"Let's go to Dunkin' Donuts," I said.

The wheels screeched, Lillie made a sharp right turn, and we pulled into the deserted parking lot.

"I'd like four dozen Munchkins," I told the clerk.

"What kind?" he asked, gesturing to the wire containers behind him.

I paused. I felt as if I was making a very important decision.

"Just give me some of all of them," I said.

"Will that be all?" he asked.

I looked at Lillie. She shrugged.

"And two chocolate milks," I said, grabbing them from the refrigerated case by the counter.

He rung me up, then handed me the two cardboard boxes with handles that contained my forty-eight-plus donut holes. Lillie and I sat at one of the tables, each opening a box.

I popped a donut hole in my mouth. It was doughy and delicious. I laughed out loud. Lillie looked at me inquisitively, as if she had missed the joke.

But here, sitting at a Dunkin' Donuts as the counter clerk mopped the floor around us, I had found the freedom I had been looking for. For the first time in as long as I could remember, I felt like I had control.

I felt a surge of motivation, possibly due to the sugar-rush of twenty-five donut holes, rushing through my bloodsteam.

I love judo. And I want to do judo because I love it. I want to do it for me. The realization washed over me. It was a feeling I hadn't had in a long time.

The next day, I went to practice because I wanted to. I trained harder than I had in a long, long time.

Not only did I look forward to training, but I wanted to train as much as possible. In addition to Hrbek's, one of the best clubs in the area was run by Jason Morris. Jason had won a silver medal in the 1992 Olympics. He was a member of the US national team coaching staff. He opened his own "club," where aspiring Olympians would come to live and train. Or at least that's how he spun it to their parents.

The dojo was actually just the basement of his house with a judo mat thrown down. Space was so tight that when everyone was on the mat, you were constantly bumping into other people and taking care not to get slammed into one of the walls. Still, the level of training was decent and they practiced every day.

Jim Hrbek had been Jason's coach, helping Jason develop and succeed. Then their relationship fell apart.

One day after practice, Jim called me aside. "I know you're training at Jason's," he said. "That's your choice. But if you're training there, you can't train here."

It was an ultimatum. I do not respond well to ultimatums.

"Got it," I said, without saying anything else. But the only thought that went through my mind was, *I'm going to train wherever the hell I want to train.*

I finished practice.

I told Jason what Jim had said.

"*I'm* not going to tell you where to train," Jason said.

Two days later, I was training at Jason's when Lillie came by. She had an uncomfortable look on her face.

"What's up?" I asked.

Lillie looked down at her Converse.

"It's just with everything with Jim and Jason and all that. We've just been with Jim a long time." She sounded apologetic.

"I've got your stuff in my car," she told me.

"You're kicking me out?" I asked.

"We didn't really know how long you were going to stay, and my mom..." she trailed off.

"I get it," I said.

I got my stuff out of her car and brought it into Jason's club. I looked around. I had nowhere else to go and no idea what I was going to do.

PEOPLE AROUND YOU
CONTROL YOUR REALITY

When you and everyone around you are immersed in one small community, it is easy to mistake it for the whole world. But once you break away, you realize that no one outside your tiny circle gives a shit about the stupid stuff that was at the center of your little world. When you understand that, you discover there is a much bigger, better world out there.

After Lillie drove away, I dragged my bags into Jason's house.

It was a three-level house. Jason and his wife lived on the third floor. There were a couple of bedrooms on the second floor, with two to three athletes in each room, and then two to three more people crashed in the living room. In the basement was the judo room.

As the newest member of the house, I was assigned to the living room, where I slept on a futon on the floor.

Jason marketed his club as an elite training center. For admittance, you needed high potential (optional) and parents with deep pockets (mandatory). My roommates were a bunch of good-not-quite-elite-enough athletes who wanted to make the

Olympic team, but not as much as they wanted to drink, hang out, and hook up. As far as I was concerned they were just a bunch of users. Then again, it seemed like everyone was using someone. Jason and I were certainly using one another—since I was actually winning at the international level my affiliation with his club made him look good and, in exchange, I had a place to live and to train.

I wasn't getting a free ride either. I was receiving a small stipend from the New York Athletic Club, where I was a sponsored member, and an even smaller stipend from USA Judo.

All of the mail went through Jason first. He had a long silver letter opener and opened every letter, addressed to every resident of the house.

"I do it so the envelopes lie flat in the recycling," Jason explained. "If people rip the envelopes open themselves, then they won't stack flat."

In the morning, the athletes who lived in the house would race out to get the mail, trying to get to their own letters first. But often, Jason beat us to it. Any checks for me, he took as payment for lodging or other expenses. Jason intercepted and deposited every single one of my checks from USA Judo and the NYAC the entire time I was there. I didn't even know what was coming in or what the cost of anything was. I just had to take everything at his word.

Even worse, I didn't feel myself getting better at Jason's. He wanted every fighter to fight exactly like him—that was his coaching strategy. He does very straight standup judo and little matwork, with an emphasis on timing over strength. I excelled at matwork and used my strength as an asset on the mat. I tried to find a balance between our two approaches, but Jason's style didn't fit my body type, didn't fit my personality, and just didn't fit me.

At Big Jim's, any input I tried to offer was dismissed. At Jason's, my input wasn't just dismissed, it was ridiculed. I was treated like I was fucking stupid.

"What are you doing?" Jason shouted at me one day during practice.

I stopped what I was doing, an *o-goshi,* which is a relatively basic hip throw that worked well for me as a left-handed fighter when I went up against right-handed opponents.

"O-goshi," I said.

"Ooooh o-goshi," he said, condescendingly. He adopted a high, lilting voice with a joker-like smile and started waving his hands in the air. "Do o-goshi again. Do it again. Just do o-goshis all day."

The other fighters laughed.

Fuck all of you, I thought. I did the throws all day.

At Jason's, I was rarely alone, but I felt incredibly lonely. I hadn't spoken to my mom since I had left home three months earlier. Dick IttyBitty and I were together, but he was one thousand miles away in Chicago. I had Lillie, but things had become strained after her family kicked me out. One of the girls at Jason's club, Bee, had been really nice to me since I had arrived, but she was no Lillie.

My relationship with my housemates was cordial, but not warm. I never really fit in. I was younger than everyone and I was a better, more dedicated athlete, and my success exposed their shortcomings. But the list of clubs I was not welcome at was rapidly growing—Pedros', Hrbek's, home—so Jason's it was.

That May, Dick moved from Chicago to New York to train at Jason's club. I was at a local high school gymnasium where we were setting up mats for the Morris Cup, an annual tournament Jason had named after himself, when Dick walked in. A wave of relief washed over me. A huge smile crossed my face. I felt my cheeks blush.

Dick shared the living room futon with me. He settled right in at Jason's, and became the bridge between me and the other athletes in the house.

A month after Dick arrived, I went to Planned Parenthood to get birth control. A few days later, my phone rang.

"Your test results came back abnormal," the nurse said.

My face felt hot.

"Are you telling me I have an STD?" I asked. I could hardly get out the words.

"It could be a number of things."

"Like an STD?"

"We need you to come in for a follow-up exam."

"Sure," I said. My hand shook as I jotted down the time and date of my next appointment.

After hanging up the phone, I stormed into the other room. Dick was sitting on the couch.

"Who have you been fucking?" I screamed.

His deer-in-the-headlights look confirmed my worst fear. Rage surged through my body. Every muscle tensed.

"Uh, uh, uh," he stammered.

"Who. Have. You. Been. Fucking?"

"It was a one time thing. I'm so sorry. It didn't mean anything. It was months ago. Not since I've been here. I'm so sorry." He was on the verge of hyperventilating.

"Who have you been fucking?" My voice was cold.

"I'm so sorry. Sorry. Oh God, I want to kill myself. I love you so much."

I was not in the mood to have to repeat myself again.

"Who?" My voice was barely a whisper.

"Bee," he said.

My mouth suddenly felt dry. My face was burning. My anger mixed with embarrassment.

"Everyone knows about this, don't they?" I asked.

He nodded.

I had to leave the room. I stood in the yard. The last thing I wanted was to go back into that house. But I had nowhere to go. I had burned all my bridges and I was stuck on an island.

For days, Dick begged me to forgive him. I felt like I had no other choice. I felt like he was all I had. Soon we were sharing the futon again like nothing happened. But it was never the same. This time I knew he was no good, and I knew I was lying to myself.

A week later, after my follow-up appointment, I called for my test results.

"Turns out it was nothing," the nurse said. "Sometimes these tests come back abnormal, then we do them again and it's fine."

I breathed a sigh of relief. I had dodged a bullet, but things in my life were far from fine.

The only reprieve from life at Jason's came when I went to tournaments and training camps. I won the US national championship, Pan American championships, the Rendez-Vous, and the US Open, but winning wasn't making me happy. The low point came when I lost the 2005 world championships in Cairo, Egypt, to an Israeli girl who had no business beating me.

Compounding everything, I was struggling to make weight. I was establishing myself as one of the world's best fighters in my division, but I had grown two inches since making my senior-level debut at sixteen and getting down to sixty-three kilos was getting tougher.

Then one night, as I lay next to Dick, a third roommate stretched out on the nearby couch, his leg dangling over the side, it hit me. I was with a guy who cheated on me in a house full of people who knew about it and said nothing. I was training under a coach I couldn't stand and who was taking my money. I was starving. I was not improving.

"What the fuck am I doing here?" I asked myself out loud.

The next day I called my mom.

"Hello?" I wanted to cry at the familiar sound of my mom's voice. There had been so many times in the intervening eight months that I had wanted to talk to her.

"Hey, Mom," I said, casually. "It's been a while."

"Well, I'm sure you've been busy," my mom said.

Through her network of judo gossips/informants, my mom had been tracking my movements since the day I left home. She had heard about Dick's cheating. She wasn't going to make it easy.

"I was thinking about the holidays," I said. "The Ontario Open is the day after Thanksgiving, but maybe I could come home after that."

"You're always welcome here," my mom said. I wasn't sure if she meant it. Still, relief swept through me. I didn't realize how much I'd missed home.

A few weeks later, I won the Ontario Open and caught a flight back to L.A. My mom met me at the airport. I had hoped she would be happy to see me, but instead her brow was furrowed in disapproval.

"Thanks for picking me up," I said.

"Yeah, Maria had to fly back on the red-eye for work. Jennifer is flying back to San Francisco tonight to go back to college, so I'll get to make the trip again," she said.

"Fortunately traffic doesn't seem too bad," I said, in an attempt to make small talk.

"Well, there's noticeably more traffic than when you slip out of the house in the middle of the night and ditch out on your family and head to the airport, but it's not too bad."

"Look, I feel really bad about that, but it was just something I felt I had to do."

"Oh, well that makes everything better," my mom said sarcastically. "Do you know how bad I felt to wake up and find that you had left? Just left everyone? Me. Your sisters. Your cat."

"Beijing never liked me anyway," I said, half-joking.

"Maybe she knew you were planning to abandon her," my mom said, without missing a beat.

At our house, I grabbed my two duffle bags and lugged them to the front door. "I'm home," I said cheerfully as I threw open the front door.

Silence.

I was hoping my little sister, Julia, would be home. I expected everyone else to be mad at me, but Julia, who was only seven, would be glad I was back.

Jennifer was packing her bag in the living room. She stopped and glared at me.

"You're wearing my shirt, take it off," she said, coldly.

"Nice to see you too," I said with a forced laugh.

"Take off my shirt," Jennifer repeated.

"God, Jen, why do you have to be such a bitch?"

"Well, at least I don't have genital warts!" Jennifer said. My abnormal test results had come to my permanent address and Jen had drawn her own conclusions. She shot me a smug look and something inside me snapped.

"I do not have genital warts!" I shrieked.

Jennifer ran in the only direction she could, to a dead end in the kitchen. I chased her. Jennifer screamed. My mom, who was two steps behind me, coming in the door, grabbed me from behind, catching me in a choke and giving Jennifer enough room out of the kitchen. I threw Mom over my shoulder and chased after my sister. Our longtime housekeeper, Lucia, a small Mexican woman, came in with the laundry. She dropped the basket and blocked me from getting to Jen. Mom caught up to me and tried to restrain me as Jennifer ran up the stairs and locked herself in the bathroom. Mom grabbed my shoulder and shook me.

"What the fuck is your problem?"

"Me? She's the one who started it," I protested. "Do you know what she said to me?"

"What are you going to do, beat her up? You can't just be attacking people because you don't like what they say." My mom was irate. "If that was the case, people would be punching people in the face all the time."

Lucia, looking shell-shocked, picked up the laundry basket.

"I'm sorry, Lucia," I said as she walked past.

She looked at me, then my mom, then back at me as if to confirm the fight was over.

Later, my mom recounted the events of the afternoon to Dennis. I had never seen him so angry. "You are so lucky Julia was not here to witness that. If that happens again, you can't live here."

You're right, I thought. *There's no way I can live here.*

That night I texted Dick in Chicago.

Come here, he texted back.

"Maybe," I replied, although my mind was already made up.

Our family was going to St. Louis to visit extended family for Christmas. Two weeks before the trip, I told my mom that I would be flying from St. Louis directly to Chicago.

My mom's brow stayed furrowed in disapproval up until I left for Chicago. But this time leaving felt different. At least, I'd gotten the courage to tell Mom I was leaving even if she didn't want to hear it.

I moved into Dick's parents' house. (I know, one more, huge, blaring, warning sign that I missed: Any guy in his mid-twenties living with his teenage girlfriend in his parents' basement is not the kind of guy you want to date.)

His parents welcomed me with open arms. His mom was a hairdresser and would take me to the salon where she would do my hair. She would do my makeup and dress me up. She was always pulling practical jokes and had a hilariously dirty sense of humor. There wasn't a single day where she didn't try to pants me in the house.

His dad was equally warm and caring, even as he suffered from terminal cancer.

"Sure, I'll teach you how to drive," he said. (I took that to mean "I'm probably dying anyway, so I have no fear of death.") He would have me drive him around and play the Beach Boys. Even when I almost got us hit by oncoming traffic or turned the wrong way down a one-way street, he was calm and cool. He introduced me to everyone as his future daughter-in-law.

We were getting close to the two-year point, and I began noticing things about Dick that I hadn't seen before. For the first time I could see just how dumb he was. I remember thinking, *I'm a teenager and you're in your twenties, and wow, I'm way more intelligent than you.* No matter how hard I tried to explain to him there was a difference between *woman* (singular) and *women* (plural), he did not get it and used the two words interchangeably. It drove me insane. Then I realized he had no original jokes. He would just quote movies all the time, and he would quote the same lines over and over. He had a set playlist of stories he would tell, whipping them out the second someone who hadn't heard them before was in earshot. Everything he said grated on me and I couldn't stand being around him.

Then I saw something new: his cruel streak. "God, she's hot," he'd say while we were watching a movie or, worse, while we were out together. "Look at her body," he'd say as a beautiful woman would walk by. It wasn't a direct comparison at first, but soon he was telling me how their bodies were better than mine. Then how they were thinner than me. Then how I was fat.

He would grab the skin at my sides and say, "Boy, you're getting fat," then he'd grin, pretending that it was a harmless joke.

I was already struggling to make weight. Now he preyed on my insecurities. I had never felt pretty. I had cauliflower ear. I regularly got ringworm, a gross but common fungal infection in wrestling and judo (for some reason, my skin seemed especially sensitive to it). I was bulky and thick, even though it was muscle. I had gone from being teased in middle school for having biceps that were "too big" to now having a boyfriend who told me I was "about a six." I wanted to be as perfectly tiny as those girls smiling out from the magazine covers that papered the airport newsstands.

But what ate at me the most was how two-faced he was. We'd be hanging out with people and he'd be cool, and the second they walked away he would talk badly about them. It got to the point where I could not look at him without thinking, *Wow, you're a real fucking dickface.*

When we first got together, I had felt special; now I just felt stupid. I had spent almost two years with a total asshole, and I was still with him.

I found solace in competition. I trained intensely, determined to emerge fiercer, stronger, and more focused than ever. That's when I started stepping onto the mat with a certainty that I had never had.

In April 2006, I won the World Cup tournament in Birmingham, England, the first World Cup that an American woman had won in nine years. I returned to the States and won the senior nationals in Houston three weeks later. In May, I took silver at the Pan American Championships in Argentina.

In July, Dick and I flew to Florida for a series of tournaments, including the Junior US Open in Fort Lauderdale and the Miami Youth International. I had known for a while that I wanted to break up with him, but I didn't know how. Then in Florida, the opportunity presented itself. Dick and I were staying at the tournament host hotel, as was my friend Marina, whom I had first met at Jim Hrbek's and became close with after we competed on the same team at a tournament in Belgium earlier that spring.

After the first tournament, a guy friend and I went for a walk on the beach, and as we were walking it hit me. *I think I kind of like this guy. I'm going to give that a try. I've just got to get rid of this fucker, Dick.* That was all the push I needed.

I texted Marina, who was also on the dump-Dick bandwagon (who wasn't?), then went up to the room Dick and I were sharing. My stuff was scattered all over. I threw it in my duffle bags and moved into Marina's room.

Dick was out so I sent him a text message: *When you get back we need to talk.*

Are you breaking up with me? he wrote back.

Just get back here, I replied.

You're breaking up with me, aren't you?

I sent one more message: *Yes.*

Then I lay down on the bed in Marina's room and ignored the dozens of messages from my now ex-boyfriend, until the panicked and apologetic messages got to be too much.

"I've got to deal with this," I said to Marina, exasperated.

Our hotel was round and hollow in the middle, so that if you were in the center of the circle, you could look up and there were rooms with balconies all around it.

"Please don't do this," Dick begged. "You can't break up with me. I can't be without you. The thought of it makes me not want to live anymore."

I rolled my eyes. He cried harder.

"I mean it," he said. "I will throw myself off the balcony. I'll kill myself."

I lost it.

"Fuck you!" I screamed. "Don't fucking joke about suicide. Your back isn't deteriorating. You're not fucking dying. Are you becoming a quadriplegic? No, you're just becoming a pussy."

He cried harder. I couldn't even stand to be in the same room. I left.

He headed down to the bar and stayed there for the rest of the trip.

Now, if I ever make a bad decision, my mom simply reminds me, "Look, of all the bad decisions you've made or could have made in your life, at least you didn't marry Dick IttyBitty." And that puts everything in perspective.

THE END OF A FAILED MOVE
IS ALWAYS THE BEGINNING OF
THE NEXT ONE

When I was sixteen, I had an epiphany about my matwork. Until then, I had just been memorizing different moves. I would think, *OK, the person's here, I'll try this. The person moves this way, I'll try that.* All the moves were separate in my head.

Then, one day, I went in for an armbar, and my opponent shifted, making it impossible for me to execute the move. I got stacked, then I realized that in defending against my attack, my opponent had perfectly positioned me to carry out a different type of armbar. It was like I just landed in the middle of another technique. I picked up from the middle of that move. I called it the Juji Squish Roll.

That was the first time I linked two different techniques on the ground, and then I realized you could do that with everything. From that moment on, I was constantly looking at ways that I could connect seemingly unconnected moves. Instead of being frustrated by what most people saw as a failure, I looked at it as an opportunity to create something new.

Dumping the dirtbag was one of the best decisions of my life, but I went from having nowhere *else* to go to nowhere to go.

While I was in Miami, I bumped in to Corey Paquette, who competed for Canada and whom I knew from various training camps. I mentioned that I was without a place to live. He mentioned that he was in search of a roommate to split the cost of renting a dorm room in Montreal.

Corey headed back home while I stayed for the next tournament. A few days later I messaged him through Facebook, *Does the offer still stand?* He had a bed ready for me by the time I touched down in Montreal.

My portion of the rent was two hundred Canadian dollars a month. The affordability aspect was important. I had aged out of the Social Security payments and was dependent on the USA Judo funding. The organization guaranteed $3,000 a month in funding to any athlete who won an A-level tournament. The catch was, for years, no one had. Then I came on the scene and USA Judo started having to pay up. But the checks were always late, and I had to repeatedly call to see when I could expect the money. One month in the spring of 2006, I called and the receptionist told me, "We ran out of money for that program."

"You ran out?" I was incredulous.

"We didn't think anyone would get an A ranking," she said.

Fuck USA Judo, fuck all these American coaches, fuck Dick, I thought. *I'm going to go up to Canada, handle my shit on my own, and compete better than I ever have.*

I had saved up a fair amount, but not enough to live off of for very long. The US dollar stretched further in Canada.

My first morning in Montreal, I found the only gym remotely close to us with a sauna, which was essential for cutting weight. Still I had to take a bus and a train to get there. Corey would get up in the morning and go to classes; I got up and headed to the gym. I did the elliptical and lifted, then took a sauna. After my workout, I showered and walked to the nearby Subway. I ordered a six-inch Veggie Delight sandwich, a Diet Coke, and a chocolate chip cookie. That was the one sweet I allowed myself all day. Aside from my Subway lunch, my diet consisted of corn bran cereal with milk, Nesquik, wheat bread with Nutella and peanut butter, and pita bread with hummus.

In the evenings, Corey and I would take the train together to the Shidokan. The Shidokan was the Canadian version of Olympic Training Center, except, unlike its US counterpart, the best judokas in Canada really did train there. I had been there several times before for camps. While they would let me in the door and everyone was stereotypically Canadian friendly, none of the coaches could coach me because I was on a rival national team. Not only was I "the American," but I always beat all their girls in tournaments, and their girls at both sixty-three kilos and seventy kilos were really good. In that way, having me there on a daily basis so they could train with me and study my tendencies was beneficial. The sense of competition that came from having good girls to train with kept me working hard.

The practices at the Shidokan were more grueling than any practice I had ever experienced back home. They would do a day of golden score where for two hours you would keep practicing nonstop until someone scored on you. The person who got scored on would be out, while the other person would keep going. I would be out there for an hour, no one able to score on me.

I made up for the fact that I didn't have any coaching with extra work. I thought about what I needed to do; I wasn't dependent on somebody else giving me orders. I would ask myself, *What can I do to improve now?* I never had to put that kind of thought into my own training before.

After practice, while everyone else showered and changed, Mike Popiel and I would spend hours just making shit up on the mat. We would try moves that no one had ever used in competition and that no coach would ever condone. Most of the moves were completely impractical bullshit, but sometimes, we stumbled upon something brilliant, and a few of those could actually be used in competition. Everyone would be going back home, and we'd be like, "What about this? What about this?"

At the end of the night, Corey and I took the train back to the dorms. When we got home, Corey called his girlfriend and they would talk for hours, while I lay in my twin bed, thinking up more cool moves I wanted to try after practice the next day.

Messing around in the gym and inventing moves developed my ability to think for myself. I went from just doing what the coach says to being able to think independently. That meant in a match I could strategize in the moment. Some athletes are amazingly talented, but can only do what their coaches tell them. They can't think for themselves.

ANYTHING OF VALUE
HAS TO BE EARNED

When I was starting judo, there were national tournaments I could have easily won, but my mom said we were not going. I hadn't yet worked hard enough to earn the honor of going. I was annoyed at the time, but I got far more out of not going than I would have if she had taken me to the tournament and I had won.

No one is ever going to give you anything of value. You have to work for it, sweat for it, fight for it. But there is far greater value in accomplishments you earn than in accolades that are merely given to you. When you earn something, you never have to worry about justifying that you truly deserve it.

During my time based in Canada, I won the US Fall Classic and the Rendez-Vous in Canada. The success set me up as the favorite to win the 2006 Junior World Championships again. In Santo Domingo that October, I breezed through the opening rounds. Then I faced a Cuban girl in the semifinal. The match was scoreless, and time was running out. I decided to go for a sacrifice throw that would put me on my back. The referee did not see the throw correctly and appeared to believe the girl threw me. He called an ippon for her.

My opponent knew she had not thrown me, but she got up and started jumping up and down as if she had done something to win the match. My hands shook with rage. It took all the strength I had not to scream. It was so fucking unfair. I stormed off the mat and threw my gi jacket on the ground as hard as I could.

I had been robbed because of someone else's screwup, and it cost me the championship and the opportunity to be the first American to win the junior worlds twice.

My bad day was about to get worse. USA Judo saw my breach of etiquette as an opportunity to make an example out of me. Instead of holding me up as a successful American athlete, the USA Judo brass was constantly looking for ways to punish me.

I had barely stepped off the edge of the mat when the USA Judo officials at the tournament got together and decided they were going to suspend me from competition for six months. But they needed something to hide behind, like a respected referee blasting me. So the USA Judo representatives went to Carlos Chavez, a big-deal referee from Venezuela. They asked Carlos what should be done to punish me.

Carlos looked at them with disbelief, unable to comprehend why a national governing body was so eager to punish its most promising athlete. Usually when organizations like USA Judo came to him, it was to appeal on an athlete's behalf. Carlos took a diplomatic pause.

"Ronda felt that she had been wronged," Carlos said. "Correctly or incorrectly, she believed that. She's very passionate about judo and very passionate about winning. In the moment, she was upset. This is what we want in judo: athletes who are passionate about the sport. She's young, and we're not going to do anything."

With tears still streaming down my cheeks from my loss to the Cuban, I battled back in the repechage bracket, and in the bronze medal match I beat the Israeli girl whom I had lost the world championship to the year before, becoming the first American in history to get two junior world medals. No one from USA Judo said anything to me about punishment, and it was only after all the officials had congratulated me that I learned about the attempt to have me suspended.

I won the 2006 US Open in Miami a week later. From there, I headed across the Atlantic for the Swedish Open. I won the Swedish Open, which came with a much-needed 1,000 euros in prize money. The victory was empowering and I was still on a celebratory high when I made an impromptu decision to compete in the Finnish Open the following weekend and booked a ticket on the ferry.

I don't know what it was but that night, after I got back to my hotel room in Boras, I was overcome with a desire to go home. I was sitting in my hotel room, and the feeling swept over me.

It's time, I thought. I felt like I had done enough. I wasn't going to be going home with my tail between my legs. I was proud of what I had accomplished on my own. I placed an international call home.

"Hello?" my mom answered. I paused for a second, trying to calculate the time difference.

"I won the Swedish Open," I told her.

"That's great," she said. She sounded genuinely happy for me.

"I want to come home again," I said. "I want to talk everything out. I'm going to go to this tournament in Finland, but I want to come home after that. What do you think?"

"Of course, you can always come home." I didn't expect for her to be so warm and welcoming. I was taken aback, but it reinforced my belief that the timing was right. I felt like things had changed.

I got bronze at the Finnish Open, but for the first time in my life, I wasn't devastated by a loss. I felt optimistic. I flew back home to L.A. with my two duffle bags. My mom picked me up at the airport.

"Hey, kiddo, how was your flight?" she asked as I slid into the passenger seat.

"Good. Long, but good," I said.

As we pulled out of the terminal, it felt different this time around.

I was tired of the fighting and the anger and the hurt, and I missed her. When I went to Canada, I felt like it was me versus everybody else, and I was going to prove them all wrong. I was going to win completely on my own. It was me versus the whole fucking world. I had taken a risk and I had survived. Now, I felt like I could do anything.

EVERYTHING IS AS EASY
AS A DECISION

One of the few ex-boyfriends I had who was not a total douche bag told me this story. It changed my life.

Say you're sitting in a cubicle and you hate your job. It's terrible. Everyone around you is an asshole. Your boss is a dick. All of your work is just mind-numbingly soul-sucking. But in five minutes you are about to leave for your first vacation you've had in five years. You're going to be gone for two weeks at this beautiful Bora Bora seaside bungalow. It's literally the most lavish thing you've ever done in your entire life.

How would you feel? You would feel great.

Now imagine that you are in Bora Bora. You're on this beautiful beach with amazing people, and you've had so much fun. In five minutes, you're going to have to put down the piña colada with the little umbrella in it. You have to say goodbye to these people. You will go back to your terrible job and won't take another vacation for another five years.

How would you feel? You would feel terrible.

Now, think about it. You're sitting in the cubicle at the job that you
hate and you feel awesome. And you're sitting on the beach with
a drink in your hand and you feel terrible. How you feel is entirely
in your mind. Your mind has nothing to do with your environment.
It has nothing to do with anyone around you. It is entirely your
decision.

Making a change in your life is as easy as making a decision and
acting on it. That's it.

Shortly after I got back to L.A., I decided at the last minute to
compete in the USJA Winter Championships. I didn't even bother
cutting weight. The morning of the tournament, I stepped on
the scale. Seventy-three kilos came the reading. I had expected
to blow past sixty-three kilos, but I had exceeded the weight
limit for seventy kilos, the division above mine. I competed at
seventy-eight kilos, a division thirty-three pounds heavier than
my typical division. I won anyway.

Little Jimmy just happened to be at the tournament as well.
I hadn't seen him since before I had left for the tournament in
Germany where Big Jim had kicked me out.

"Ronda," he said, giving me a big hug. "You looked great out
there."

"Thanks," I said, caught slightly off guard.

"It's been a while."

Yeah, maybe because you guys kicked me out, I thought. But
as much as I wanted to be angry, I was tired of being mad at
everyone.

"You've been doing really great," Jimmy said. "I've been following your wins."

"Thanks," I said.

"Things are really different back at the club," Jimmy said. "We've got a lot of good people training out there. We've got a house where all of the athletes are living. It's going really well. We would love to have you come back out and train with us."

A smile crossed my face. Sure it wasn't the groveling, tearful, we-made-a-huge-mistake apology I had played out in my head, but having Jimmy ask me to come back was pretty damn gratifying. I felt vindicated that I went out on my own and did better than I ever did with them.

"That would be cool," I said.

But I was also hesitant to return to Massachusetts.

My whole day revolved around eating or, more accurately, not eating. I was constantly thinking: *What is the most I can eat and not gain weight?* Often, the answer was "nothing." I tried everything to suppress my appetite: water, black coffee, sucking on ice. And the highlight of my day was what I ate. It wasn't that I had discipline issues or self-control issues or that I was a weak person. It was that I was so dissatisfied with my life that the best part of my day was what I ate. Things were looking up, but life wasn't completely better.

I had been battling bulimia since living at Big Jim's two years ago. I wouldn't have admitted it at the time or called it by its name, but I was struggling with the eating disorder.

When I moved up to competing in the senior division as a sixteen-year-old, I fought at sixty-three kilograms (138.9 pounds). Four years later, I was still fighting in the same weight class despite having grown from five-three to five-seven. But all I saw was the scale tipping ever heavier.

It got to the point where my actual weight was around 160 pounds, and I needed to cut twenty-two pounds ahead of competition. The toll of trying to take off that much weight that you don't have to lose was getting to me mentally and physically.

No matter how hard I trained, it was getting harder and harder to make weight. The idea of eating and then just throwing it all up is an unfortunately common approach to cutting and maintaining weight, especially among lighter-weight fighters and wrestlers.

My approach to making weight was a combination of deprivation and purging. Ahead of tournaments, I would go as long as a week without eating an actual meal. I was constantly tired, not only physically exhausted but sleepy. Thinking of eating consumed me. Other times, I ate, then forced myself to throw up. Even with these extreme measures, I struggled to make sixty-three kilograms.

I had been hiding this secret ever since I had left Big Jim's. I went through phases where I would try not to throw up, but eventually, it seemed like the easiest approach. I was just so hungry, and I backslid right into it again.

But this time around, it had been different. After I moved back home, I started seeing a guy named Bob. (His name wasn't really Bob, but my mom calls all of her daughters' boyfriends Bob. The only way a guy gets called by his real name is to marry into the family. "Why waste time learning his name if he's not going to be sticking around?" she says.)

One day I collapsed onto the couch beside Bob, starving and exhausted. We had never addressed my issues with eating, but he saw what was happening. He asked why I didn't stop dieting.

"It's not that easy," I said defensively.

"It's as easy as making up your mind and making a decision not to," he replied.

Then he told me the Bora Bora allegory and it was like a switch flipped on in my brain. I decided in that moment that I needed to stop forcing myself to throw up. The decision was the best possible move for my health, but when it came to cutting weight, things got worse. Without purging, my weight became even more unmanageable. But I was convinced I could make it work.

In January 2007, I returned to the Pedros. I moved into the athlete house and actually felt like I fit in. I was older and the group of athletes training in Massachusetts were more dedicated to the sport than Jason's crew. Everyone welcomed me, and Big Jim, whom I had only exchanged very brief hellos with when we crossed paths at tournaments, seemed glad to have me back in his own Big Jim way. There were seven of us living in the house, six of us doing judo—four guys and two girls—plus one of Mikey Pedro's friends. I had my own room, with an actual bed. I was moving up in the world.

One of my housemates, Rick Hawn, was working at Home Depot as part of a program where the company hired aspiring Olympians. I signed up and got myself a Home Depot job as well.

Bob and I were giving the long-distance thing a try. I had left my family on good terms. For the first time in a long time, everything was going great. I was happy.

At the end of January, I headed to Europe for another round of tournaments on the European circuit.

The first tournament was the British Open.

Weigh-ins at European circuit tournaments were chaos. Unlike at the Olympics or the world championship, where only one or two divisions fight a day, at other elite tournaments, everyone in every division fights on the same day. That means dozens of hungry girls from every division, wanting to weigh in at once. And there is no decorum. I was standing in an open room, filled with girls covering themselves with nothing but their passports. The athletes were waiting around, some preparing their post-weigh-in drinks and food, everyone just waiting for the weigh-in to officially start.

The female official in charge announced them open.

Every naked chick in the room ran toward the scale. It was just titties and passports everywhere.

The officials started grabbing passports out of the sea of athletes who were waving them in the air and began calling the names of their owners. Girls were pushing up against each other. Caught in the fray, I eventually pushed myself to the front.

I used to be really shy about being naked in public, but in situations like that, you lose any self-consciousness real quick. When you starve for a week, you're dehydrated as fuck, and the only thing standing between you and a bottle of water is a bunch of naked bitches, you will rub titties with any country in the world in order to get on the scale first.

I made weight, then chugged a bunch of water and Gatorade. The cold fluids gave me the chills, and later on I was still shivering under a blanket at the venue with my teammate Justin Flores.

Justin ran a couple of sprints up and down the mat, trying to get warm. Suddenly, he turned and ran through a side door leading outside.

"What happened to you?" I asked when he returned.

"I puked everywhere," he said. "But I feel a little better. What about you?"

Throwing up after a weigh-in is common, as athletes who have been fasting for days eat or drink too much too quickly. But I never threw up after weigh-ins.

"I'm fine. I'm fine," I told him, my body still shaking.

"Well, you look like shit," he said with a grin.

I felt like shit. But the officials were calling my name, so I pushed everything else aside. I won my first three matches. There was supposed to be a break before the semifinals. *Thank God*, I thought. *I just need a little time to recover.* But when I looked at the schedule, I saw that one semifinal had moved up before the break: mine. "Motherfuckers!"

My next opponent was reigning European champion Sarah Clark from Great Britain. It was no secret that cutting weight was killing me and that making weight for this tournament had been especially rough. The British Open tournament organizers saw an opportunity to give their girl an edge.

Halfway through the semifinal match, we tumbled to the mat. I landed on my stomach and Clark landed on top of me. I felt like someone had jumped on my stomach. Before I could even clench my jaw, I threw up on the mat. I was afraid that I'd be disqualified, which is what happens if you puke on the mat. But I was lying facedown in my own vomit with my arms crossed, and I managed to wipe it up before anyone saw.

The match came down to golden score (sudden death), when I pulled out the win. I walked off the mat, and Justin reached out to give me a hug.

"I had no idea you were so amazing," he said as he pulled me toward him.

He wrinkled his nose, adding, "And you smell like vomit."

"Yeah, I threw up," I said, sheepishly.

I won my next match and the tournament, but I couldn't enjoy the win because I was already dreading making weight at the Belgian Open the following week.

Over the next several days, I ran the equivalent of several marathons while wearing plastic sweats, which increase sweating. I starved and dehydrated myself. I sat in the sauna watching flames jump off the heated rocks. I ran out of the sauna to escape the fire, only to learn it was a heatstroke-induced hallucination.

I made weight in Belgium, but didn't even place in the tournament. My body was breaking down, but I refused to cave.

The Super World Cup in Paris was the following week. It was the circuit's biggest tournament. When I arrived in Paris a few days before, I hadn't eaten an actual meal in a week. I hadn't had more than a few sips of water in days. I stepped on the scale to see what I weighed. I was 66.6 kilograms. I stared at the number, devastated.

I went upstairs to turn on the hot water in my bathtub to try to sweat it out, and the whole hotel had run out of hot water because all the tournament athletes were there cutting weight.

I found a gym with a sauna and sat on the top level, as close to the heater as possible, my head against the wood-paneled wall. I could smell my hair burning, but I wasn't sweating.

I gave up. I called Jimmy Pedro back at home.

"I can't do it," I said over and over. "I can't make the weight."

"No, you're going to make weight," he said. "You need to do this. Get back in there. You need to do it again."

It was the only time in my entire career that I said I couldn't make weight. I had never even admitted to the struggles I was going through in the process. I finally brought myself to have the courage to say something and got shot down.

Fuck it, I thought. *There's no way I can drop over three and a half kilos.*

I ate all the snacks—fruit, trail mix, granola bars—that I had been saving for after the weigh-in. Then I went and met up with Bob, who had flown out to Europe to watch me compete. He was staying in a Parisian apartment, and had bought some groceries, and I made myself a cheese sandwich, skipping weigh-ins and the tournament. But I was already looking ahead and couldn't even enjoy the meal. I was ashamed and embarrassed for failing, but I believed if I won the next tournament in Austria all would be forgiven.

I arrived in Linz in the afternoon. Linz had been host to the annual Austrian World Cup tournament for decades; my mom had competed here. I checked into the hotel. I had less than twenty-four hours to lose nearly ten pounds and be ready to compete.

In judo, you make all your own arrangements and travel alone with no coach, putting up the money yourself, as you circle the globe representing the United States. Sometimes, USA Judo would reimburse you months later, sometimes they wouldn't. I booked my room at the hotel that had been the tournament hotel in years past.

I arrived in Linz and got to my hotel early. I pushed through the glass doors and surveyed the lobby for other team sweats, duffle bags featuring national flags, other athletes. The reception area was largely empty.

Great, maybe I can get an early check-in, I thought.

The desk clerk motioned me to the counter. "Hallo, welcome to Linz," she said in a thick Austrian accent, pronouncing her *w*'s as *v*'s.

"Thank you," I said. "I have a reservation for Rousey."

She typed something into the computer.

"Yes, we have you staying with us for six days," she said.

"Yeah, I'm here for the tournament," I said.

"That's nice," she said in a tone that made it clear she had no idea what I was talking about.

Well, not everyone is a sports fan, I thought to myself.

She handed me my room key.

"Is there a shuttle?" I asked.

"A shuttle?" Now she looked confused.

"Yeah, usually, there's like a shuttle to take you to the tournament."

"I'm not sure what you mean," she said.

"Um, OK, well, maybe there's someone else you could ask." Clearly there was some kind of language barrier. I had not eaten anything in nearly forty-eight hours and my patience was wearing thin.

"Of course," she said with a smile. She turned to the other reception clerk. Their brief conversation in German ended when her coworker gave the internationally recognizable "I have no clue what you are talking about" shrug.

"I'm sorry," the receptionist said to me. "I do not know about this tournament."

I had a sinking feeling in the pit of my stomach. Something was not right.

She handed me my room key.

"We hope you enjoy your stay with us," she said cheerfully while eyeing me like I was mentally unstable.

Up in my room, I dropped my duffle on the floor, pulled out my laptop, and Googled: Austria World Cup. Nothing but soccer sites.

I typed in: Austria World Cup judo. I clicked on one of the pages, reading as it loaded. The tournament was being held in Vienna.

"Fuuuuuuuuuuck!" I screamed at the top of my lungs.

I started bawling and called my mom.

Her voice was groggy. I had woken her up but even then her mind was a steel trap—she had just happened to read that there was no one competing for the United States in the division up from mine that weekend.

"Here is what you are going to do," she said. "You are going to call up Valerie Gotay. [Valerie was at the tournament and competing in the women's lightweight division.] You are going to tell Valerie to go to the coach's meeting tonight and move you up to seventy kilos. Linz is not that far from Vienna. You are going to go to the airport in the morning and get a ticket. You will go to the tournament, and everything will be fine."

"But they'll all be bigger than me," I said, still crying.

"Well, no, apparently, they'll all be seventy kilos, which is what you are now," my mom said.

I didn't know what to say.

"You might feel like this is a terrible thing, but this isn't the worst thing that could happen," my mom continued. "You've been in the top ten at sixty-three kilos for years, so all these girls are training for you. Nobody at seventy kilos is expecting you. Just go out and fight. There are no expectations."

Her logic was calming.

"And get something to eat because you've been trying to kill yourself making weight," she added.

I got off the phone and ate the entire minibar. It was delicious.

Suddenly all the pressure disappeared. I had spent so much time feeling guilty, like I had let everyone down, like I had failed. Now, I realized that I had always had the option of making a change. It was just up to me to make that decision.

The next morning, I ate breakfast, flew to Vienna, and headed to the venue. I made weight and won the tournament. It was one of the best tournaments I ever fought.

I stepped on the mat and was only seconds into my first match when I realized, *These girls are not any stronger than I am.* They were fifteen pounds heavier than the girls I had been fighting, but not any stronger. It was only then that I understood how much I had weakened myself at that lower weight.

What was more, for the first time in as long as I could remember, I was enjoying myself. I realized that the making weight part of competition had become the whole tournament for me. Once that wasn't an issue anymore, my focus was just on competing and having fun. I actually had a lot of fun the day I won the Austria World Cup. I had no expectations for myself, or for anybody else. I didn't feel like I had to live up to anything. I just had to do as well as I could do.

I used to say all the time, "Changing things is not that easy."

But it is just as easy as making up your mind. You can always make a decision. And if that decision doesn't work, you can make another decision.

WHEN DO YOU CROSS THE MAGICAL BOUNDARY THAT STOPS YOU FROM DREAMING BIG?

As kids we're taught to dream big and to think everything is possible: Win the Olympics. Be president. And then you grow up.

People talk about how I'm so arrogant. They don't realize how much work went into getting where I am. I worked so hard to be able to think highly of myself. When people say, "Oh, you're so cocky. You're so arrogant," I feel like they're telling me that I think too highly of myself. My question for them is: "Who are you to tell me that I need to think less of myself?"

People want to project their own insecurities on others, but I refuse to allow them to put that on me. Just because you don't think that you could be the best in the world doesn't mean that I shouldn't have the confidence to believe I can do anything.

When I got back from Vienna, I was happy. I wasn't starving myself anymore. I was winning tournaments. I had a wonderful boyfriend. I lived in a house with a bunch of people I liked. And while practices were grueling, sometimes they were even fun.

I looked forward to Thursday practice all week, then when Thursday actually came, I counted the hours down until training. Since retiring from competition, Little Jimmy was around the club less, and on Thursdays, Big Jim worked at the fire station, so Rick Hawn ran the senior practice. One Thursday, Rick suggested we do a round of no gi grappling (matwork without a gi jacket to grip on to) at the end. It was the most fun any of us ever had at practice. From that practice on, we only did no gi grappling on Thursdays. We would get to the gym, Rick would turn on music, and the dozen or so of us at practice that night would just grapple. Big Jim knew we were doing no gi on Thursdays, but a lot of the stuff we were doing translated over to competition, so as long as we were working out, he didn't care.

Afterward, we would go to Chili's. Having just turned twenty-one, I always ordered a strawberry margarita and sipped it slowly, enjoying the sweet cool drink and the camaraderie.

We had just gotten back from Europe when a guy from Pedros' invited us over to watch a fight at his house. There had been a big MMA event on Showtime that he had recorded while we were gone. We occasionally all got together to watch fights at people's houses and just unwind. There was beer and pizza, and I helped myself to a slice. We piled into the living room as the fight was cued up. It had taken place on February 10, the same day I missed weight in Paris. I was not that into MMA, but my judo teammates loved it. It was all guys except for me and my housemate Asma Sharif. We were laughing and relaxed.

The undercard fights were on. They were fun to watch, but unmemorable. Then Gina Carano and Julie Kedzie entered the cage. I was stunned; I didn't even know women fought in MMA.

When the fight came on, the entire room went quiet. I leaned in toward the TV. It was an all-out brawl. The house was going wild. I watched their every move. I kept seeing all the mistakes the girls were making, all their lost opportunities, and I knew, even then, even though I had never done MMA, that I could beat both of them.

But what stuck with me even more than the girls' performance that night was the way the guys in my house reacted to it. They were in awe. The girls were beautiful, yes, but the guys didn't talk about them like they did the ring girls—the girls in bikinis holding up cards that say the round number—who they talked about as if they were strippers. When the guys were talking about the female fighters, they talked about their physical appearance with a level of admiration. The look I saw on their faces was respect. I had never gotten that kind of reaction from these guys, guys whom I trained with and sweated with every single day.

Gina Carano won the fight in three rounds by unanimous decision and by the end of the fight, every guy in the room was talking about what badasses these girls were. And they were awesome, but I was also convinced that I could beat the crap out of both of them.

I didn't dare say that out loud. I knew everyone would laugh at me. So I kept it inside.

I was training for the Beijing Olympics. I still wasn't over my loss in Athens, this time I was going to take home the gold. Training was the focus of my every waking moment. So, when thoughts of MMA popped into my head, I just pushed them out.

Then, one morning in the spring of 2007, I was walking to Home Depot in Wakefield, Massachusetts. Usually I'd grab a ride with Rick, but when our shifts didn't overlap, I made the mile-and-a-half walk listening to pop music. Trees were starting to sprout leaves, but the New England winter hadn't fully given way. Even though the sun was out, the air was brisk. I pulled the hood of my sweatshirt over my head. I carried the store's signature bright orange apron in my hand, unwilling to put it on until I absolutely had to. Walking under the I-95 overpass, I bobbed my head to "Peanut Butter Jelly Time." I envisioned the dancing banana from the YouTube video, and without realizing it I started choreographing my MMA victory dance as "It's Peanut Butter Jelly Time. Peanut Butter Jelly Time" thumped through my headphones. My celebratory shuffle wasn't all that different from the banana's pixelated shimmy. "Where ya at? Where ya at?"

Cars zoomed above me and I walked faster to the beat. It felt good. In judo, you could never do a victory dance, just a proper little bow. God forbid you do a fist pump after you win. A victory dance would have given the entire arena a coronary. But MMA was different. MMA seemed like the kind of sport that would appreciate a good victory dance.

I imagined fighting, winning, and being embraced by my cornermen.

I tried again to push it out of my head. It was a ridiculous fantasy. I redirected my thoughts to something more practical, winning the Olympics. I focused on standing atop the podium, a gold medal around my neck.

I imagined the American flag being raised, the sound of "The Star Spangled Banner" echoing through the stadium. But as I summoned the sounds of imaginary cymbals smashing out "And the home of the brave," I couldn't help but give one shimmy to the sounds of "Where ya at? Where ya at?" actually coming out of my headphones.

I gave up trying to fight it, and let my mind drift back to standing in the center of the Octagon, my hand raised as the crowd cheered around me. I imagined my teammates watching me on TV, cheering me on through the screen.

If you can't dream big, ridiculous dreams, what's the point in dreaming at all?

PEOPLE APPRECIATE EXCELLENCE NO MATTER WHO YOU ARE

I have been booed in thirty countries. I have been booed following UFC victories. I'm more used to being booed by a crowd than I am being cheered. I have never been a fan favorite. Pretty much my entire competitive career has been defined by people hoping to see me lose.

In the UFC, I've embraced the role of the villain. I don't shy away from controversy. I don't hold back when it comes to speaking my mind. That doesn't always endear me to the masses. In a world that loves to root for the underdog, I'm always the favorite—and I always win.

But there are moments where no matter who you are or what you represent, people will be so impressed by what they see that they will forget everything else. If the performance is great enough, nothing else matters.

My mom says that to be the best in the world, you need to be able to beat anyone twice on your worst day. She's right, of course. But some days you wake up and you just know no one is going to fuck with you. That's how I woke up in Rio de Janeiro the morning of the 2007 World Championships. I woke up ready to kill somebody.

We had arrived in Rio a few days before, checking into El Motel—the Brazilian equivalent of Super 8. Some of my teammates were complaining about the rooms, but I didn't need anything too fancy and, unlike at most tournaments, USA Judo was at least paying for my room.

The day of competition I got up early so I could take the first shuttle to the weigh-in. I checked myself on my scale: seventy kilos on the dot. I was close, but was going to make weight without issue. On my way down to the lobby, I ran into Valerie Gotay. Valerie was lighter than me and had already fought.

"Did you hear what happened?" she asked.

I had no idea what she was talking about.

"Some guy at sixty-six kilos was running last night to make weight and he got stabbed," she said.

"Oh shit," I replied.

"Speaking of which, I'm heading out," I said.

"You know about the scale, right?" she asked.

My eyes narrowed.

"No, what?" These words right before a weigh-in are never followed by good news.

"The ones we have are light," she said, meaning the US teams' scales were giving a reading that was less than one's actual weight. The official scale was .4 kilos heavier, meaning I was nearly a pound overweight. If you step on the scale at the weigh-ins and miss weight, you can't compete. You don't get a second chance.

"You have got to be fucking kidding me!" I shouted, throwing my bag on the hallway floor. Several heads in the lobby turned.

I started to head back to my room.

"Where are you going?" Valerie asked.

"To my room!" I shouted over my shoulder. "It looks like I'm running to the weigh-ins, incompetent USA Judo motherfuckers."

I stormed into my room and pulled on my plastics, a pair of sweats made out of thin plastic. The suit prevents sweat from evaporating, keeping your body warm and making you sweat more. Then I layered my regular sweats over and pulled up my hood and headed back through the lobby, past the shuttle bus waiting to take the athletes to the weigh-in, and started running the mile to the tournament host hotel for the weigh-in.

It was September in Rio, and the sun was already beating down. Sweat dripped down my face. I could feel the hot condensation building up on my skin inside my plastics. I was running fast, when it dawned on me this was the exact stretch of road where the sixty-six kilo guy had been stabbed the night before.

If anyone tries to stab me today, they are gonna die, I thought. I was not in the mood to take shit from anyone.

I had turned a corner when I saw a sign for the host hotel and a sprawling nine-star resort spread out behind it.

"No fucking way," I said out loud.

This was the hotel where the USA Judo executives had booked themselves. I ran up the long manicured drive to the lobby doors. A burst of cool air hit me in the face as the bellman pulled the door open. The weigh-in room was not yet open, but there was a scale in a room across the lobby where athletes could check their weight. I walked in and pulled off my sweats and wet plastics. I stepped on the scale. 70.2.

I growled. There is no worse physical sensation than putting on plastics again after you have already sweated in them. It is like pulling on a wet garbage bag, only it's not dripping with water, it's dripping with sweat and it sticks to your skin. I pulled my sweats over my plastics, headed back outside into the beating hot tropical sun and ran down Shank Road again, then I stormed back inside.

As I walked back through the lobby, I saw the Japanese girl in my division coming out of the elevator. The Japanese team was staying here at the Hotel Deluxe Riviera Ritz. She was walking with two coaches, who had undoubtedly watched hours of her opponents' footage, which they were likely discussing with her at that exact moment. She was wearing her sponsored designer sweats with her matching sponsored designer bag. But what pushed me over the fucking edge was that she was carrying a little tea kettle with a matching sponsored designer tea kettle warmer slipped over it.

I about lost my mind.

USA Judo had barely provided us matching sweats, so I sure as shit didn't have a matching tea kettle warmer, and even if I had, I wouldn't have it with me because it would have been back at El Motel and I would have to run back along Shank Road to go get the goddamn thing. The hairs on the back of my neck were standing up as every muscle in my body tensed. I caught myself grinding my teeth. My fists were balled up so tightly that my nails were digging into my palms.

You're my first match, I said to her in my head. *I'll deal with you then.*

At the unofficial scale, I peeled off my plastics for a second time: seventy kilos. Now I had to go weigh in across the lobby. I looked at my pile of sweats on the floor. There was no way I was putting them back on. I wrapped myself in a towel and marched into the lobby. It was filled with athletes, tournament officials, coaches, referees, a few tourists. All heads turned as I passed by. I held my towel with one hand and looked straight ahead. If I could have walked through there with my middle finger up in the air and not have risked getting in trouble for violating some tournament rules of conduct, I would have.

I walked into the room where the official weigh-ins were underway. Because it was the world championships, the organizers had everyone lined up. I was near the end of the line. I stared down each girl who walked by on her way out the door after making weight, making a mental note to destroy her when the tournament began. Finally, it was my turn. I weighed in, got some water, took the shuttle back to the hotel to get my things for the tournament and got ready to make these bitches pay.

A favorite joke in judo circles is the Americans always have the worst draw, because it's better to have an easy fight first and get warmed up. People always laugh when an American draws a Japanese in the first round. Judo started in Japan, and the Japanese take judo very seriously. It is not that hard to be the best in the United States in judo. To be the best in Japan, you have to be solid. Japan almost always dominates. The draw is posted at the coaches' meeting the night before the tournament starts. Some people will map out their entire potential pool. I just took it one match at a time, never looking ahead to see who I might face.

Gonna have to beat 'em all anyway, I figured.

My match against the Japanese girl was early, so the stadium was only about a quarter filled. Still, I could hear the Japanese cheering section in full effect. Their cheer coordinator shouted something out, and as always, the Japanese fans returned the cheer. I never let the crowd impact me, but the crowd often influences the referees. I always made a point to gauge the atmosphere in order to know what the referees might be thinking, then I tuned the noise out.

I stared across the mat at her.

Fuck your tea kettle warmer, I thought.

I made the match a brawl, which is the worst possible matchup for a Japanese fighter. They're very traditional and focused on proper technique. I was hustling on the ground, spinning her off balance, throwing her all over the place.

I wiped the mat with her, throwing her twice and winning by a *waza-ari* (half-point) and a *yuko* (roughly a quarter-point). She was scoreless.

Next, I had Ylenia Scapin, a two-time Olympic medalist from Italy. We had never met before, so I didn't know what to expect. The second you grab someone you feel the strength on them; it was immediately apparent that she was the strongest chick I had ever faced. Strong fighters present a different set of challenges. It's much harder to break grips against them. Their defense is a lot better.

Offensively, I wasn't really scared of Scapin, but she was harder to grip with and harder to throw. Being strong doesn't necessarily make an opponent more threatening, but it makes them more difficult to control.

I threw her for a waza-ari in the first minute of the match. She couldn't score on me either.

Then, I had Mayra Aguiar from Brazil, the hometown favorite in the quarterfinal. The arena had been steadily filling up and was now closing in on three-quarters full. In contrast to the Japanese fans with their cheer coordinator, the Brazilian fans were the complete opposite. Unadulterated pandemonium. The Brazilians were the craziest, most passionate crowd I had ever experienced. They were blaring blow horns and flying flags. One section was covered by a massive Brazilian flag the fans were holding up.

They booed me as I walked onto the mat, chanting "You're gonna die" in Portuguese. I noted the noise, assessing the impact it might have on the referees. I was going to have to win more definitively. Up against the roar of the crowd, I took her to the mat and pinned her for ippon with thirty seconds left on the clock. The Brazilian fans booed me viciously as I walked off the mat.

I had made it to the semifinal. It would be a matchup between me and Edith Bosch, the reigning world champion. She was a six-foot Dutch chick with an eight-pack. I looked like a hobbit next to her.

Bosch and I had fought for the first time at the German Open a month earlier. I was declared the winner of the match when she was disqualified for doing an illegal armbar on me. She had dislocated my elbow in the process.

If I had a nemesis during my time competing at seventy kilos, it was Edith Bosch. You know how in movies where the hero fights off like five guys and is taunting "Is that all you got?" then turns around to find himself eyeball to belly button with a giant? Edith Bosch is that giant.

I knew Bosch would be happy with the matchup. She thought she got an easy draw. I wanted to make sure this would be the last time she was ever glad about having to face me.

The referee said, "*Hajime*" (begin). And what does Bosch do? The exact same move that got her disqualified in Germany *again*. And *again*, she dislocated my elbow. Only this time, the referee didn't see it.

I glanced at my limp elbow, then back at Bosch with a look that said, *Are you fucking kidding me?* I could not believe she had pulled this shit again. I could not believe she was going to get away with it. I looked back to the referee. Nothing.

I wanted to scream. But arguing was pointless. A shooting pain quickly brought me back into the moment. I had never forfeited a match in my life, and I sure as hell wasn't going to quit in the semifinal of the world championship.

I braced myself. I tensed my left arm and took a deep breath. With my right hand, I grabbed my forearm just below the dislocated elbow and pushed as hard as I could. *Pop.* The joint snapped back into place. The manipulation hurt like a bitch, but as soon as my elbow was back where it belonged, the sharp pain dulled to a barely tolerable ache.

I glared across the mat at Bosch. She showed absolutely no remorse, which only made me angrier. Looking straight at her, I shook out my arm, and thought, *Fuck you, bitch, I'm going to keep going.*

Bosch scored on me about halfway through a five-minute match, putting me behind. She tried to avoid any contact with me over the next two minutes, hoping to stall long enough to run out the clock. Her plan was working.

There were thirty seconds left. I said like nineteen million prayers. I looked up toward the rafters and had what felt like an incredibly long conversation with God.

"Please, God, help me," I pleaded. "Please help me figure this out, this one match."

The clock was ticking down.

29 seconds. *Please God.* I went in for a grip.

28. *Please God.* Bosch pushed me off.

27. *Please God.* I went in to grab her again.

26. *Please God.* Bosch moved like she was going to attempt to throw me.

25. *Please God.* She did not have a chance in hell of throwing me.

24. *Please God.* I made my move. I timed it perfectly.

23. *Please God.* I grabbed Bosch, one-handed with the arm of the elbow she had dislocated.

22. *Please God.* I turned, the leverage pulling Bosch off the ground and over my head. She went sailing through the air, in front of God and everyone.

21. *Please God.* Bam! She landed on the ground on her back for ippon. I had won instantly.

20. *Thank you, God!*

Bosch lay facedown on the mat for a moment, as if she could not believe she had lost.

The place exploded. The entire arena had been watching our fight, and everyone in the building lost their minds after seeing my David-and-Goliath moment. The whole crowd erupted, cheering for me.

The applause had nothing to do with who I was or where I was from. In that moment, they didn't care—they had seen something amazing happen.

My match against Bosch was the only time I got cheered for in judo. It was the most exciting moment of my judo career, but the elation was shortlived as I tried to block out my throbbing elbow and my focus immediately shifted to the final.

I faced Gévrise Émane of France in the championship and got called for a bullshit penalty in the first minute, which put me immediately behind. She scored on me a few seconds later with a throw that was questionable at best as far as whether it was a legitimate scoring takedown. I scored on a throw halfway through the match, bringing me within a minor score of tying the match—that is until the referees conferred and reversed the decision giving the score to my opponent. Firmly ahead on points, she spent the rest of the match running from me. She got a stalling penalty with less than a minute to go, then sprinted away from me in the final seconds of the match.

The world championship had slipped through my fingers. Every time I closed my eyes, even to blink, I saw Émane throwing her arms in the air in jubilation. I had no one to blame but myself. I had let it come down to points. I had failed. It hurt to breathe.

After the competition had ended for the day, I walked up into the stands where the crowd had been cheering for me so loudly hours before. I had to call my mom back home, but I couldn't do it yet. Making that call would require finding the strength to say: I lost. My gut twisted. I climbed to the very top of the seats. The arena was nearly empty. I settled myself at the end of a row of seats, up against a corner, pulled my knees up to my chest, and cried harder than I ever had since Dad died.

A LOSS IS STILL A LOSS,
BUT IT'S BETTER TO GO OUT
IN FLAMING GLORY

I've always gone for the finish, giving my all until the very end. The idea of losing while playing it safe is appalling to me. I just can't stand the idea of not leaving everything out there. I would rather take a big risk and throw a Hail Mary, hoping it will work, instead of playing it safe in those last few seconds and losing the decision. I wouldn't be able to live with the regret that would come from wishing that I'd tried something crazy at the end instead. I don't gamble on the hope that maybe it could go my way with the judges. I throw everything on the line while it's still in my hands.

I will never be OK with losing, but losing in the wrong way, losing with regret, can take your pride away. I've never chosen to lose that way.

After Rio, all of my energies shifted toward Beijing. The Olympics were less than a year away. When I wasn't training for the Games, I was thinking about them. I knew there wasn't a single person in my division that I could not beat, but some competitors would be tougher than others. Bosch would be among them. Cuban players always posed a challenge. The Cuban team was deep, so I wouldn't know who I was facing until their Olympic team was announced, but each one of their girls at seventy kilos was amazing. Collectively, the team was known for diving at your legs repeatedly to attempt a takedown. Their strengths played to my weaknesses. I dedicated myself to eradicating any area of vulnerability.

From the moment I stepped off the mat in Athens, I had been driven by a singular goal: Win the Olympics. It consumed me.

A lot had changed since my Olympic debut. Heading into Athens in 2004, I had about four months to prepare mentally and physically. Back then, I was largely unknown on the international scene. I had been considered a dark horse to make the team up until I won the senior nationals that April and I was coming off of knee surgery. By contrast, I spent four years preparing for Beijing. One of the top five in the world in my division, I was no longer under the radar. I had built up an impressive résumé of international wins, compiling a record rivaled by only one other woman in the history of US judo: my mother.

In 2004, the question people were asking was "Can Ronda win the Olympic Trials?" In 2008, the question became "Can Ronda win the Olympics?" No American woman had even medaled in the Olympics since judo became an official sport in 1992. I was America's best chance.

The first thing I noticed when we stepped out of the airport in China was the smog. The air felt thicker as you inhaled it, and at the end of the day, it was as if you could feel an invisible layer of grime on your skin. The heat made it worse.

Every stadium and every building was state-of-the-art. In Athens, it was obvious they got to a point where they had to cut corners. A dirt patch where a garden would have been. A half-dug trench originally mapped out as an artificial river. The Olympic Village at Beijing was pristine. There wasn't a flower petal out of place. The athlete dorms were imposing yet inviting high-rises that resembled luxury apartments.

At times, it seemed almost too perfect, artificial. If you walked through the city and glanced behind large billboards constructed in odd locations, you would catch glimpses of abandoned, trash-filled lots hidden behind brightly decorated facades.

The Opening Ceremonies were hot and humid, and the US Olympic Committee decided to outfit us in blazers, long-sleeved button-up shirts, pants, newsboy caps, and ascots. When my teammates and I tried to take our scarves off, a Team USA official reprimanded us.

"Put them back on, Ralph Lauren is watching," she hissed as if we were small children in trouble.

"Seriously, though, did he not know that we were going to be wearing these outfits in China in the summer when he designed these?" I asked.

She shot me a dirty look. I really didn't care. I wasn't there to win friends or fashion accolades. I was there to win Olympic gold.

My opening match I faced a girl from Turkmenistan. I had never heard of her, but that can be dangerous. We stood in line with our coaches and basket holders, and Israel Hernández, the only member of the USA Judo coaching staff that I had any respect for, turned to me.

"*Todo es fé*, Ronda." My Spanish is limited, but I heard him say this a lot: Faith is everything.

"I know," I said.

I threw her in the opening seconds of the match, then pinned her to win by ippon in a little over a minute. I was just getting warmed up.

Next round, I had Katarzyna Pilocik from Poland. I was not going to let her get in my way.

Two minutes into the match, she came in for a throw, but quickly dropped to her knees in an effort to prevent me from countering her attack. I saw my opening and jumped on top of her so she was on all fours on the mat with me on her back. I reached down to grab her left arm. Knowing what was coming, she pulled her arm in, clinging to it.

I rolled, flipping her onto her back. She struggled, trying to get up and break free, but I was not letting go. She turned her torso, so her face was against the mat. She tried to stand up. I shoved my leg across her chest. She twisted, but I held on. She made another attempt to escape, but I pushed her leg out of the way, rolling her again onto her back. Sensing the end was near, she tried to lock her hands together. With one leg across her neck and the other across her chest, I pulled on her left arm. Her hands started to slip apart. I pulled harder. Her hands broke apart. I threw my body backward, her arm between my legs and started to arch my back. She tapped quickly.

I was headed to the quarterfinal.

I walked off the mat to check the bracket for my next opponent. The name was written in block lettering: Edith Bosch.

It had been eleven months since our world championship showdown in Rio.

And so we meet again, I thought to myself in my best James Bond villain voice.

The referee had barely finished saying "Hajime" when Bosch grabbed me by the collar and straight up punched me in the face. It stung, but I know how to take a hit. She was pretending like she was going for a grip, but she launched a straight jab at my face. Then she punched me in the face again. And she punched me in the face again. The referees didn't care. They let it go. She came in again and I grabbed her hand, pushing it away from my head. Our match was under way. Over the next five minutes, I gave it all I had. I went after Bosch relentlessly.

After a scoreless regulation, we went to golden score, a five-minute overtime where any score wins the match. If no one wins in golden score, it goes to a judges' decision.

There was a minute and some change left on the clock. The match was close. And I didn't trust the referees to give me the fight. In the back of my mind I could hear Mom saying, "If it goes to decision, you deserve to lose because you put it in somebody else's hands."

There was time for one or two more exchanges before time ran out. I went in for an attack. Bosch got away. I went in again, this time attempting a throw.

Bosch tried to counter.

We tumbled to the mat.

The crowd roared. For a moment, I thought it had gone my way. Then the referee called a score for Bosch. We bowed out and turned to walk off the mat. She pumped her fist victoriously. I took a few steps, willing my legs to support my weight. I reached the edge of the mat and paused, not certain I could go on. Israel stretched out his arms. I stepped off the mat and collapsed into him.

I went back to the warm-up room and sobbed, hot tears running down my face. I felt like my heart had been ripped out of my chest. Then something clicked and I went from devastated to fucking furious. It was as if all the cells in my body had realigned—everything changed.

I decided I was not leaving that motherfucking arena empty-handed.

I battled my way back through the repechage bracket. My first opponent was from Algeria. She had lost to Bosch on points in regulation. I wasn't going to let our match get that far. I threw her in the opening minute, scoring a yuko, which is a partial score. I was ahead, but I wasn't content. I was out there to win. Thirty seconds later, I took her to the mat and pinned her. She writhed trying to escape, but I had her flat on her back. She kicked her legs a few more times, then she stopped. For the next five seconds, she just lay there pinned, accepting the loss before it was called. Then the referee called it: Ippon. The win did not soothe the pain of losing to Bosch, but it did force me to focus.

My next match was the semifinal for the bronze medal. I threw this Hungarian chick so hard that I bruised every single knuckle on my hand. I threw her so hard that my mom heard her land from across the arena. I didn't just want to get an ippon, I wanted her to hurt. I wanted her to hurt as much as losing the gold medal had hurt me.

Only one more person stood between me and the bronze medal, Germany's Annett Böhm. Böhm had taken bronze in Athens and unquestionably wanted to medal again. This match was going to end one of two ways: with me on the podium or dead on the mat. Walking on to the floor, I was like an evil robot, programmed to destroy. I locked in on Böhm. The referee said, "Hajime." Böhm and I were familiar enough with each other from various European and international tournaments and training camps that we didn't need to go through the get-to-know-you dance that can start off a match. We got right into it.

Thirty-four seconds into the match, I tossed Böhm over my

hip for a yuko. It should have been at least a waza-ari, I was up, but the match was far from over. If there was ever a time to be a points fighter, this was it. There were four minutes and twenty-six seconds standing between me and my medal, and all I needed to do was skip around the mat, making half-ass throw attempts before dropping to my knees. But getting ahead by a small margin and trying to protect that lead is totally against everything that I've ever done. I had lost a piece of my soul en route to this medal, but I wasn't going to sell my soul to get it. For the next four minutes and twenty seconds, I was as relentless and aggressive as I had been in the opening seconds. I held my lead on my terms. Then, with seven seconds left, the referee called for us to break. I glanced at the clock. I did the calculation in my head. If I dropped to my knees and took the penalty, I could run enough time off the clock to guarantee my win. If I engaged, there was a chance that Böhm could catch me with a last-ditch effort. The referee signaled us to resume.

I ran.

I may not believe in hiding behind the rules as an entire fight strategy, but I also don't condone being dumb. With three seconds left, I got called for a stalling penalty. Then time expired.

The timer buzzed. A wave of joy and relief came over me. I fell to my knees. And suddenly the arena rushed back in. I could hear the crowd roar. A chant of "USA! USA!" rose in the stands from about eleven people, but it was still deafening to me. The arena seemed brighter, as if someone had turned up the lights in the venue.

The referee raised her right hand in my direction. Böhm and I shook hands. As my opponent walked off the mat, I raised my hands victoriously, then bent down and kissed the mat. I ran off the mat and jumped joyously into Israel's arms.

I looked to the stands for my mother and found her across the arena waving an American flag. It was so big she could barely hold it open.

After thirteen years, the American flag that had been placed on Dad's coffin at his funeral had been unfurled and was fluttering in the arms of my mother.

My dad had always believed I would shine on the world's biggest stage. And for one moment, seeing Mom holding that flag, I felt like we were all together.

I had not won a gold medal, but there was a sense of accomplishment I would have never believed could come from third place. Of all the third-place finishes in my career, the bronze in the Olympics was the only one I took any satisfaction in.

But still, there was a void. I had not won the gold I had dreamed of.

That Olympic loss still eats at me. It will follow me forever. But, I'm not ashamed of how I lost. I don't wonder about what I could have done differently. I have no regrets about the match. I had to do a haymaker at the end. I made the right decision. It's just sometimes even the right decisions don't work out.

THIS IS MY SITUATION,
BUT THIS ISN'T MY LIFE

When you're in the middle of the hustle, there are going to be times when your life is complete shit and you've got absolutely nothing to show for the effort you've put in. I don't just mean tough times, but the moments when you have to swallow your pride and check your ego. I'm talking about the kind of times where, if it were happening to someone else, you would silently be thanking God that it wasn't happening to you. There were times when I knew that I was in a terrible situation, but I also knew that it wouldn't last forever. Those are the moments when you have to remind yourself that this experience is a defining moment in your life, but you are not defined by it.

I stood on the medal stand and watched as the American flag was raised into the third-place position. The Olympics were over for me, but I was not over the Olympics.

The day after I won my medal, I was sitting in my room in the athlete village. It was late morning and I was just sitting on the bed, when my heart started beating fast out of nowhere. I couldn't catch my breath. I was overcome with guilt and anxiety, but I couldn't figure out why. I felt like I had done something terrible, but I couldn't remember what it was. The wave of panic passed, but I couldn't shake the feeling that something had gone very wrong, that I was an asshole.

I got back from Beijing with a bronze medal and no home, no job, no prospects. I quickly learned I had no boyfriend either.

Bob and I took a break before the Olympics. It was his idea, and came completely out of left field. He said the long-distance thing wasn't working out and we would pick up where we left off when I moved back to L.A. after the Olympics. I was devastated. When I got back home I called him and he told me he and his girlfriend had been cheering for me. I felt like the wind had been knocked out of me.

It felt incredibly unfair.

I had gotten $10,000 from the US Olympic Committee for earning a bronze medal, which came out to roughly $6,000 after taxes. I used all of my Olympics money to buy a used, gold, four-door Honda Accord, and I still had to finance half of it. I was crashing at my mom's house while I looked for a job.

I finally found a bartending job working at a pirate-themed bar called The Redwood. It was something, but before I'd made it through my first two weeks I was on thin ice. I had been late one day, so my shifts had been cut for the week. Then the manager asked me to come in that weekend. The message was clear: If you don't, you're fired.

I had promised the guy who ran the judo club in Baldwin Park, the club where I first started judo, that I would grand marshal a local parade. He was a friend of my mother's and had wrangled me into doing it.

I didn't want to get fired, especially over a parade I hadn't really wanted to do in the first place. I told my manager I would be there. I told the parade people nothing. Every time their number came up on my phone, I sent it straight to voicemail. I was hoping they would give up. Then, Blinky Elizalde, my first judo coach, called. I explained the situation to him. He understood, but no one else did.

When I got off my shift Saturday afternoon, there were six missed calls from my mom. I was putting my phone back in my pocket when she called a seventh time. I hesitated, then answered. She ripped into me, demanding to know how I could think of ditching out on the parade.

I had a knot in my stomach. I couldn't answer her. She was fucking pissed. Mad enough that I didn't want to go home. I drove to Hollywood and went to a bar. I drank by myself and realized that I couldn't go back to my mom's house. But I had nowhere else to go.

I am a homeless Olympic medalist, I thought to myself.

After several hours of drinking, I walked to get a pizza and ate it in the back of my car. Then I curled up in the backseat. The next morning the whole car smelled of pizza and I had a crick in my neck.

It was midday. I just lay there, sweating in the backseat, staring at the ceiling.

I camped out in the car for a couple of nights until I got paid. I deposited my money in the bank and set out on my mission to find a non-automotive home. By the end of the day, I had signed the lease on an apartment.

The apartment was a step up from the car, a baby step. My first apartment was a twelve-by-twelve-foot, first-floor studio. The only sink was in the bathroom and it constantly fell out of the wall.

I picked up two more jobs just to make ends meet; even

then things were tight. I was a cocktail waitress at The Cork in Crenshaw, and on Sundays I'd work till the predawn hours, then crash for a few hours before working a morning bartending shift at Gladstones, a fancy restaurant in Malibu.

On more than one occasion, sewage would come up out of the toilet and shower, and I'd come home from work to an apartment filled with shit. I didn't think I could get any lower. Some days I would come home, look around and promise myself that this was temporary, remind myself that I was better than this moment. I knew I would make something of myself. I just had to decide what that was going to be.

YOU CAN'T RELY ON JUST ONE THING TO MAKE YOU HAPPY

For years after Claudia Heill beat me in the 2004 Olympics, I harbored all this animosity for her. I convinced myself that if only I had won the medal, everything would have been better.

Years later, Claudia jumped off a building and committed suicide. Her death hit me hard. The main reason I was so angry with her is that I felt like she had robbed me of not just an Olympic medal, but of happiness. When I lose, I feel like that win, that happiness, is still out there and that the person who took it from me is walking around with it. But Claudia had that medal and whatever was making her unhappy was still there. By the time she died, I had my own Olympic medal. And I had quickly realized just how little happiness it brought me.

When I came back from Beijing, I decided to take a break. I spent a year doing everything I could to destroy all the work that I had put into my body. I didn't know exactly what I wanted, but I knew that I needed things to change. Building up my body and chasing the Olympic dream had made me unhappy. I wanted to have a normal life. I wanted to have a dog and an apartment and to party.

From the end of 2008 well into 2009, I did not aspire toward anything. My plan involved drinking heavily, not working out, and cramming everything I thought I had missed into as short a time as possible. I was going to take a year off from judo, from structure, from responsibility. I was going to do what *I* wanted for a change.

One of the things that I wanted was a dog. I had my heart set on a Dogo Argentino, or an Argentinian mastiff. They're a big, white, beautiful breed and the kind of dog you don't have to worry about hurting if you accidentally step on it on the way to the bathroom in the middle of the night. I didn't have many requirements; I just wanted a girl.

A breeder in San Diego, a married couple, sent me an email with photos of two girls from a recent litter; they were too big to be show dogs, so they were being offered at a discounted price.

I clicked on the first attachment. "That's the one," I said. "That's my dog."

I didn't even look at the other photo. There wasn't a single doubt in my mind. I just knew. I went out that afternoon and bought her a crate, bed, the best dog food they had, and a couple of chew toys.

Three days later, I drove down to San Diego to pick her up. The breeders lived in a subdivision out in the suburbs. They were waiting for me in the open garage with the puppy's mother. She was a gorgeous dog.

Then the wife brought out my puppy and without even realizing it I cooed aloud. This was her. This was definitely my dog.

"You can hold her," the breeder said.

I scooped up the puppy. She sleepily opened her eyes, then

nuzzled against my chest, settling back to sleep. She was a big, fat, white puppy.

"You're not too big," I whispered to my dog. "You're absolutely perfect." I named her Mochi after the Japanese ice-cream balls covered in rice cake, and true to her name, she is the sweetest dog, not to mention loyal and loving and one of the most grounding and comforting presences in my life. I instantly fell in love with Mochi, but being in charge of another living thing took some getting used to.

The night I took her home was her first time away from her mom. She cried all night. I relented and let her sleep in my bed.

"Don't get used to this, Mochi," I said.

She slept in my bed for the next few weeks. Then one morning, I rolled over sleepily and opened my eyes. Mochi was already awake next to me, resting her head on her paws.

"How's my little puppy?" I asked in a baby-talk voice.

She lifted her head when she saw I was awake, opened her mouth, and threw up a pair of my underwear she had eaten out of my laundry basket.

I had gotten a dog with absolutely no understanding of how much responsibility it would actually be. But I committed the first $35 of every shift I worked to pay for her doggie daycare. That was probably the only responsible decision I made that year.

I started my morning with a smoke on the way to work. Camel menthols were my cigarette of choice. After I dropped Mochi off at doggie daycare, I smoked menthols up Pacific Coast Highway on my way to Malibu. When I got to Gladstones, I would go behind the bar and start my day with a concoction I called "Party Like a Barack Star." Obama had just been elected, and the drink was a mix of dark and light ingredients. It tasted like the most delicious iced mocha with vodka in it. I would sit and drink that all morning.

PARTY LIKE A BARACK STAR

2 shots espresso
1 shot (or 2) Stoli Vanilla
1 shot Kahlua
½ shot Baileys
1 tablespoon cocoa powder
2 shots ice cream milk (half-and-half and simple syrup
*   can be used as a substitute)*

Combine ingredients with ice. Shake. Blend. Enjoy. (Unlike I did, please enjoy responsibly.)

BARTENDER TIP: How much is a shot? Pour and count to four.

On Sundays, these two hip-hop producer dudes would pedal up on Tour-de-France-caliber racing bikes and order surf-and-turf and Cadillac margaritas. They tipped me thirty dollars in cash and enough marijuana to get me high for several days. During the week, one of the regular bar patrons sold Vicodin to servers and would slip me one or two for passing the cash and pills between him and the waitstaff, without our boss knowing.

I would gaze out at the ocean while rolling on Vicodin, drinking whiskey at noon, and watching dolphins in the waves. The TV over the bar played an endless loop of SportsCenter. I was riveted by the MMA highlights.

"I could totally do that," I would say out loud.

Everyone at the bar kind of nodded to humor me. It was

obvious that no one believed me. The fact that I was doing absolutely nothing with my life was apparent to everyone.

I had endured so much to get to the Olympics. All along the way, I told myself that the result would be amazing; that it would all be worthwhile. But the truth was that it had been amazing, but it hadn't been worth it. Realizing that crushed me. I had dreamed of the Olympics since I was a little girl. I won an Olympic medal, and yet I felt like I had been let down.

My disappointment haunted me. I didn't know how to cope with it. I was trying to drink myself into contentment, but I still wasn't happy and I didn't understand why. I spent that whole year lost. I couldn't figure out what it was, but there was something missing.

DISREGARD NONESSENTIAL INFORMATION

When I am in a fight, my brain is picking up a million things at once. The volume of the crowd. The brightness of the lights. The temperature of the arena. Every movement in the cage. Any pain my body is feeling. A lesser fighter would be overwhelmed.

I take all the information in, but I only process the pieces that matter. The distance between my back and the cage. Every move my opponent makes. The effort in her breathing. The impact of my fist as it hits her face. Anything occurring around me irrelevant to whether I succeed or fail is completely disregarded.

Everything in the world is information. The information you choose to acknowledge and the information you choose to ignore is up to you. You can let outside factors beyond your control throw off your focus. You can let aching muscles hold you back. You can let silence make you feel uncomfortable. By choosing to focus only on the information that is necessary, you can tune out every distraction, and achieve far more.

I was trying to figure out my life. I wanted to be content with being a bartender, but pouring cocktails for the next several decades was definitely not it.

Judo hadn't made me happy. But not doing judo wasn't making me happy either. I worried nothing would ever make me happy, that I had missed my chance at happiness. I just tried to get through each day. Now that I was no longer doing judo, I learned quickly who my real friends were. One of those true friends was Manny Gamburyan. We had done judo together since I was eleven, and Manny was the one who opened the gym and spent hours working with me after my knee surgery. He was good at judo, but hadn't pursued it. Instead, he went into MMA. After the Olympics, Manny would call me occasionally to check in.

"You should come out and grapple with us," Manny said.

"OK, I'll come," I said. I needed the exercise. I looked like someone had taken a bicycle pump and inflated me to a larger version of myself.

"I'll meet you at Hayastan," Manny said. It was the same club where we had developed my matwork after my ACL repair years before, but it had moved to a new location. Still, walking back into the club felt familiar. It smelled the same: sweat and an ocean of cologne. The place had gotten a facelift, but many of the faces were the same. Several guys I knew from youth judo were there doing MMA. They were bantering back and forth in Armenian. I dropped my bag by the side of the mat, surveying the room. A dozen guys were already grappling. There wasn't a girl in the place.

"Ron, you came!" Manny said. He gave me a hug. "You ready?"

"I was born ready," I said. We wrestled for over an hour. Manny came at me full strength. I met him with the same energy.

By the time practice ended, I was covered with sweat and had a few burgeoning bruises.

"Not too bad, Ron," Manny said. "Lucky for you, I took it easy."

"You wish," I said, laughing. Being back on the mat felt good.

After the first workout, I decided to get back to grappling with Manny regularly. I loved it just as much as I had before.

I grappled on Tuesdays, but between work and heading out to Hayastan in Hollywood, I would swing by doggie daycare, pick Mochi up and take her to the dog park.

Mochi was now four months old, and I had just started taking her to the park. I saw Dog Park Cute Guy there most days, but I never spoke to him. He was a tall, dark, handsome, tattooed surfer guy who made a little voice in my head say with a French accent, *Ooh la la*. When I caught myself staring, I would quickly avert my gaze and pretend I had nothing but a laser focus on Mochi.

One day, his dog came over and started punking Mochi. Mochi ran behind my feet to hide and Dog Park Cute Guy had no choice but to come over. Privately I was screaming, *Oh my God, Dog Park Cute Guy is coming over here.*

We got to talking about our dogs, then we made the kind of small talk that you don't remember later. Eventually, he invited me to come surfing. Yes, he was cute, but I wanted to learn how to surf, honestly. It was one of those things on my bucket list. After so many months of drinking and smoking, I was craving a physical challenge, and the ocean seemed strong enough for me to take on.

"Cool," he said. "We leave at five a.m."

I couldn't even speak; I was too afraid, "Five a.m.?! Are you fucking kidding me?" would slip out.

"Cool," I echoed, while I did a happy dance in my mind.

The next morning, I arrived at his house before the sun. I was nervous, but excited. We drove up north along the Pacific Coast Highway in his old Pathfinder. The windows were cracked and the air was humid and cool. We drove in complete quiet.

He knew I had no idea how to surf, but when we got to the beach he handed me a surfboard and wetsuit and said, "OK, then." And that was it; he headed out into the water. I watched him paddle out into the ocean and then dragged my board over the sand into the freezing-ass water.

Bam. A wave knocked me off. I tried to get on again. As soon as I laid myself on top of the board—*bam.* Freezing salt water surged through my sinuses, and I came up coughing and gasping for air. Another wave. *Bam.*

I felt like I was in a washing machine with a surfboard tethered to my ankle.

I got my ass handed to me by the ocean for over an hour. Then Dog Park Cute Guy caught one last wave and paddled in. I waited a minute or two so I didn't look overly eager to get out of the water, then I ungracefully hauled myself and the board to shore.

We loaded the boards back into the car, then drove home in comfortable silence. I had no idea whether he was interested in me or not. But I was interested in him and I really did want to learn to surf. We planned to surf again in two days.

I still didn't have any idea of what I wanted to do with my life, but the drinking and smoking was getting old. *I'm supposed to start training again in August,* I reminded myself. But instead of being motivated by a potential return to the sport I had dedicated my life to, the idea of staging a comeback made me miserable. Regardless, I decided I should get back in shape.

After a half dozen of our silent surf dates, I asked DPCG to run hill sprints with me. He said yes, but the night we were supposed to meet, he didn't show. I waited for almost an hour, checking my phone, convincing myself he got stuck in traffic. For a moment I almost let the self-pity creep in, but instead I called another guy who had recently given me his number and set up a date for the next weekend, and then I ran the sprints. With each hill, I cycled through a new emotion.

Hill 1: Denial. *He'll be here. He's just running late. Maybe his car broke down.*

Hill 2: Sadness. *I really liked him. I can't believe he didn't show.*

Hill 3: Confusion. *Could I have gotten the wrong signal? Did he see me in the friend zone? Was it something I said?*

Hill 4: Rejection. *He doesn't like me. It was ridiculous for me to ever think he would.*

Hill 5: Anger. *You know what? Fuck that guy.*

Hill 6: Apathy. *Whatever. I'm over it.*

Just as I was finishing up, DPCG pulled up at the top of the hill. His car was crammed full of white garbage bags that looked like they had been hastily stuffed with various belongings. His dog, Roxie, was wedged between bags. He couldn't even see out the back window. I was midway up the hill when he got out of the car and stood next to it, waiting for me. I reached the top of the hill and stood with my hands on my hips as I caught my breath.

"I got kicked out of my place," he said. It wasn't an apology, just an explanation.

Then DPCG went AWOL. Two weeks later I saw him at the dog park. When he looked my way, I pretended he didn't exist. He came over anyway. "I wanted to apologize. I'm going through some shit right now."

"Uh huh," I said coolly.

"Do you still want to hang out?"

I did. I couldn't help it. I was drawn to him. So we made a date, and then it was on. We started spending all our time together. I never even called back my replacement date. I never gave him an explanation.

DPCG and I resumed our surf dates, but this time there was no longer silence. I would drive to the house where he was staying with a friend, smiling the entire way there because I was so happy to be seeing him. Driving up the coast and back, we talked and listened to music. He took me to hang out at his friends' houses, where sometimes we watched MMA fights. He was always interested in my observations. He asked me questions and respected my analysis. I mentioned I was interested in doing MMA. "Yeah, girl, go for it. You should do it," he said.

We went to Trader Joe's and brought home food that he would cook. We took Mochi and Roxie to dog parks around the city, then home where the two of them would lie on the floor, exhausted. But mostly we would shut ourselves away in his little room, which we referred to as "the cave," and lie in bed and talk. We discussed bands and movies. We had a similar sense of humor and we would laugh for hours. We talked about our lives. He told me about his son. I told him about losing my dad. He told me about his recovery from heroin addiction, five years clean. I confided in him about the devastation I had felt after losing the Olympics. With him, I felt understood.

One day, I woke up next to DPCG, looked into the brown eyes that I had grown to love and realized I simply could not bear to leave his side. I called the bar and told them I was sick. Gladstones' policy was that if you called in sick on the weekend, you needed a doctor's note to return. When I returned without a note, I was told I could not work again until I had one. I never went back.

I had spent the last year searching for something that would make me happy, and maybe I had finally found it. With DPCG, days would go by, weeks would go by, and we would be so happy we wouldn't even notice. We tuned out everything else.

RELATIONSHIPS THAT ARE EASILY RUINED WERE NEVER WORTH MUCH

I expect that if someone is overseeing such an invaluable and important part of my life as my career, they should give a damn about me.

You need a coach who actually cares about you and not just about their own statistics. Many people find a coach who's great at their job but doesn't care about them as a person. When people who don't care about you make decisions that impact your life, those decisions generally end up being bad ones.

The longer you're in a relationship, with a coach or anyone, really, the harder it becomes to walk away. A lot of people stay places too long because they don't want to have those difficult conversations or risk ruining relationships. But if the people around you aren't willing to accept what is best for you, your relationship with them wasn't as meaningful as you thought. A relationship worth anything will endure the process.

I decided I would make a comeback in judo, but on my terms. I had told everyone I was only taking a year off, and that year was up. I hadn't worried about losing my job at Gladstones, because I would be returning to judo. Funding as a judo athlete could even allow me to train MMA.

For four months, I traveled extensively as part of my judo comeback. During a trip to Japan, I was sitting in the athlete dorms at a training facility when it hit me: I was miserable, and I was going to be miserable doing this every day of my life for the next three years until the Olympics. I thought back to winning the bronze medal and how fleeting the happiness that had accompanied it was. I didn't believe that a gold medal was going to make me much happier. I didn't want to be miserable anymore. I cut my trip to Japan short and returned home.

When I got home, I wrote up this crazy training schedule totally unique to MMA or judo that would allow me to change around what I was doing every day. It was on two-week cycles, so I would make sure to hit all the disciplines, but I would be able to have options to change things up. For example, in any given fourteen-day span, I would have to do eight judo practices, four boxing practices, four grappling practices, two strength and conditioning sessions, and a couple wildcard workouts, which could be anything from running sand dunes to surfing. If I didn't feel like going to judo one day, I could go do something else. If I felt like surfing, I could go surfing. It didn't matter if I went to judo eight days in a row or every other day as long as I got in the required number of workouts in the cycle. For the first time in my life, how I trained was up to me.

After taking a year away, I had changed. I had spent all this time just living for me, trying to figure things out on my own.

I was the one making the choices, not always great choices, but my own choices. And now, I was choosing for things not to go back to the way they always had been.

In May 2010, I flew to Myrtle Beach for the senior nationals for judo. It was the first time I'd competed in a major tournament since the Olympics, but there was no question I was going to win. Everyone was excited for my comeback, believing it marked my return for the 2012 Olympics.

Little Jimmy and I were standing on the warm-up mat next to each other. He had helped train me since I was a sixteen-year-old kid. I had looked up to him most of my life: as a sports idol, as an Olympic teammate, and as a coach. Now, at twenty-three, I wanted Jimmy to train me for MMA.

I told him about my plan to transition to MMA. He was really quiet. I plowed ahead with the little speech I had rehearsed.

"USA Judo will benefit way more from someone from judo like me becoming a world champion in MMA and proving that it's a legitimate martial art for self-defense," I said. "That would get more attention for the sport of judo than anything else, including me winning an Olympic gold medal."

Jimmy narrowed his eyes, nodding his head. I knew I was talking fast, but I didn't want my voice—or my confidence—to waver. I told him I didn't want to move back to Boston. I told him I wanted to follow my own training schedule.

"I want to do judo, but I also want to do MMA," I told him.

When I finished, Jimmy looked at me, as if deciding between rage and hysterical laughter. "What do you want me to say to that? That I support your decision? Because I don't. You want me to tell you that I'll help you with this ridiculous plan? I won't. You're wasting your talent. If you don't want to do judo, don't do judo. Quit wasting everyone's time. But unless you are one hundred percent devoted to this sport, you will not be getting any judo funding. I will make sure of that.

"Good luck to you," he said in a condescending tone. "You're going to need it because this plan of yours is never going to work." Then he turned his back on me and walked away. Jimmy had just brushed me off like I was nothing.

Stunned, I watched him go. Then a little bubble of rage formed at the edge of my brain, but, before it could boil up it was replaced with resolve. *You are going to rue the day we had this conversation. I'm going to be the one athlete you regret losing for the rest of your life.*

I was ready to walk away from Jimmy, but not judo, not yet. I traveled to Tunisia for the Tunisia Grand Prix in May. I won my first match by ippon, but lost my second match. I came home, planning to head to a tournament in Brazil. I dropped my passport off at the Brazilian consulate to get my visa, but as I was driving away I realized I was already dreading going to the tournament. By the time I got home, I had made the decision to cancel my trip.

My relationship with judo, like my relationship with Little Jimmy, had come to an end.

SOMEONE HAS TO BE
THE BEST IN THE WORLD.
WHY NOT YOU?

"Someone has to be the best in the world. Why not you?"

My mom asked me a variation of this question every day.

"Why not you?" she said. "Seriously, why not you? Somebody has to do it. They're handing out Olympic medals. They're literally handing them out. Why don't you go get one?"

Her question was not rhetorical. She knew what it took to be the best in the world. She had been a world champion. Being the best in the world is not easy, but it is completely achievable—if you are willing to put in the effort. My mom taught me to expect that I could be the best.

"Damn, Ronda, if you did MMA, you would beat all of these chicks out there," Manny said. We were sitting on the mat, taking a break during grappling practice.

Among the guys at the gym, my skills earned me respect. I

wasn't just good for a girl, I was better than almost anyone in the gym. He was saying aloud what I had known since I had watched Gina Carano and Julie Kedzie's fight years earlier. Having people around me acknowledge this fact broke open a dam that I hadn't even known existed.

"You know, I think you're right." I eased into the conversation as if the idea had never crossed my mind. "I think I can beat these other girls."

"No question," Manny said.

I asked a few other guys from practice who happened to be standing around. It was unanimous: No girl would stand a chance against me in MMA.

Soon, I started asking, "Do you think I should fight? Do you think I should really do it?"

Everyone said, "No." Everyone thought that I could do it, but no one thought that I should. They all thought it was a dead end. They didn't think that winning anything in MMA would ever be worthwhile for a girl. The respect for women's MMA wasn't there and a career in women's MMA wasn't there.

"Why would you want to do it anyway?" Manny asked me. "You know you're the best in the world, and proving it will gain you nothing."

He was right and wrong. I knew I was the best in the world and I understood that I wouldn't be able to make a living out of being the best until the MMA world changed radically. Where we disagreed was that I thought I could change the entire MMA world, and he didn't believe it could be changed.

"Somebody can do this," I said. "You can't tell me it's not possible. Who on the fucking entire planet earth is more qualified than I am?"

Manny shrugged.

The next step was to get some fights. I needed a fight manager. I asked the head coach at Hayastan, Gokor Chivichyan, if he knew any fight managers, and he recommended Darin Harvey, who rented a small office space at Hayastan, where he tried to pick up fighters to represent. Darin was just some guy in his forties who came from a rich family, did some martial arts as a hobby, and decided he wanted to get into sports management. He claimed to be involved in the success of fighters like former UFC heavyweight champion Bas Rutten. I asked Darin if he would be interested in being my fight manager and he said he would.

The pieces were falling into place, but there was still one thing I had to do: tell my mom. For a few weeks, I danced around the subject, trying to work up the nerve. But I was resolved to tell her about my plan. I wanted her blessing. I didn't want to run away and do something she didn't approve of again. I had worked so hard to fix our relationship, I didn't want to take any steps back.

A few days later, I made my move.

My mom was sitting on the living room couch. I positioned myself seven feet away, close to the kitchen. That was the maximum distance I could put between us while maintaining visual contact. As I stood between the kitchen table and the oven, I realized that she was between me and the apartment's only exit if things went really wrong.

For a few seconds, we just faced each other. Then I looked away. She didn't know what I was going to say, but she knew she was going to disapprove. I shifted from foot to foot, waiting for her to break the ice, but my mom wasn't going to make it easy.

"Mom," I said, then paused.

"No," she said.

"But I haven't even said anything yet," I said.

"I know, but clearly it's going to be something I'm against," she said.

How does she do that?

I realized I was holding my breath and let myself inhale.

"Mom, I know this doesn't sound like the greatest idea. But you're always asking me about my plans for the future. I think I have it figured out, although I know you're going to be against it. I really want to give this MMA thing a try. And if it doesn't work out after a year, I'll go join the Coast Guard or go to college or whatever you want. But I feel like I have a real shot at making something out of this. And if I fail, then I'm completely content to say you were right and go be a responsible adult. Just give me a year."

My mom said nothing. She sat there for a moment. Her face wasn't angry; it was unreadable.

"It's the stupidest fucking idea I've ever heard in my entire life," she said, repeating herself for emphasis. "The stupidest fucking idea I've heard in my entire life."

She spoke in a cool voice that was far worse than if she were screaming at me.

"And when I say the stupidest fucking idea that's saying something, because you have had some really dumb ideas," she added.

"But, Mom, it's my dream," I said. "I—"

She cut me off. "We have seen you through two Olympics. I kept my part of the deal. I did whatever I could to support you. Everyone in our family made sacrifices for you for over eight years. Now, it is time to buckle down and get a job and be a grown-up. It is not time for 'I have a dream to do MMA.'

"I am not going to be one of these parents who has a thirty-year-old kid living in their house and eating their food, because you have a dream. I have a dream too. My dream is to

retire someday, and I am an old woman. I'm not going to be supporting an able-bodied adult. It's a stupid idea. You should go to college and get a real job and quit all this stupid shit."

She paused for air. I opened my mouth to respond, but she wasn't finished.

"Not to mention the fact that this is exceptionally stupid because there really is no such thing as professional women's MMA," she said. "Yes, I know there are guys who make a living as a professional fighter, but all of them are in the UFC, and last I checked, they don't have women fighting in the UFC, nor have I heard of any plans to have women fighting in the UFC."

"I'm not asking for financial support," I said. "I just want your blessing to give this a try."

"Well, you're not going to get it," my mom said. "But I'm sure you will pursue this ridiculous fantasy anyway, because you have already proven that you don't give a damn about my approval."

I didn't speak to my mom for two weeks. She left me a few messages, but I avoided her calls.

I checked my voicemail.

"Ronda, this is your mother. I know you are intentionally not answering my calls. If you are hoping that I've changed my mind and no longer think this MMA thing is a stupid idea, I have not. Call me back anyway."

Waiting her out was not going to work. I invited her to dinner with Darin and Leo Frincu, my strength and conditioning trainer, to prove to her that my MMA ambitions were more than a pipe dream.

We met at the Enterprise Fish Company. Darin, Leo, and I sat at our table waiting.

"It's really an honor to meet you," Darin said when Mom

arrived. "Ronda has said so many great things about you."

"I bet."

Darin gave me a smile that said, *Don't worry, I'm just warming up.* I gave him a look that said, *You don't know my mother.*

"Ronda has the potential to be a star," Darin forged ahead. Mom rolled her eyes.

"You don't believe me?" he asked.

"I'm skeptical," she said, her voice tight.

The waitress arrived to take our order. All conversation at the table stopped abruptly. While my mom looked at the menu, I shot Leo a pleading look from across the table.

"Ronda is an incredible athlete," Leo jumped in, as soon as our server had walked away. "She's one of the best athletes I've ever worked with, and we've only scratched the surface. She has amazing potential.

"I know what it takes to be the best in a sport," he added. "I was world champion in wrestling."

"You were?" A flicker of respect crossed my mom's face.

"Yeah, 1994, I competed for Romania."

My mom nodded.

"She hasn't even reached her peak," Leo said. "She's still young. Ronda is just coming into her prime. She could be the best in the world."

"I don't disagree with you," my mom said. "But my question is, 'Yeah, and then what?' From what I can tell, there isn't any market for women MMA fighters. Am I wrong?"

Leo hesitated. Darin jumped in.

"Not yet, but we're going to change that," Darin said. "Ronda is going to be huge. We're going to get her some fights, and then really, from there, the pieces are just going to fall into place. I have a really great feeling. There's just so much energy around her."

"I'm a statistician, so I operate based on facts and data instead of energy. I hope you'll understand why I'm skeptical," my mom said.

"Completely." Darin nodded a bit too emphatically.

The waitress brought our entrees. Mom grilled Darin about his qualifications, his fighters, his experience.

He didn't help his case and my mom hummed dismissively as he rambled. He tried to name-drop some reality TV stars and a few other D-list names. He was sinking fast.

"But those people aren't fighters," my mom pointed out.

"Uh, well, no."

"So you understand why I'm skeptical?" she asked once more.

"I do," Darin sputtered. "But we have a plan. We have it all mapped out. It's not going to happen overnight. But I think in four years, if she has the right kind of support…"

He paused and looked at my mom, apparently expecting her to jump in and offer that support. My mom looked at him with a combination of disgust and disbelief.

"Oh wait, are you saying that we should financially support her?" my mom asked with a laugh.

"I can support myself," I interjected.

"I'm putting a lot of money into her career," Darin said.

"That's great," my mom said, condescendingly.

I wanted to slip under the table, and run as far from the restaurant as possible.

"I'm not arguing Ronda's ability as an athlete," my mom said. "I am questioning the whole 'She's going to be a star and make lots of money,' when as far as I can tell, there's not a real demand for women MMA fighters."

Darin was silent.

"So you understand why I'm skeptical?" my mom asked yet again.

Darin nodded.

"And what do you get out of all this?" my mom asked him. "I just want to see Ronda succeed," he said.

"Do you have a contract?"

"We have an agreement," he said. "But if Ronda is ever not happy with the job I'm doing, I'll just walk away."

My mom narrowed her eyes.

"It's not about business," Darin said. "Ronda is like family to me."

"Business is always about business," my mom said, then turned to me. "And I've found the only people who are like family are your actual family. Look, if this is something you really want to do, you can do it, but you're doing it on your own. I'll give you a year. That's it. One year."

Joy surged through me. I did a happy dance in my brain. It was the closest I was going to get to her approval. It wasn't complete acceptance, but it would do.

When we had finished eating, Darin made a big show of paying the check.

"Well, Leo, it was nice to meet you," my mom said.

"One year," she said to me.

She gave Darin a once-over and said nothing.

She called me later that night.

"Hey Mom, what's up?"

"One year," she said, skipping over any salutation. "And I don't trust that Darin guy."

This is really happening, I thought.

This was my dream, and my mom was giving me a chance to pursue it even if she didn't really believe in it. I was OK with that.

If people don't believe you when you say something, then you have to prove it. I promised her I would prove her wrong.

FINDING A COACH IS LIKE FINDING A BOYFRIEND

When I am looking for a coach, I shop around. It is a lot like dating. Sometimes you might meet a great guy, but he's just not the one for you. When you find the right coach, something clicks. It just feels right. If you don't have that feeling, you don't have the right coach.

Fighters have to search for a coach with potential, just the way coaches have to search for fighters with potential. After all, it's a relationship you build over time.

I believe it's very important for a person to stick with consistent coaching throughout a career instead of bouncing around. Over time you develop a rapport and a way of communicating. Coaching is all about communication and being able to get information from one person to another fairly quickly. If you can find all these things in one person, you'll have a long, happy life together.

When I made the transition to MMA, I knew I could submit anyone on the planet. Striking was a different story. I'm sure it's that way with any career change. You bring the skills you have, but you also need to develop new ones. To improve, I had to find a striking coach. I went to a couple different gyms, but I just wasn't clicking with anybody.

I remembered the advice my mom had given me when I was searching for the judo coach who could take me to the next level. "There isn't a best coach; there's a best coach for you."

By early 2010, a few of the guys I trained with over at Hayastan were also working out at Glendale Fighting Club (GFC), which was owned by Edmond Tarverdyan. Edmond was younger than most trainers, not even thirty, but he had been running his own gym and training fighters since he was sixteen. The guys from Hayastan said good things about Edmond as a striking coach, so I went over to see the place.

When I first went to the GFC, it was filled with dudes speaking in Armenian who turned and stared at me when I walked in, as if I had landed from an alien planet. I couldn't understand what they were saying, but I was pretty sure I knew what they were thinking: *Who the hell is this girl, and what is she doing in our gym?* They knew that Edmond "didn't train girls," that he was "never going to train a girl."

Manny introduced me anyway. Or I assume that's what he did because the actual conversation between him and Edmond was "[Something in Armenian], Ronda. [More Armenian.]"

Edmond did not even look in my direction.

There were ten to fifteen guys in the club at any given time: hitting the bag, doing drills, riding the bike, hitting mitts in the ring with Edmond, and sparring. Then there was me, this blonde chick with absolutely no idea what she was doing when it came to striking. Manny started working out, and I was alone, standing there listening to the whir of the exercise bike, the smacking of mitts being hit, and Armenian music playing over the speakers. No one spoke to me—not in Armenian, not in English.

I put on my gloves and started hitting the heavy bag. I knew my technique sucked, and no one took the time to correct me. I felt stupid; I looked stupid; but I got down to work. As I worked out, I watched Edmond give Manny instructions inside the ring. Even though Edmond was giving instruction across the gym in a foreign language, I understood him better than I had ever understood a coach. I watched the corrections he gave Manny and I started making the same corrections myself.

I came back the next day. And the next. And the next. GFC became the part of my day that everything else revolved around.

I got to the gym between eight-thirty and nine, which is like Armenian early. The doors were locked. I didn't have a key.

I called Manny, who told me to call Roman, who told me to call Edmond and gave me Edmond's number. "Hey, is someone going to come open the gym?" I asked when Edmond answered.

"Yes, someone is going to come," Edmond said, exasperated. "Sevak will be there soon."

I sat on my bag outside the backdoor to the gym and waited. Sevak's sedan pulled into the GFC lot. I stood up and bounced from foot to foot.

"Morning," I said cheerfully as he unlocked the doors.

Sevak held the door for me. At twenty-one, he was a couple of years younger than me, but had been training under Edmond since he was fourteen and had been teaching at GFC for a couple years. He largely followed Edmond's lead when it came to dealing with me, but he at least acknowledged my existence.

Sevak turned on the lights, then sat behind the desk. The gym was spotless, a result of Edmond's OCD-level obsession with cleanliness. I walked through the door, the boxing ring on my right, a large mural of Muhammad Ali and Edmond in boxing stances painted behind it with the words "Nothing Is Impossible" in big red letters.

I wrapped my hands, shaking my head at the amateur job I did on my wraps. I did the best I could, then went to work, hitting the bag. Slowly, the place came to life as fighters trickled in.

Edmond showed up between ten and eleven in the morning. He said something to Sevak in Armenian and shouted for whoever was up first to train, hopped into the ring, and got to work.

His first training session of the day done, Edmond slipped out of the ring and walked to get something out of his bag. I went up to him.

"Edmond, will you hold mitts for me?" I asked for the umpteenth time.

"No, I'm busy," Edmond said, not even looking up.

"Maybe you could give me a drill," I said. "I really liked the footwork one you gave me a couple of days ago."

"Just go hit the bag," Edmond said, giving me a dismissive wave.

I walked over to the heavy punching bag and started hitting it. I felt like an idiot. I heard two guys across the room laughing and felt the back of my neck turn red. I knew my form was a joke. I hit the bag harder and kept hitting the bag. I wanted Edmond to see that I was doing what he told me to do. I watched Edmond for tips as I worked out, but it was hard to do both at once.

When Edmond stepped back into the ring to train the next guy, a boxer I recognized named Art Hovhannisyan, I took a break from my workout and bounced back and forth on one of the tires that looked into the ring.

Edmond and the fighter were moving around the ring. *Bam. Bam. Bam.* The sound of Art hitting the mitts echoed throughout the gym. *Bam. Bam.* Edmond slipped to his left. I watched Art as he came in with another series of blows. *Bam. Bam. Bam.* Edmond bobbed and weaved. Art started to come in again, when Edmond stopped him. Edmond started talking in rapid-fire Armenian as Art listened, nodding that he understood. Then Edmond punched at the air a few times, still rattling off feedback. Art replied in Armenian and Edmond shook his head as if to say, "No, that's wrong." He did the move again, after which Art said something else in Armenian and Edmond nodded emphatically. Then the two of them squared off again in the ring. *BAM. BAM. BAM.* The sound of the punches hitting the mitts was noticeably louder. Art did it again. *BAM. BAM.*

"Shot lava!" Edmond shouted, which I imagined to mean, "Yes, yes, that's it!"

I took a few weak swings into the air, committing the combination I had just seen to memory to try out on the bag later.

I was learning to read body language really well. Edmond might refuse to give me private lessons, but I was learning more simply from observing him with other fighters than I had learned from all the other English-speaking striking coaches I had worked with. I turned my focus back to the training session in the ring. I fixed my stare on Edmond, narrowing my eyes as if I just concentrated hard enough I could will him into working with me.

This went on for a good three months. Every day, I kept coming, and Edmond let me come in for free. Being broke made me even more driven. I was determined to work harder than anyone else. I started going to Alberto Crane's gym in the Valley to train in the morning and do MMA sparring before heading to Glendale. I would leave that practice a little early so I could get to GFC.

Even then I was still the first person at the gym in the morning, which meant daily calls to Edmond asking if someone was coming to open the gym.

This happened so many times that Edmond got annoyed with me and gave me a key. He wouldn't train me, but I had a key! This was when I realized that annoying Edmond was the best way to get what I wanted. I decided I would just annoy him until he gave in.

I would watch Edmond train everybody else and continue to ask him to hold mitts for me. I kept asking every day, and every day, he would say no.

On the morning of July 16, 2010, I opened up the gym at GFC. I'd been going to Edmond's club for four months and Edmond still pretty much pretended I wasn't there. Fighters started showing up to work out, and the gym came to life. I was sitting behind the front desk wrapping my hands when Edmond walked in with Art, who unbeknownst to me was weighing in for his next fight later that day. Art jumped on the elliptical machine and started working out without saying a word.

"Edmond, can you hold mitts for me today?" I asked.

Edmond didn't even look at me. He just said, "No. I don't want to sweat in this shirt," and kept walking.

My mouth dropped open. Rage shot through me and I thought, *What? You don't want to sweat for me in your shirt? Like the way I sweat for you every day trying to impress you? Like how I was sweating at the gym I was training at before I came over here to beg for some of your time? By the way, we're at a gym. Oh, and you can change your goddamn shirt.* I didn't say all that, but suddenly, all of my crazy came out. "THIS IS FUCKING BULLSHIT!" I yelled in the middle of the gym. The whole place went silent.

Edmond spun around in total disbelief. His tone was cold. "Don't you ever swear at me in my gym."

Fuming, I grabbed my bags and left. I was fighting back tears.

I was never going to win Edmond's respect with hard work. I gave up. I was exhausted from training at a place where I wasn't accepted. I was going to have to figure out how to train on my own.

I drove off. But less than a mile away I realized I had forgotten my gloves at the gym. I couldn't afford another pair. *Fuck!*

My phone rang. It was Edmond. I hesitated before answering, then flipped my phone open.

"Hello?"

"Ronda, it's Edmond. Drive back here and take me to the bank. We'll talk."

I made an illegal U-turn and headed back to the gym. I wasn't sure what to expect, but, at the very least, it meant I could grab my gloves.

What I had not realized was how Edmond would react to the state of my car. Do you know those air freshener commercials where they fill a car with trash, put it in the sun, and then bring people in blindfolded to show how well their product works? My car was kind of like that without the fresh scent. Imagine an overflowing laundry basket of dirty gym clothes. Then mix that with a dog kennel. Now imagine if that same car had little cheap plastic toys glued all over the inside—in part to give it a little character and in part to distract from the zombie wasteland of my backseat. I had not washed my car in over a year. I only had one working window and no air-conditioning. It was summer in the Valley, and the temperature in Glendale that day was almost one hundred degrees.

I pulled into the gym parking lot feeling apprehensive. Edmond walked out, but when he caught a glimpse of my car, a look of disgust crossed his face and he hesitated before reaching for the handle. Somehow he managed to slip into the car without touching any of its surfaces—it was as if he was just hovering over the seat.

"Go straight, then take a left," Edmond said reluctantly.

I nodded. I had said everything I had to say back at the gym.

"When you came to me, my mind was on Art," Edmond explained in his thick Armenian accent. "I just said I don't want to sweat because I wanted to help him make the weight. I was not thinking about my words."

Edmond explained that Art had been sick and drinking water and was way heavier than he was supposed to be. Art had come to the gym to try to sweat the extra pounds off in an effort to make weight. If anyone was going to be sweating, Edmond wanted it to be Art. Edmond added that it wasn't about his shirt, but that was the shirt he was wearing to the weigh-in, and he didn't have a change of clothes.

"I didn't mean to say it in the way I said it," Edmond said.

It was a very Edmond apology. He couldn't just say he was sorry for brushing me off. In fact, this wasn't an apology at all. This wasn't even Edmond telling me that he didn't want me to go. This was Edmond letting *me know that he was right* to not train me that day.

We pulled up to the bank. Edmond got out of the car, while I looked straight ahead. He took a few steps, then doubled back and leaned in the rolled-down passenger window.

"Don't leave me, OK?" he said. "I'll be right back. Don't drive away. OK?"

He paused, unsure whether I was going to peel away from the curb or not. I couldn't help but crack a smile.

"I'll be here."

A few minutes later, Edmond emerged and got back into the car. "Look, Ronda, I have seen that you have been practicing," Edmond said. "I see you training really hard."

I nodded.

"Maybe I haven't really been working with you," he continued.

"Yeah." I summoned all of my inner strength not to whip out a sarcastic reply.

"But I will put in more time training with you," he said.

"Yeah?" I said. It was the only word I could choke out while holding back what I really wanted to say, which was, "That won't be very hard considering you've put in absolutely no time so far."

"Maybe hold the mitts," he said.

"That would be great," I replied.

"You got a fight coming up?" Edmond asked.

"My amateur debut is next month."

"OK, I'll make sure you're ready for that," he told me.

We were back at the gym. Edmond flung open the door and all but jumped out of the car, putting as much distance as possible between him and my dog-hair disaster of a car.

"OK, see you on Monday," Edmond said.

"Monday," I agreed.

As I pulled away, I broke into a huge smile. I was halfway home when I realized my gloves were still at the gym. I would just have to get them on Monday.

Monday morning, I smiled the entire drive to the gym. I could hardly contain my excitement. This was the day.

I got there early, before even Sevak, and let myself in. About an hour later, Edmond walked through the door.

"Hey, Edmond, you said you would hold mitts for me today." It wasn't a question.

"Yeah, yeah," he said. "After I train some guys."

A training session with Edmond could be an hour if he was really into working with the person or he might only hold mitts less than a round (a professional boxing round is three minutes) and then move on. It depends on the mood Edmond is in and whether or not he likes you. I didn't know how many guys he was planning to train first, and I didn't care. I was not leaving that gym until Edmond held mitts for me.

For the next hour, I waited around, warming up and bouncing around. I wanted to be limber so that I would be ready to jump in the ring as soon as Edmond said, "OK, Ronda, now." Then he called my name.

I tried not to look overly excited as I stepped into the ring. I wanted him to understand that I was serious and focused. I didn't say a word. I had learned from Big Jim that coaches really like when you shut up and do what they say.

He worked with me for a few minutes on basic footwork. Then he told me to throw a left jab.

I threw one. I was trying to stay relaxed, because if you're stiff you can't punch for shit, but I was way too stiff because I was all amped up and my jab was awful. He had me throw a few more jabs, and then as soon as I felt like I was loosening up and doing a good job, Edmond said, "OK, we're done."

We had been in the ring for less than twenty minutes.

Years later, I heard Edmond say in an interview that the morning I yelled at him was a turning point, because he saw that I had the balls to say something. In that moment, he saw how much I wanted to train and it made him realize I was worth training. In that moment, I found my coach.

YOU WILL BE TESTED

I have lost tournaments. I have lost friendships. I have lost my
father. I know that I can deal when things are bad. I can come
back when things are at their worst. I'm not afraid of losing all
my money or losing my career, because I know I'm capable of
living in my car and rising up. Once you've conquered the worst
things that could happen, there is no need to fear the unknown.
You are fearless.

My MMA career was getting off the ground, but I needed another
job to carry me through until fighting started paying the bills. I
hustled to find work. My sister Maria called a friend from high
school and got me a job working the graveyard shift at 24 Hour
Fitness. The job sucked, but every time the resentment welled
up, I imagined the backseat of my Honda as my bedroom.

A few weeks later, I got a second job teaching judo at a club on
L.A.'s Westside. I picked up a third job working as a vet assistant
at an animal rehabilitation clinic. It was piecemeal employment,
but it was enough to pay (most of) my bills. Besides, I was so in
love with DPCG that, as long as he was with me, nothing else in
the world mattered.

But you can only live in a bubble for so long before it pops.

After almost a year of being nearly inseparable, DPCG called me as I was leaving grappling practice.

"I need to see you," he pleaded.

When I got to his place, he was sitting on his bed, crouched over. Roxie was cowering in the corner of the room, more frightened than I had ever seen her. I set my purse down next to the bedroom door.

"I drank," he said.

I didn't know what that meant. "It's not the end of the world. You drank today. It's one lost day. We will move on. Just talk to me about everything that's going on with you."

He had drunk a forty-ounce bottle of malt liquor before I arrived and he pulled out a six-pack of beer that he drank as we sat there. *He's going to drink for today,* I thought to myself. *Just let him get it out of his system and we will move on tomorrow.*

A few hours passed. He slipped into this other place. His pupils were so dilated that his eyes looked black. I couldn't get him to focus on me.

"I gotta go on a journey," he told me. His voice was flat.

"What is wrong with you?"

As a bartender, I was used to seeing people who had too much to drink, but this was unlike anything I had ever seen. He was starting to scare me.

"I gotta go on a journey," he said again.

"Talk to me. I'm right here." But he was somewhere else. He kept staring into space, then he got up to leave.

"You're not fucking leaving this room." I didn't raise my voice, but I stood blocking the doorway.

Looking right past me, he tried to move me aside as if I was a chair that happened to be in his way. I planted my hands on his chest and pushed him onto the bed. He tried to get back up. I shoved him again and he hit his head against the wall. My stomach dropped. I thought I'd hurt him. But he shook it off, unfazed, then tried to get up again. I shoved him once again, more gently this time. He didn't fight me. He just sat there for a few seconds, then tried again as if he had forgotten what had preceded. We must have danced this strange dance a dozen times. Each time he tried to stand, my muscles tensed, preparing to go another round. And each time my heart sank deeper. DPCG was slipping further away from me, and I could not pull him back. Finally he sat on the bed.

I ran into the kitchen, found his keys on the counter, and hid them in a cupboard before running back into the bedroom in case I had to intercept him again.

I sat down beside him, feeling exhausted and sad. A little while later, he got up like he was going to the bathroom, then made a sharp turn for the front door.

I headed him off, and for the next hour, I sat guarding the door, blocking the apartment's only exit.

"I'm sorry," he said finally. "I'm sorry. Let's lie down. Let's just lie down."

I was drained. It was past three a.m. and I had been guarding him for hours. We got into bed in silence. I looked into his eyes and he seemed present again. It looked like he was finally sobering up. We lay there together, and he held me in his tattooed arms. Slowly, I relaxed, and eventually, I drifted off to sleep.

I woke up in the morning, alone. The contents of my purse were strewn all over the bedroom floor. DPCG was gone along with my car.

I called his phone, but he didn't answer.

I called everybody I could think of. I called his friend Mike. I called his friend Luke. I called his friend Jack. I called his mother. I called my mother. Everyone said the same thing: Call the police and report your car stolen. They'll look for the car and they'll find him.

I felt ill and my hands shook as I dialed 911. The dispatcher did little to reassure me.

"If you report this car stolen and he tries to resist, then you know, they have license to shoot him," he said. "Do you want that to happen?"

"No!" I said appalled. "I don't want you to shoot my boyfriend!"

They sent a squad car over to the apartment. There were two officers—one a head taller than the other. I invited them inside. They were very nice. The tall one gave me a forced smile, then his partner took out a notepad and flipped it open. I told them my story, and the knowing looks on their faces made it clear that they'd heard this all before.

"Are you really going to shoot him?" I asked.

The officers looked slightly confused.

"No," the short one said. "We're going to drive around to different motels, looking in the parking lots. We'll try to find him for you."

His partner gave me a sympathetic look.

"Here is a number where you can reach us," he said, handing me a business card. Then they set out to look for him.

I sat on DPCG's living room floor, leaning against the wall, and barely moved. His dog, Roxie, lay at my feet.

"What the fuck did you get yourself into?" I asked myself aloud.

I had no idea what to do. I kept checking my phone, turning it over and over in my hands. Willing it to ring. Then it did. It was his mother. We had met in passing, but were not close.

"What exactly happened?" she asked.

I recounted the events of the night before.

"You let an addict drink?" she said, her tone accusatory. "How could do you that?"

"I...I...I thought he had a problem with heroin, not alcohol," I stammered.

"Unbelievable. They're all connected," she said. "I know you don't want to hear this, but this is your fault. You encouraged him.

"Let me know if you hear from him," she said, and hung up. Fifteen minutes later, she called again. I let it go straight to voicemail.

An hour passed, and I heard someone at the door. I jumped up. Roxie started barking like crazy. The door opened. It was his mother.

"No word?" she asked. She seemed less angry at me. I shook my head.

"This is why you shouldn't get involved with an addict," she said.

She pulled out her phone and started making phone calls. I sat there in the kitchen, shell-shocked. She went into his bedroom and started throwing clothes into a bag. Her phone rang. We both jumped.

"It's not him," she told me, looking at the caller ID.

Late that afternoon, DPCG just walked back into the house. A wave of relief washed over me. He looked like shit, but he was OK. He threw himself down on the bed and started crying.

"I'm so sorry," he choked out between sobs. I'd never seen him cry before. He confessed to taking my car downtown to score heroin. All he could find was crack. So he spent the morning doing crack, then just drove around. As he started to come down, everything hit him at once. He was low. Lower than I'd ever seen him. He couldn't even look me in the eye.

The situation was so fucked up, I didn't even know how to process it.

His mom took control with an amazing level of organization; she had been down this road before.

"Get in the car," she said, firmly. "You're going back to rehab."

He stood up slowly but didn't argue. She led him out to her car, a luxury sedan. I followed them, Roxie close behind me. DPCG slid into the back and I sat next to him. Roxie lay down at his feet. It was a forty-five-minute drive to the rehab center, and it was silent all the way there.

"I'm sorry," he said once we stepped out of the car.

I tried to force the kind of smile that tells a person it's going to be all right, but I couldn't get the corners of my mouth to turn up.

DPCG signed his admittance papers with a shaking hand.

"I'm sorry," he said again. "I'm so sorry."

His mom and I got into her car. I needed to go back to his place to get my car. She looked tired and worried. We pulled onto the freeway.

"I can't believe you let him drink," she said again. I said nothing.

"God, who lets an addict drink?" She wasn't even looking in my direction. She was quiet for the next few miles.

"I knew when he met you, he would be back here, but I still can't believe we're going down this road again." She wasn't talking to me this time. She was clutching the steering wheel so tightly her knuckles were white. I glanced back at Roxie, who was still lying on the floor in the backseat.

We kept driving.

"You need to leave him," his mom said to me, breaking the silence. "He's no good for you, and you're no good for him. You can't be with someone who is running around doing this kind of shit."

She continued like this in bursts, the entire way home. She never took her eyes off the road, and I never said a word.

She dropped me off at the house and drove away without saying goodbye. I stood there with Roxie, who stared up at me looking scared and lonely. I realized I felt the exact same way. I reached down and scratched the back of her neck.

"Come on, girl," I said. She followed me to my car. I opened the back door and tossed my purse on the floor. I tried to get Roxie in the car, but she became frantic, pulled away, and ran down the street. I slammed the door and ran after her, catching her halfway down the block. Holding tightly to her leash, I walked her back to the car and went to pull open the door. It was locked. I had to laugh. I could not have possibly imagined that the day could get any worse. I called AAA, and then sat on the curb to wait. Roxie would not settle down, and I yanked hard on her leash.

"Roxie, calm down," I said firmly.

A guy I had never seen before walked across the street in my direction.

"How would you like it if someone jerked you around like that?" he asked me.

"Motherfucker, you don't have any idea what's going on today. Do not fuck with me!" I snapped. He looked at me like I was crazy, then walked away.

It took more than an hour for AAA to come.

By the time they arrived, it was too late to pick Mochi up at doggie daycare. I didn't know how I was going to afford paying for two overnight stays. When I finally got home, my apartment was cold. Money was tight, and I had decided that while electricity and water were necessary utilities, gas for heat was not.

My room was dark and I just climbed straight into my bed.

I didn't have sheets (they cost money that I didn't have), just a sleeping bag. It was so cold. Roxie climbed up onto my bed. I covered her with my sleeping bag and wrapped my arms around her. We spooned all night for comfort and warmth. Tears poured down my face.

While DPCG was in rehab, he would write me long hand-written letters filled with apologies and declarations of love. I'd lie in my sheetless bed reading them and spooning his dog, and crying, thinking, *He loves me, that's all that matters.*

I missed him a lot. I had been around him every single day for months. I had actively started pursuing my MMA dream, and he was the one person I felt really believed in me. I wanted him back.

I went to see him on visitors' day about two weeks after he had been there. He looked a million times better than when we had dropped him off. The light was back in his eyes. We sat on a little couch in the visiting area holding hands, then he took me on a tour of the well-manicured grounds. He was embarrassed that I had to see him there, but happy that I had come. I had been there for an hour and then it was time to leave. As I walked out the door, I realized I wasn't ready to go. I wasn't ready to let him go.

A few hours later, I pulled into the parking lot of 24 Hour Fitness in North Torrance. I sat in my car, trying to muster the strength to walk in. It had already been an emotionally draining day, and of all the jobs I was working, this was my least favorite and the most thankless. I closed my eyes.

"Just wait," I told myself, launching into the internal pep talk I pulled out whenever I needed some cheering up. "I'm going to be super successful one day, and I'm going to write a book. It's going to be a kickass autobiography. And this is how it always happens in the book. This is just that part of the book where the character is going through hard times. This is that sucky part of the story. Just get through a few more pages, and it's going to have an amazing ending."

I took a deep breath, stepped out of the car, and walked into the gym. I sat behind the counter and spent the next several hours jerking my head back as I tried to keep myself from nodding off.

"I hope you fucking die," Eileen spat at me, snapping me out of a semi-sleep.

"Huh?" I shook my head slightly, pulling myself back into the moment.

"I hope you fucking die," Eileen repeated.

I put on my best customer-service smile.

This is just the sucky part of the book, I reminded myself. *And you,* I thought, turning my attention to Eileen, *will be one of the villains.*

The last person I wanted to deal with was Eileen, an alcoholic lady who lived in her car. She reeked of booze and her dirty blonde hair looked like it rarely saw a comb. She had bags under her eyes and a cluster of pimples along her jawline. She scowled at me, and though she was probably in her mid-thirties, she looked closer to fifty.

I had less than an hour until I could clock out. The air conditioner kicked into full blast at five every morning and I was freezing cold. I just wanted my shift to be over.

Eileen would wish death upon me every week when she would put the tip of her finger, where the finger and nail meet, on the scanner and, of course, her print wouldn't register. *Tap. Tap. Tap.* I would hear the angry tapping of her fingernail on the scanner's glass.

Eileen would glare at me. "It's not working! It's not working!" she shouted. "Just let me in."

She would always fight with me. She'd scream that I was stupid and I would calmly explain that she had to place the pad of her finger down, but this morning I just couldn't bear to guide her through the process again.

She kept jamming her finger into the scanner. Finally, by chance, she got it right and the machine registered her print.

"You're all set," I said in an overly cheerful tone. "Have a great workout." Eileen stormed into the workout area.

As the clock slipped from 5:59 to 6:00 a.m. I grabbed my keys and headed to the car in the cool November air.

"Damn it!" The gas gauge was on empty. I was surprised, somehow I was always surprised, but the empty tank was strategic. The cheapest gas in L.A. was right by the 405 freeway entrance near 24 Hour Fitness. I would time it so that my tank was at the absolute emptiest point when I had my shift. *It will be fine,* I told myself, it was only a short drive.

But the whole way there I leaned forward, praying that the smallest amount of momentum would be enough to propel my little Honda to the ARCO station.

As I stood there pumping the gas, I was so tired and cold that my hands were shaking as I put the gas in my car.

I put my whole minimum wage paycheck into the tank and my heart sank. I wasn't taking home a single penny after having worked all night. I wanted to curl up and sleep right there in the gas station parking lot. *Keep going,* I told myself. *In twenty minutes I'll be home and in bed.* I was doing strength and conditioning training on Mondays and I had to train in a couple of hours. But if I got home by six-thirty, I could sleep for three hours before I had to work out. I got in my car and turned the heat on full blast.

I pulled onto the freeway, ready to zoom home. Gridlock.

Bumper-to-bumper as far as I could see. I forgot it was a holiday weekend. Everyone who had tried to avoid the return-to-L.A. traffic on Sunday was coming home at dawn on Monday.

The traffic was slow. The heat was on. I was so tired. My car was so comfortable.

BOOM!

I woke up when my face smashed into the steering wheel. I opened my eyes. The accident didn't knock me out. It woke me up.

I had rear-ended a silver Toyota Solara.

I pulled over. When I touched my face my hand was covered in blood. I was edging toward hysteria. My breathing was quick. Tears were burning my eyes. I couldn't think. I didn't know what to do. I called my mom.

"I just got into an accident on the freeway, and I don't know who to call. Do I call 911?"

She told me emphatically yes.

Cars crawled past and I could see the passengers staring at me. Neither car was badly messed up, but the accident would have to go through the insurance. I started to worry again about money. My insurance rate would go up and I was afraid I wouldn't have enough for rent.

The woman in the Toyota walked up to me, and I watched as the color drained from her face when she saw me. She kept asking me, "Are you OK?"

The paramedics came. The guy looked me over and told me, "You have a broken nose and maybe a mild concussion. That sucks. Go home." He may have used more medical terminology, but that was the gist.

When I fell asleep at the wheel, I smashed my nose on the steering wheel and deviated my septum; now my nose is a little deformed. It's one of the reasons why when I get punched in the face, my nose goes flat. If you look up my nose, you can see it's off.

Since both cars were drivable, the highway patrol officer said we were free to go. The paramedics left. Highway patrol left. The Solara driver drove off. I sat in my car on the freeway for another few seconds. I don't know what I was waiting for. I was just waiting. I wanted to close my eyes again and wake up and be anywhere else. To wake up in my bed, rested for the first time in God knows how long. And not sore for the first time in God knows how long. And certainly not looking like I'd been whacked in the face with a baseball bat.

I felt beat down. My face hurt. I was shaken up from the crash. I felt myself teetering on the edge, struggling to find my footing. Everything seemed to be falling apart.

This is the part where I wish I could say that I reached deep down and screamed. That kind of primal soul-cleansing, "Is that all you got?" kinda scream. Where the sun started to break over the horizon, and I saw the beauty and meaning of nature. Where maybe a bird flew overhead as a sign. Then I could say that I knew in that moment that everything would be all right. That did not happen.

Instead, I cried, heaving body-racking sobs. The salt of the tears and the iron taste of blood pooled in the back of my throat. In the rearview mirror, I could see the mess of clotting blood and slimy snot, streaked by tears. I didn't even care enough to wipe it away.

"I'm so fucking tired," I said aloud, feeling blood drip down my face. Cars kept passing me by and I let them.

Hands trembling, I called my mom again.

"Hello…" Hearing her voice, I choked up even more, and—on

the verge of hyperventilating and much to her confusion—the words burst out, "I fucking hate this part of the book."

I was being tested, and while I knew in my heart that I was going to pass, in that moment, it felt like I was failing.

CHAMPIONS ALWAYS
DO MORE

Every time I step into the cage, I am absolutely confident I will win. Not only am I a superior fighter. Not only do I want it more. But I have worked harder than she ever will. That is what truly sets me apart.

Growing up, Mom hammered into me how much harder champions worked than anyone else. When I complained about going to practice or when I hit the snooze on the alarm instead of getting up to go running, my mom would say casually, "I bet [whoever my archrival at the time happened to be] is training right now."

She had me stay after practice and work on drills. Whenever I pointed out that no one else's mother made them stay, she simply informed me, "Champions always do more."

Exasperated, I whined, "Mom, I've been here for an extra fifteen minutes. Everybody's already left. I've already done more."

She simply told me, "Champions do more than people who think that they've done more."

Tuesdays were the hardest day of the week.

I worked the graveyard shift at 24 Hour Fitness on Saturdays and Sundays, so on Monday mornings, depending on how tired I was, I either headed to my apartment for a few hours of sleep or drove directly to strength and conditioning training with Leo. Leo was in Sherman Oaks, which is completely across L.A. from both 24 Hour Fitness and my house. I worked out with Leo, lifting weights and doing circuits, then showered at the gym (it had free conditioner!). Afterward, he let me sleep on the couch at his house for a few hours before we drove to wrestling practice. I relished that quiet time alone where I didn't have to be going from one place to another and could rest. We went together to wrestle at SK Golden Boys, which was a makeshift wrestling gym in a garage where Martin Berberyan ran practice. The level of competition made up for the thrown-together practice facility. I would go up against all the guys in wrestling, and when I didn't one-up them, I at least held my own. The garage was built to hold cars, not wrestling practice, so it was poorly ventilated and stiflingly hot. It was humid and smelled like sweat. I showered there, in the added-on bathroom, but the minute I stepped out of the shower, the heat was so overwhelming that I immediately started sweating again. We got back to Leo's after eight p.m. and it took me another hour to drive to DPCG's house, where I spent almost every night. He wasn't working, so he watched Mochi for me. After back-to-back overnight shifts and a double workout, I collapsed into bed.

On Tuesdays, DPCG and I woke up at seven-thirty a.m., then drove to the Coffee Bean in the Santa Monica business center. I loved waiting in line with his arms around me.

Then Mochi and I were off to Glendale to train. I took the 405 North to the 134, glad to be going against traffic My car's air-conditioning was still broken and I still only had one working window. I had a pair of laundry baskets in the backseat of my car, one containing clean clothes, the other dirty. Mochi liked pulling the dirty ones out and rolling around on them. The smell of dirty laundry, sweat, and dog slobber was overwhelming. I was pretty sure a new super pathogen was being bred in my backseat, and when Mochi started developing a rash, I considered that proof.

I got to GFC around nine in the morning, before Sevak, and let myself in. Mochi was supposed to stay on the slab of concrete by the door, but she refused to listen and climbed up on the corner of the ring. I warmed up until Edmond came. When he walked in and saw the dog in the ring, he could not hide his disgust, but it wasn't until months later that he politely asked me to stop bringing the dog to the gym.

"What should I do today?" I asked Edmond.

Then I did whatever exercise Edmond told me to do.

Hitting the bags, the little speed bag, the hulking heavy bag, the double end bag. Shadow boxing. Jump roping. Bouncing on the tire. Working with the medicine ball. Doing drills. Going under the little ropes, working on agility. There were hundreds of different things there I would do.

I did whatever Edmond assigned me to do until he realized that he had forgot I was still there doing it, far longer than he had intended me to do it. I never lessened the level of intensity that I put out. Then Edmond told me to do something else.

I spent three hours a day at GFC, and occasionally, if he was in a generous mood, Edmond held mitts for me, not even for twenty minutes. But on these days, I made the most of every second.

Whenever he called my name, I jumped up, ducked under the ropes, and stepped into the ring, where he had me throw a left jab. A jab is a quick, sharp blow, not the kind of power punch where you can throw a knockout with one hit. For months, every session was jab, jab, jab. Sometimes it was a double jab. That was all Edmond let me do in the ring for a very long time.

We worked on how to throw jabs and how to match them. Edmond hit me with thousands of punches and showed me how to block. If I looked tired, he hit me harder. Once he hit me so hard in the body that it knocked the wind out of me. I moved to take a knee, to catch my breath; he grabbed me with one hand and pulled me up.

"You're not taking a knee," he said. "If you take a knee, I'm going to hit you more. You don't have the choice to get hit or not get hit. You have one choice. You can get up and get hit or I can hit you down there." That was the last knee I ever took.

He kept throwing punches. I brought my hands down, as if to say, *Hit me in the face. I can take a punch.*

Edmond looked me in the eye and threw a jab right to the body. I fought not to double over.

"I'm not fucking stupid," Edmond said. "You give your head to me and expect me to hit your head. No, I'm going to hit your body."

I learned to never expect my opponents to just do what I wanted. I would have to make them do what I wanted.

I had to rush out of GFC to make it to the animal rehabilitation clinic where I was a vet assistant. I loaded into the car covered in three hours' worth of sweat to drive back across L.A. when the sun was at its highest point in my hotbox of a car. With Mochi settled in the back, I made the forty-five-minute drive home blasting indie dance music and singing and grooving in my car.

I would stop at my apartment and run in to shower. The water pressure was so pathetic that only a dribble came out.

DPCG lived right down the street from the clinic, a fifteen-minute commute from my place, and I swung by his house to drop off Mochi.

"Be a good girl," I said, leaving my dog behind to go care for other people's. I gave DPCG a big kiss, and he slapped me on the ass as I ran out the door to work.

I spent the next several hours hoisting dogs into and out of pools where they walked on an underwater treadmill, holding them down for physical therapy and acupuncture. I watched injured animals recover and aging animals deteriorate; I tried to keep a detached distance but always failed. In between appointments, I chatted with the clients about how I was training to be in MMA, until my bosses got tired of hearing people asking me how my fighting was going and banned me from talking about anything but dogs while I was on the clock.

I got a lunch break in the late afternoon and drove over to DPCG's house, where he would already have all my training food cooked— vegetables and chicken grilled with my favorite sauce from Versailles, a local Cuban restaurant—and waiting for me. I inhaled the food, leaving us a few minutes to enjoy each other's company before I raced back to work. I would finish my shift, but my day wasn't yet finished.

After thirty minutes stuck in the tail end of rush-hour traffic, I taught adults judo on L.A.'s Westside. I went through the motions, but felt an odd detachment from the sport. I stuck around to do the Brazilian Jiujitsu class afterward. Back at DPCG's house, he made this little tuna concoction— tuna, mayonnaise, Parmesan cheese, and Balsamic vinegar—that I loved and that we ate with toasted bread or tortilla chips.

Before climbing into bed, I peeled off another sweaty layer of clothes to shower. My body was noticeably slimming down, my muscles firming up. I was covered in bruises and mat burns and dog scratches. Sore was just a state of being. It wasn't as if I was not sore and then I became sore. I was sore just like I am blonde.

I stepped into the shower, letting the water pour down on me. Then I adopted my fighting stance and shadowboxed in the shower, throwing punches at water droplets.

I toweled off and collapsed into bed.

The days were all soreness, sweat, the stench of my car, and constant wet hair. I didn't mind it. I was in the middle of the hustle, and I understood that in order to be successful this was what I needed to do. I needed to practice more than anyone on the planet. I needed to be smarter and stronger and go longer. I needed to be at the gym when other people were merely thinking about going to the gym. I needed to go beyond what anyone else thought was reasonable and then go beyond that. Every day I did that, I moved one day closer to achieving my goal.

At night, I slept soundly, absolutely certain that I could not have done any more.

PLAN OUT THE FIRST EXCHANGE

People ask me all the time what my game plan is for an opponent. I never have a strict game plan. I plan the first exchange, then I improvise based upon everything that follows. Then I sketch out different possible scenarios. If she charges, I'm going to throw her forward. If she runs, I'll throw her backward.

You have to stay flexible. You have to be ready for anything. But I always plan the first exchange. By making the first move, I control the first action, which causes all the reactions.

I went from having no one willing to coach me to having no one willing to fight me.

In the beginning of my MMA career, the hardest part was getting fights. Darin would call and tell me he had a fight lined up. Then a few days later he'd call again to tell me that the girl's coach said she wasn't ready, or that I wasn't the right opponent.

The first few times I had been disappointed. By the fifth time it happened, I was just pissed. These girls supposedly wanted to be fighters, but they were unwilling to take a fight that they weren't absolutely positive they could win. It felt like no one was ever going to take a fight against me.

I took my frustration out on the punching bag and pounded it furiously, over and over and over.

I wanted to fight.

I wanted to win.

I wanted to beat someone up.

I told myself it was only a matter of time, and that when that time came, I was going to be ready. These girls would have to face me eventually, and I would make them regret giving me time to improve.

Darin called again. He had a potential fight lined up.

"There's just one thing," he said. "She will only take the fight at one-fifty."

I was now walking around at about 145 pounds. "Tell her we'll take it," I said.

There were two weeks until the fight. My excitement grew each day as the fight edged closer, but I was afraid to get my hopes up after being let down so many times.

The day before the fight, Edmond held mitts for me at GFC. He wasn't enthusiastic about training me, but he had kept his word about helping me prepare.

"Getting better," Edmond said.

I nodded.

"You ready?" he asked.

"Born that way," I said, punching the mitts.

He looked at me slightly confused, lost in translation. His English had improved dramatically since he started working with me, but like my striking, it still had a long way to go.

"Don't go in striking," Edmond said. "Do judo. Use judo to beat this girl."

I felt a surge of adrenaline.

"You think I'll win?" I asked. I knew I was going to win, but a sense of pride came from knowing that Edmond believed in me.

"Fighting girls? Not that hard," Edmond said with a shrug.

Edmond was noncommittal about cornering me. Darin said he would give him a call.

Darin and I left L.A. late morning on August 6, 2010, making the hour-long drive up to Oxnard. Edmond had agreed to come, but was going to drive up on his own later.

As we drove, Darin attempted to make small talk, but I preferred quiet before I fight. I was mentally preparing myself to fight the entire way up.

We pulled into the parking lot of the gym where the fight was being held. It was a completely random gym in Oxnard. Because it was an amateur fight, the weigh-in was the same day as the fight. We checked in and stood around waiting. My opponent had yet to arrive.

Just be ready, I told myself.

Then Hayden Munoz walked into the gym. There is very little ceremony to an amateur weigh-in, so they just had us hop up on the scale. She went first.

"One hundred and fifty-four pounds," the official running the weigh-in declared.

Everyone looked at me. Now, it was up to me. I could fight her or she would have to forfeit. I expected her to look disappointed, but I could see relief in her eyes. It would be short-lived.

"I'll fight anyway," I said.

I had never been more ready for something in my entire life. I changed in the gym's locker room and walked over to the warm-up area, which was just a sectioned-off part of the floor with some mats thrown down. Other fighters were starting to warm up, stretching, doing some light sparring. I lay down and closed my eyes. People started trickling in, most of them friends or family of the fighters. Gokor came over to where I was resting; he had agreed to be one of my cornermen. Edmond was nowhere in sight.

A few guys from Hayastan were milling around. I was flattered. My mom, Jennifer, and my old coach Blinky arrived. My mom made sure I saw she was there, but kept her distance, knowing that's what I like the day of a fight. Edmond still wasn't there. I accepted the fact that he might not come. I didn't need him there. The girl could have had forty pounds on me, and I was still going to beat her. Then about an hour before the fight, Edmond walked into the gym.

I felt a surge of happiness. Edmond cared enough about me as a fighter to come and corner me. He was reluctant to hold mitts for me and less than enthusiastic about training me, but he saw something in me that made him at least willing to take time out of his day to be there for me.

"You warmed up?" he asked.

I shrugged. I didn't need to be warm. I could be ready to go at a second's notice.

He took me over to the corner of the warm-up area, where he wrapped my hands, then had me throw jabs.

Energy was pulsing through my body. I was excited and calm.

"Relax," Edmond said.

I wanted to do more.

"Look, this girl is a kickboxer," Edmond said. "She's going to try to kick you right away. Step in, catch her leg, and take her down. Use your judo, nothing else. Just your judo."

I nodded.

"Munoz, Rousey, you're next," the fight organizers called out.

I walked into the cage. It was as if a switch was flipped, as if the entire world did not exist outside of the chain-link walls. I locked in on my opponent.

I stomped, then jumped, then smacked my shoulders. The referee looked at Hayden.

"Ready?" he asked. She nodded. He looked my way.

"Ready?" he asked again. I gave a nod.

Fight.

We approached each other in the center of the cage. She kicked. I grabbed her leg and took her to the ground. I threw myself on top of her and reached in for her arm. She fought to get away, but she never stood a chance. I grabbed her arm and cranked. She tapped. The entire fight lasted twenty-three seconds.

The referee called stop, and suddenly the whole world came back into view. Only this time, it was a better world. The crowd was cheering, screaming and whistling, and they were cheering for me. I raised my fist in the air, making a victory lap around the cage.

I felt a level of joy that I had never experienced before. It wasn't merely the victory; the joy came from a place much deeper, from an understanding that this was only the beginning.

On the way home I blasted Matt and Kim's "Don't Slow Down."

My next two amateur fights were a part of a well-run amateur show called Tuff-N-Uff. They were held at the Orleans Hotel in Las Vegas, about a mile off the Strip. My fights were so far off the radar that I did not even make it onto the event's promotional flier. I looked at it and thought, *One day my name will be on there.* Neither fight lasted a minute.

Five months after my amateur debut, having gone 3–0, I announced my decision to turn pro. With my amateur career behind me, I was one step closer to achieving my goal of being the world champion. The next leg of the journey was about to begin.

I am often asked if I could have ever envisioned achieving all that I have accomplished since I stepped into the cage that night. People are often surprised to learn that the answer is unequivocally yes. Everything that has happened since that moment is exactly what I had in mind when I executed that first exchange.

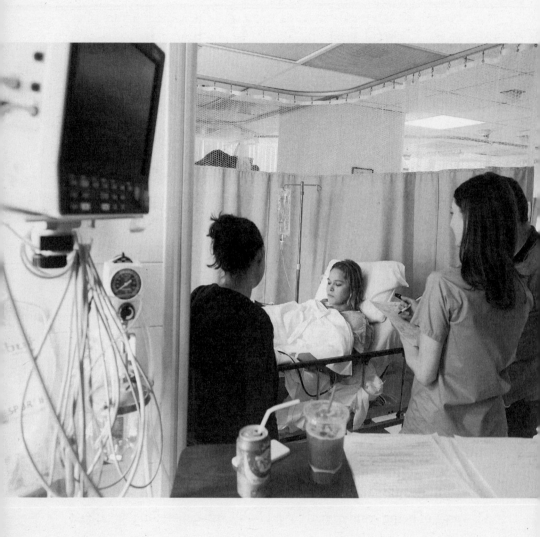

NOTHING WILL EVER
BE PERFECT

You can spend your entire life waiting for perfect. The perfect job. The perfect partner. The perfect opponent. Or you can acknowledge that there is always a better time or a better place or a better opportunity and refuse to let that fact hold you back from doing everything to make the present moment the perfect moment.

I'm not undefeated because I had the perfect circumstances leading up to every fight. I'm undefeated because, regardless of circumstances, I still win.

I had made the jump to the professional ranks, but aside from my record being reset to 0–0, not much had changed. I was still working three jobs. I was still living in a rundown place I found on Craigslist (although I was now renting a room in a house on the verge of being condemned). And fights still kept falling through.

Darin lined up my professional debut against a fighter named Ediane Gomes. As part of the deal, he was paying for her flight (which is not standard for a low-level pro bout). It was scheduled for March 27, 2011, at a country club in nearby Tarzana.

Each fighter would make four hundred dollars for showing up, with the winner getting double.

I pulled up all the information and videos I could find of her previous fights. She had a record of 6–1 and was creaming people. *She'll do,* I thought.

The way my fights kept falling through, Edmond had been working with me more regularly, but we were focusing on building up my skills as opposed to preparing for any single opponent.

"It doesn't matter who you're fighting," Edmond told me. "It doesn't matter if they give you one day's notice, you're going to win."

I nodded in agreement.

The week of the fight, I allowed myself to believe it was really going to happen. I could not wait.

"What do you want your walkout song to be?" Darin asked me a few days before the fight.

"'Sex and Violence' by The Exploited," I replied. The song consisted of the words *sex* and *violence* repeated over and over.

Two days before the fight, I was lying in my room thinking about how I was going to destroy this girl when I heard a commotion in the living room. Mochi had been playing with my roommate's dog. Now they were fighting.

Porkchop, a sixty-pound pitbull, was on his back and Mochi, who had grown to eighty pounds, had him by the neck. Mochi looked like she was going to kill him. Without thinking, I gave Mochi a swift kick in the ribs. She jumped back, leaving Porkchop flailing about. Still in fight mode, he bit me twice—once on the foot and once in the shin. I felt his sharp teeth break through my skin and sink into my muscle.

Before my body even registered the pain, I began to worry about what the injury would mean for the fight.

I collapsed on the living room floor and pulled off my sock. There was a hole in the arch of my foot. Flesh was hanging off the base of my toes. A split second later, blood filled the holes and started gushing onto the carpet. I grabbed my cell phone off the floor where it had fallen during the chaos and dialed Darin's number. I needed to go a doctor and I needed for nobody to know about it.

As I waited for Darin to find me a doctor, I pulled myself up off the living room floor. My foot was swelling up. I hopped into the kitchen, leaving a trail of blood droplets. There wasn't any ice, but there were several open packages of frozen vegetables. I hopped to the bathroom and wrapped the bags of vegetables around my foot with an Ace bandage.

In the living room, my phone rang. I hopped back to answer it, frozen peas and carrots spilling out behind me.

"Get a pencil," Darin said.

He had a friend who was a fancy plastic surgeon in Beverly Hills who was willing to see me off-the-record.

I called DPCG. "I need you," I said.

"I'm on my way," he told me before I could even explain the situation.

I had moved to the kitchen, because it would be easier to clean blood off the tile.

Fifteen minutes later, I heard DPCG rush into the house.

"Where are you?" he called.

"Follow the blood and carrots!" I shouted.

He came into the kitchen, a look of concern on his face. Without saying anything, he scooped me up and carried me to his car.

I put my foot up on the dashboard and stared at the blood that was seeping through the bandage. DPCG had one hand on the steering wheel as I squeezed his other hand. Tears ran down my cheeks.

"It's going to be OK," he said.

The spa-like waiting room was filled with wealthy women seeking Botox and boob jobs. They all turned to stare, but the woman behind the reception desk looked completely unfazed.

DPCG took me into the exam room. The doctor looked at the bloodsoaked bandage and thawed vegetables.

"Do you mind if I take this off?" he asked.

He unwrapped the bandage, "Wow, this looks pretty bad. You're definitely going to need stitches."

I started to sob. I was terrified I would not be able to compete. *No,* I thought. *I am not going down like this.*

I wiped away the tears and looked at the doctor. "The only thing I need to know is will I permanently hurt myself if I fight on this?"

He paused, taken slightly aback. "Well, no. I mean, you'll rip the stitches, and it'll take longer to heal, but you're not going to do any permanent damage."

I took a deep breath and said, "OK, then, sew me up."

He looked at me, uncertain as to whether he should be impressed or have me committed, then slowly said, "I can do that, but you're going to burst your stitches open in the first round. You'll bleed all over everywhere and everyone's going to know."

"It's OK" I said. "I'll just have to win faster than that." He took out a kit to sew me up. He picked up the needle.

"Do you want the stitch knot from the outside?" he asked. "If I stitch it from the inside, it won't scar so badly. But if I stitch it from the outside, it'll be stronger."

"Fuck the scar," I said. "Do the one that's stronger."

The doctor finished stitching me up. There were three stitches on the side arch of my foot, six over the top.

"That's the best I can do," he said, looking at his work. "But you better win fast."

"I will," I promised.

DPCG carried me back out to the car.

The next morning, my foot was throbbing even worse. I had iced it overnight and took Advil and the antibiotics the doctor prescribed, but it had swollen up considerably. Still, I had no doubt in my mind that I was going to beat this girl. The real challenge was going to be getting through the weigh-in and the medical check. If you have stitches, they won't let you fight.

It took nearly all of my energy not to limp into the building for the weigh-in.

The doctor performed a cursory exam. "Hop on one foot," he said.

I hopped on my right leg.

"Now the other."

I shifted all my weight to my left foot and hopped with a stoic face. I could feel the stitches bulge under the weight.

"Everything looks good," the doctor said.

You have no idea, I thought. Now, we just had to weigh in.

Then the athletic commission representative dropped a bomb on me.

"Shorts or underwear only," an official announced. "So shirts, shoes, socks, they all need to come off."

No socks? My pulse spiked.

The only thing racing faster than my heart was my mind.

Then I had an idea.

Here's the thing about making weight. If you're comfortably within your weight, you might weigh in wearing underwear or fight shorts. But if you're close, you can weigh in naked. When that happens, members of your team hold towels around you so that you're not giving the public a free show.

"I think I drank too much water," I announced loudly so anyone in the general vicinity could hear.

"I'm paranoid that I'm not going to make weight," I told Darin. "I'm going to weigh in naked."

"What?" he asked me as if I had lost my mind. "Why? It doesn't matter. She's overweight. You don't need to." My opponent had shown up overweight and had been upfront about it. I had been starving myself to make 145 pounds.

"I'm getting naked," I blurted out.

I started ripping off my clothes while my team rushed to find towels to hold up in front of me. Everyone was confused and scrambling, and in the pandemonium, no one noticed that I had jumped on the scale with my back to the room and took off my socks last. I weighed in at 145.5, three and a half pounds lighter than the other girl, and while everyone was busy trying to figure out why I had suddenly decided I needed to weigh in naked, I put on my socks before anyone noticed my mangled foot. By the time I'd pulled on my underwear, I knew I'd be fighting the next evening.

On fight night, I slipped an ankle sleeve upside down over my foot to cover the stitches. My foot hurt so badly that I was limited in my warm-up.

"You better make this quick," Edmond said.

"I know," I said.

"You're crazy," he told me.

I just smiled. He was probably right.

I watched as Gomes walked into the cage, the hip-hop beat of her walkout song blaring through the venue. She danced around the cage.

You won't be dancing when I'm done with you, I thought.

The drumbeat of "Sex and Violence" came over the speakers. I marched out, the pain in my foot suddenly irrelevant.

The referee clapped his hands and the bell rang.

I came forward with a jab and a left hook and we clinched. I tried to throw her forward, but she resisted. I instinctively changed direction and swept her left foot with a *kouchi-gari* judo throw. As the stitches on the arch of my foot collided with her heel, signals of pain flared. I ignored them. She hit the ground and I mounted her immediately. I punched her in the face several times; the blows focused less on inflicting damage and more on forcing her to react. She turned to her side: There it was! I spun into my favorite *juji gatame* armbar, and she tapped. The bell had barely stopped ringing. The entire fight lasted twenty-five seconds.

I raised my hands above my head. I had won. For a split second, it felt amazing.

The joy of that first pro victory was slightly tempered by the pain receptors kicking back in, my brain letting me know that my foot hurt like a motherfucker.

I was 1–0, and I was impatient. A week after my win, I took nail clippers and cut the stitches out of my foot. The doctor had been right; the scar was noticeable. I thought it looked badass. I was ready for another fight.

Darin told me he had one lined up in Calgary against a fighter named Charmaine Tweet. She would only take the fight at 150 pounds, but I was desperate for an opponent. We booked our plane tickets. I was going back to Canada. But from the beginning, the match was jinxed. When I told Edmond the date, he furrowed his brow; his son was due right around then. Then, two weeks before the fight, I was at Rite Aid with Jennifer when Darin called.

"I've got some news," he said. "Strikeforce called. They want to sign you to a fight."

Strikeforce was the highest level professional MMA organization that had a women's division. They wanted me to fight Sarah D'Alelio because Gina Carano, who was slated to be making a comeback after two years away, had pulled out with a medical issue.

I was getting the call-up from the minor leagues to the big time. Strikeforce fights paid a lot more money than the small shows. This meant I could quit my three jobs and finally make ends meet by fighting.

I felt like the heavens had opened up and angels were singing. The biggest smile spread across my face. I actually squealed in delight, moving my feet up and down in what was a publicly acceptable happy dance.

"What is it?" Jen whispered.

"The only thing is the fight is scheduled for June 18," Darin said.

I paused.

"The fight in Canada is the night before," I said.

"But don't worry about it. We'll get you out of it."

I hugged Jennifer, who is not the hugging type.

"Jen, I'm in Strikeforce," I said.

"Great," Jen said in a voice that conveyed if she ever got overly excited about anything, this would be that kind of thing. "I don't know what that means, but congratulations."

I started putting random things in my shopping basket. An electric toothbrush. Expensive whitening toothpaste. Eyeliner. Nail polish. I didn't even know how to put nail polish on, but I threw it in with everything else. I grabbed the nice, soft toilet paper. I was going to have the money to afford a few luxuries.

We checked out and were in the parking lot when Darin called me back.

"I've got some bad news," Darin said. "She's not going to let you out of the fight."

My heart sank. I felt completely deflated. Jen and I got into the car, and as I looked behind me to pull out, I saw the white Rite Aid bag on the backseat. "Fuck, I can't afford any of this shit," I realized out loud.

I was still upset the next day at practice when Edmond pulled me aside.

"Ronda, you got to calm down," he said. "Strikeforce wanted you. You beat this girl, and I promise you, they're going to want you again. No need to get upset about it. Who else are they going to pick in Strikeforce? All you need is two to three fights. You're the best fighter they know. You're still going to get a call. I promise you, after this fight, you'll be in Strikeforce."

For the next two weeks, I trained with a singular focus: making Charmaine Tweet pay.

Darin, Edmond, and I were scheduled on the first flight to Calgary on June 16. The day before we flew out, I got a call from Edmond. His wife was in labor.

"I'm still coming," he said. "I'm just going to change my flight and meet up with you guys there."

"Congratulations," I told him.

"Thank you," he said.

The next morning, Darin picked me up at dawn and we headed to the airport. We were in line waiting when I looked at the time.

"We're super early." I was used to cutting it close when it came to flights.

"Well, we're only going to Canada, but it's still an international flight," Darin said.

The line started to move, but every single muscle in my body froze.

"Do you need your passport to go to Canada?" I asked quietly.

Darin turned to me.

"What?"

"Do you need your passport to go to Canada?"

"Yes. Why? Did you forget it at your house?"

I frantically tried to picture where in my house my passport was.

When was the last time I needed my passport? I asked myself.

I felt the blood drain from my face.

"My passport is at the Brazilian consulate," I admitted. I had left it there to get a visa ahead of the judo tournament I never attended in Brazil. I racked my brain; had it been a year ago?

We stepped out of line. Darin looked at his watch. The Brazilian consulate wasn't even open yet. He got on his phone. I just stood there, not knowing what else I could do.

"Someone is going to meet us at the Brazilian consulate and open it up for us," Darin said. He had talked to the promoter as well. They said I could weigh in at the hotel whenever we arrived. Then he got us on a later flight, and we jumped in the car and rushed to the consulate. When we arrived forty-five minutes later, a staffer was waiting for us. He handed me my passport.

"You have great timing," he said. "We only hold passports for a year. We were about to send it out to you this week and it would have been in the mail."

I couldn't help but think that the timing could have been a little better.

Passport in hand, Darin and I rushed back to the airport. We were going to be cutting it close if we wanted to make our flight.

Standing in the security line, I heard a familiar voice say, "Heeeeey you guys."

It was Edmond, still wobbly from a night out celebrating his son's birth and surprised to see us.

Thirty minutes later, the three of us were packed into a row in coach, me in the middle. Edmond passed out right away. I could smell the alcohol oozing out of his pores.

The next day, we arrived at the casino where the fight was being held. They had a craps table in the back. The warm-up mats were so dirty that Edmond had to find towels to rub down the noticeable layer of grime. Even so, when we got up after grappling, we had dirt all over our skin.

"Make this fight fast," Edmond said. "This place is disgusting. I want to get out of here."

I beat her by an armbar in forty-nine seconds to improve to 2–0. Afterward, as she was walking back to her corner, I got in her face and shouted, "You should have let me go to Strikeforce, you stupid fucking bitch!"

It wasn't my fastest finish, but it was my biggest payout so far. I earned $1,000.

After the fight, we headed back to the hotel so I could take a much-needed shower. I had just finished getting dressed when Edmond knocked on my door. I opened the door and Edmond came inside the small entry hall leading into my room.

"I have something to tell you," Edmond said.

"What?" I asked.

"Strikeforce called: You're in Strikeforce."

"Oh my God!" I shouted. I started jumping up and down. I did a happy dance.

"I told you it was going to happen," he said.

Edmond looked me over. I was wearing jeans and a hooded sweatshirt. He was wearing his immaculately ironed shirt, his nice shoes, expensive jeans, and a Gucci belt.

"Now listen, you're going to be out in front of the camera a lot and people are going to see you," he said. "There are things we have to do a bit different."

He pointed to my outfit.

"No more baggy clothes like that," he said. "I know you're a fighter and you don't care, but let's forget about the fighting for just one minute. Let's get a little bit image going on. Forget about looking fancy when you can't fight for shit, but you can fight.

"Things are going to change and you need to start thinking about that. I'm guiding you like I would to my sister. I'm not telling you these things about your appearance so you feel bad about it. I just want the best for you. You deserve it."

I was excited and flattered, but more than anything, I was hungry.

"OK, Edmond," I said. "I will do that. I will fight perfect and I will dress perfect and I will do whatever else you ask, but can we start after dinner?"

My life was going to radically change. I was going to be able to quit all of my other jobs and support myself as a fighter. I was going to prove all of the people who said I shouldn't be a fighter wrong. I was going to have enough money to fix my car windows and maybe even the air-conditioning. I might even be able to afford to move to a nicer place.

I could have done without the stitches, the false alarm, the forgotten passport, and the dirty casino. But those bumps, like all obstacles in life, forced me to adjust. I learned I could fight through anything. I learned how badly I wanted this dream and how much it hurt to have it so close and then ripped away. The experiences made me want to succeed even more and made me even more driven. The lead-up to my first professional fights might not have gone perfectly according to my plan, but, in the end, everything worked out perfectly. That's all you can ask for.

IF IT WAS EASY,
EVERYONE WOULD DO IT

People are always looking for the secret to success. There isn't a secret. Success is the result of hard work, busting your ass every day for years on end without cutting corners or taking shortcuts. It was Michelangelo who said, "If people knew how hard I worked to get my mastery, it wouldn't seem so wonderful at all."

It is not hard to figure out what goes into being successful, but it's also not easy to do.

DPCG and I broke up several times. The day he stole my car was the lowest point, but he was still struggling with his addiction. We would break up, but it always felt like the universe kept pulling us back together.

Twice, we broke up, and a few days later, I would be stopped at a light and see him in my rearview mirror. He shrugged his shoulders or shook his head, as if to say, "What are the odds of seeing you here?" We pulled over and laughed about it, and realizing how much we missed each other, we would kiss and cry and make up.

However, the relationship had changed. I was transforming and that was the one thing that really pulled us apart. Not the MMA itself, but that I got to the point where I wanted more. I was getting more and more motivated every day. I was on a mission to take over the world.

He didn't have the same drive. And though DPCG believed in me and supported my MMA dream when everyone else was rolling their eyes at the idea, he was also insecure about it.

One night, practice at Hayastan ran late.

"Hey, girl, where you been?" he asked casually as I walked in the door.

"Practice," I said. I was exhausted, sore, and wanted nothing more than a shower before falling into bed. But first, I leaned in to give him a kiss. He pulled back.

"You smell like some dude's cologne," he said. It wasn't an outright accusation.

"What are you saying?"

"Nothing." He shook his head and smiled apologetically. "Nothing."

"The Armenian guys I was training with douse themselves in cologne after practice and hug me as I walk out the door," I said, defensively.

"They're hugging you," he said. His eyebrows furrowed slightly.

"They're my friends. I've known them forever. They're Armenian. Armenians are very affectionate. I can't just tell everyone to fuck off and run out the door after practice."

"Yeah, I guess so," he said.

"Thank you," I said. "Now, I'm going to take a shower."

As I started to undress, DPCG wrapped his arms around my waist from behind. I leaned back as he nuzzled his face into my neck. Suddenly, he pulled back.

"Is that a hickey?" he asked. His tone was accusatory.

"Wha—What the what?" I stumbled over the words. I looked in the mirror.

"That's a mark from where someone was trying to choke me," I said, pointing to my neck. "And that one there, and that one there too."

"It looks like a hickey," he said.

"Well, it's not," I told him. "I've spent most of my life covered in bruises and marks. I don't even notice them. It's nothing to get worked up about. It's just normal."

But he wasn't a fighter, so he didn't see it that way. He wanted to support me, but the more driven I became, the more threatened he felt in our relationship. He didn't have a job he liked. He hadn't found something he was passionate about. He was resigned to accept his situation, whereas I was obsessed with elevating mine.

When we met, he was perfect for me. We were two people content not to aspire toward anything. But then I changed.

We broke up for the final time shortly after I had gone pro. We had been through so much after two years together. He really was one of my best friends. I knew it was different this time, because it wasn't dramatic. There was no animosity. I didn't cry hysterically. It wasn't like we were having an argument. It was more like we were really saying goodbye. And we just talked, tears trickling down our faces until we fell asleep.

He woke up before me, and slipped out without waking me. On my door, he left a message in dry-erase marker. It read: *I love you, girl. Don't ever forget, you are my heart.*

I never wiped it off.

THE ONLY POWER PEOPLE HAVE OVER YOU IS THE POWER YOU GIVE THEM

In judo, so many people care about rank and what degree black belt they are. I have never gotten caught up in that. Rank is based solely on a board of people getting together and saying, "Oh, you deserve to be such-and-such a rank." Once you give them the power to tell you you're great, you've also given them the power to tell you you're unworthy. Once you start caring about people's opinions of you, you give up control.

It's the same reason I don't get caught up in being the crowd favorite when I fight. It's why I don't read things that are written about me. One of the greatest days of my life was when I came to understand that other people's approval and my happiness were not related.

My first Strikeforce fight was scheduled for August 12, 2011, and I would be facing Sarah D'Alelio after all.

Ahead of the D'Alelio bout, I had a camp for the first

time—camp is tailoring your workout schedule so that you are at your absolute physical and mental peak when you step into the ring. The emphasis was still on building up my skills, but we started preparing specifically for D'Alelio.

I quit all my jobs and we did a four-week camp. Though we didn't have the money to bring in top-notch sparring partners, I'd never had such focused training leading up to competition.

On Monday of the week of the fight, I got a call from Darin.

"The folks at Showtime called," he said. Strikeforce had a national broadcast deal with the cable network. "It's about your walkout song."

"Same one, 'Sex and Violence,'" I said.

"That's the thing, they have an issue with the words," Darin said.

"Wait, which word? *Sex* or *violence*? Because that's literally the entire song, just a guy going 'sex and violence, sex and violence.'"

"Actually, both," Darin said.

I laughed. "But literally, isn't that what they're selling?" I asked. "Why do people watch women's fights? Sex appeal and physical violence."

"I don't know," Darin said, slightly exasperated. "You just need to choose another song."

"Fine, just pick something from Rage Against the Machine," I said.

Two days before the fight, we drove to Vegas. I rode with Darin. Edmond and a few other guys from GFC came. We met at the club and caravanned out through the desert. We could have flown to Vegas, but I liked making the drive.

From the moment we arrived and checked into the Palms—where the fight was being held—it was clear I had reached the next level. Everything just ran smoother. It was more professional.

The organizers knew who you were and where you needed to be when. The venue was bigger. The fighters higher caliber.

We had a warm-up room; not a random area cordoned off, but a room to put our stuff in and to warm up with my trainers. There were people who kept me updated on when I was going to fight and showed me where to go. I felt right at home.

I walked out to Rage Against the Machine. The song didn't feel quite right.

I stepped inside the cage. The referee sent us to our corners, then told us, "Bring it on!" I jabbed to close the space for a clinch. D'Alelio threw a straight right and missed. I took a grip that only a judoka would know. It was a grip for one of my favorite judo throws, *sumi gaeshi*, where you pull your opponent to the ground on top of you and throw her over. I instinctively jumped into the throw, but because there was no gi to grab on to, I started to lose my grip. Midair I changed the technique to an armbar and started cranking on her arm while she was still falling.

"Tap! Tap! Tap!" she started yelling as she fell to the ground, holding one arm out to keep herself from face-planting into the ground.

I knew she did not have a hand to tap and that when her hand hit the ground to catch herself, all of the weight from the fall would go through her elbow and obliterate the joint. To save her arm, I let my legs fall off as we hit the ground, but I held my position. She still didn't have a free hand to tap.

"She's trying to tap," I told the referee.

The referee called the fight.

"I didn't tap! I didn't tap!" she shouted to the referee.

The entire fight had lasted twenty-five seconds.

I jumped up, pumping my hands in the air. She went back to her corner, protesting. The crowd booed.

I looked in her direction.

"You want to go again?" I yelled in front of the crowd. "Come on, let's go again."

But once a fight is called, it's over. The referee brought us to the center of the ring.

"The winner, by way of submission, Rowdy Ronda Rousey," the announcer declared as the referee raised my hand. The boos grew louder. Interviewed post-fight, she would admit to crying out, which by the rules qualifies as a "verbal tapout."

D'Alelio and I shared a post-fight loose hug. "Don't listen to them," she said in my ear.

Though I appreciated the sentiment, my elation was tempered, not by the boos raining down around me—I had been booed all over the world— but because people were questioning my win. I didn't want anyone to ever question me in the cage ever again.

"She tapped," I said to Edmond as we walked out of the arena.

"Of course, she tapped," Edmond said. "Every person in this goddamn arena knows she tapped even if some people are acting like she didn't."

"From this day on, I'm just going to break everybody's fucking arm," I said.

Before I left the venue, they gave me my check. It was eight thousand dollars, but it felt like a million.

"Now, I can pay you," I told Edmond. The standard is for a fighter to give ten percent of their winnings to the head trainer.

"Ronda, you deserve way more money," Edmond said. "A fighter like you, you deserve a million dollars to fight."

"You really think so?" I asked.

"Absolutely."

"I can't wait to pay you that ten percent when I make millions," I said.

"Yeah, me too," Edmond said. "Because let's be serious, I am not going to take anything out of that check. You keep it." My eyes widened.

"Are you serious?"

"Of course, I'm serious," Edmond said. "You keep that. I don't need that money. You fight for a living. I understand what fighting for a living is. I fought myself. Just keep doing your thing. Now, you make a million…"

I gave Edmond a huge hug.

I'd made it into the top ranks. Now I set my sights on a championship.

Then, one day, Miesha Tate mentioned me on Twitter.

A fan asked Miesha if she would ever fight me. She included me in her response: "Sure! Why not!" (Note to Miesha: Proper punctuation in the second sentence should actually be a question mark.)

I had never heard of her, but I clicked on to her page to check her out. Turned out she was the Strikeforce women's champion at 135 pounds. I had been considering dropping down to 135 and was on the record saying I planned to be the 135-pound (bantamweight) and 145-pound (featherweight) champ simultaneously. When the champ at 135 pounds said she was down to fight me, I decided the time had come to make the move. As I saw it, two people stood between me and a bantamweight title fight: my upcoming opponent, Julia Budd, and the No. 2 fighter at 135, Sarah Kaufman. I was going to take them both out.

Budd loomed over me at weigh-ins. She had a height advantage, but I didn't care. I was still pissed off about my last victory being questioned. I was going to make an example out of this chick.

I walked out to Rage Against the Machine again, a different song, but it still didn't feel quite right.

As soon as the referee said "Fight!" I jabbed in to close the distance and pushed her back to the cage. We clinched, and I could feel she was slick with lotion. I went to throw her forward, but she was so slippery, I knew if I fully committed, I'd lose my grip. I switched direction and swept her backward.

Once I had her on the ground, all I had to do was punch and herd her into the position I wanted to set up my favorite armbar. As soon as I broke her grip and pulled her arm straight, she bridged and flipped over trying to escape. We were facedown, and I could feel her elbow joint popping, but I was not going to make the mistake of leaving any question like I had last time. I flipped her back over so the referee could see the damage. I kept cranking on her elbow, leaning back until it popped. She tried to keep going, but gave up a few seconds later. The announcer compared the appearance of Budd's badly dislocated elbow to a flamingo knee.

The fight had taken thirty-nine seconds.

In judo, I had been conditioned to be humble after victory, to be respectful of a challenger who puts up a good fight, not to celebrate after injuring an opponent. I tried to contain my elation. When I saw her rise from the mat, I allowed myself to smile and relish the victory. But my night was not yet done.

Mauro Ranallo, the Showtime broadcaster, asked me about my plans to move to 135 pounds after the fight.

I glanced over at Edmond. My corner knew about my plan.

I looked straight into the camera. I had thought about this moment.

"If Sarah Kaufman is next in line, please, Strikeforce, let me get a crack at her first. I really want to have a title fight against Miesha Tate, and I don't want to take a risk on her losing. Please give me a crack at Sarah Kaufman first, then Miesha Tate. I swear I'll put on a good show."

It was the first ever nationally televised women's callout. No woman fighter in MMA had ever really called anyone out in such a public setting. It was both a plea and a performance. It was my first attempt at being an entertainer.

Backstage, Strikeforce matchmaker Sean Shelby approached me.

"You're not going to have to fight Kaufman first," he said. "We're just going to give you Miesha right away."

"Awesome," I said.

I was thrilled. Miesha was not. She did not want to fight me, and she argued with Sean Shelby about it, but the decision had been made.

I didn't know much about Miesha Tate. I just wanted to fight her because she was the champion, so I assumed she could fight. I knew there were people who thought she was reasonably good-looking and I was reasonably good-looking. I figured that would help draw interest in the fight. I knew the fight would sell. And I knew I could beat her.

The fight game is not just about the fight. It's about the show. The athleticism is an integral part of the show, but that alone is not enough to keep people coming back. People watch fighters, but they remember characters. You have to keep them excited. You have to make them intrigued. You have to captivate them.

Two weeks later, Miesha and I made a joint appearance on the "MMA Hour" podcast to debate whether I deserved to get a title shot at her immediately or eventually.

Now, I come from a family of smart, quick-witted women. When we were younger, my sisters and I engaged in a fair amount of "verbal sparring." You had to be quick with your response or you would get put in your place. My sister Jennifer can smack you so hard with a comeback that you will need to sit down. My sister Maria has this ability to remember everything, from what she had for lunch in preschool to a random magazine article she read five years ago. She will cite five rapid-fire, airtight examples, then call you out with, "Give me a specific example." My mom has the ability to, without raising her voice, shift her tone to send a shiver down her enemies' backs. There was no opportunity in our house for "Yeah, yeah, but, but." The conversation would have moved ten steps past you at that point, and you would have to admit defeat. I had been training in this arena even longer than I had been training in judo.

In interviews she had given, Miesha had already shown that she was underestimating my abilities inside the cage. I was fairly certain she was underestimating me outside it as well.

I wanted to be ready to tear down any potential argument she could conceive of. I wanted to be ready to rip apart arguments that she hadn't even thought up yet. I wanted to back her into a corner so she had no choice but to fight me, and I wanted her to see how superior I was to her in every aspect of the fight game, in and outside of the cage.

I did the exact same thing I would do ahead of a fight: I prepared.

In the days leading up to the podcast, I spent every waking minute either fight-training or debate-training. Between practices and before going to bed, I read every article I could find on her. I scoured her social media. I watched interviews she gave. I jotted down every point Miesha had made, every argument against me she had already tried, and arguments against me that she hadn't even conceived of yet. I took notes that I typed up on a friend's computer. During breaks at practice, I would pull out the cheat sheet containing both points of view. I handed it to one of the guys at the gym.

"Say something and I'll refute it," I said.

I practiced defending against her points. I practiced arguing her points. Regardless of which side of the argument I was on, I would win. By the time I was done, I was better at arguing her side than she was.

At Edmond's urging, I had gone to the Third Street Promenade to buy some new clothes for the upcoming media appearances. It was almost Thanksgiving and the outdoor shopping mall was already decorated for Christmas.

I'll actually have money to buy my family Christmas presents this year, I realized. I was window-shopping when I realized I'd lost track of time and wouldn't be able to make it home to do the call-in. I picked a spot on the sidewalk outside of Urban Outfitters. It would have to do.

My phone rang. I felt a surge of adrenaline. I was ready to give a verbal beat down.

When the show started, Miesha took the first shot, "What happens when she gets a failed armbar and someone ends up on top pounding her face in?" she asked. "Is she going to tap out or quit? We don't know. We haven't seen that yet. I think it's kind of silly to put her in with me, because that's what I'm going to do. I'm going to take it to her."

Her logic seemed to be that because I had been so dominant, because no one had lasted even a single minute in the cage with me, I hadn't proven myself. She was grasping at straws.

I realized that I would be better served by selling the fight than defending myself. I talked about money. I talked about interest. I talked about putting on a show. It wasn't just about me and Miesha. It was about everything I had envisioned when people told me no one would ever care about women's MMA.

Miesha just wanted to talk about me. I dodged every jab she threw my way, replying with a power punch.

You should be more humble as a fighter, she said.

Fighters who lack humility get paid just the same, I pointed out.

I hadn't proven myself, she said.

I named other successful fighters who had made a rapid ascent.

You're just thinking about yourself, she said.

It's a professional sport, I explained to her, with emphasis on the professional. If she wanted it to be about ideals, I suggested she forgo the money and try out for the Olympics.

"What happens if I go out there and I just cream you?" she asked.

"That's a risk I'm willing to take," I said. "You should be willing to take some risks too."

"I'm willing," Miesha said.

Interest grew exponentially. Articles about our fight were everywhere. Fans were taking sides. Interest in a women's fight, in any Strikeforce fight, had never been higher. I responded to every single interview request, scheduling and squeezing them in between training sessions and taking calls early in the morning or late at night.

The next weekend I drove out to Las Vegas for the World MMA Awards, to party with some fighters I knew and to catch a UFC fight at the Palms. We were a few rows back from the cage, and I was several drinks into embracing the "What happens in Vegas, stays in Vegas" mantra, when Frank and Lorenzo Fertitta and Dana White, the three most powerful men in the sport of MMA, walked into the arena. The Fertitta brothers own a combined eighty-one percent of Zuffa, the parent organization of the UFC, MMA's premier organization. Dana White is the UFC's president. Zuffa owned Strikeforce.

As if someone poked me with a cattle prod, a jolt ran through my body. I sat straight up with a smile. My inner voice was screaming at full volume, "Hold it together, woman."

They walked right by us and Dana stopped and introduced himself.

"You're Ronda Rousey," he said.

My jaw nearly hit the ground.

"Hi," I said.

"Great to meet you," he said.

Then someone a few seats over called him, and Dana moved on.

Two days later, I was pulling out of the parking lot at the Palms when Joan Jett came on the radio.

"I don't give a damn 'bout my reputation..." The lyrics struck a chord with my soul.

I had found my new walkout song.

WINNING IS A HABIT

Aristotle said, "We are what we repeatedly do. Excellence then is not an act, but a habit." Winning is a habit, and so is losing.

You can get into the habit of going into a tournament, a meeting, or an audition telling yourself: This is just for practice. If I fail, I can always try again later. If you go in with your excuses already laid out for you, it's hard to shake that mindset when "later" finally comes.

Or you can go into every endeavor with the attitude that you are going to knock this one out of the park. You can tell yourself: I am bringing my A-game because that is the only grade of game that I have. I am here to win, and you can come along for the ride or you can get the hell out of the way.

Winning is a habit that means trying—and expecting—to be better than everybody in the world every day.

Everything leading up to the Tate fight was amplified. Camp was more difficult. The weight cut was harder. The attention was greater. The tension was higher. But every day I woke up with one purpose: Take the belt away from Miesha Tate.

I could have beaten her the day I called her out, but merely winning wasn't enough. I wanted to annihilate her, to embarrass her, to force her to admit that I was the greatest female fighter on the planet, to apologize for thinking she could be mentioned in the same sentence as me.

It was the first full camp we ever did, setting aside six weeks ahead of the March 3, 2012, bout in Columbus, Ohio. It marked the first time Edmond brought in outside sparring partners in addition to using the guys at GFC.

Darin got me a temporary apartment by the club so I wouldn't have to commute back and forth across L.A. I was so traumatized from losing water to cut weight in judo that I wanted to make 135 just by dieting down. I limited myself to one meal a day, which I didn't eat until night; it was a promise to myself, a prize for getting through the day.

Because I hadn't done a dramatic weight cut in more than two years, the weight dropped off right away. I was almost at weigh-in weight the first week of camp, but I was weakened. I was going more rounds of sparring than I had ever gone with no food in my body.

I was working social media as if it were a full-time job.

Coming out of camp, I was totally worn out, but I knew I didn't have to be fresh in order to be the best in the world. The Tuesday of fight week, Edmond, Darin, and I boarded a plane for Ohio. I took my scratchy airplane pillow, rested my head against Edmond's shoulder, and slept the entire flight.

We landed and made our way to the hotel. I woke up the next morning with a sore throat and a fever. Edmond took my temperature, and it was 101.2. For the next two days, I stayed in bed.

Friday, we went to the arena for the weigh-ins. I made weight. Then they had Miesha and I face off, our faces just inches apart.

She leaned forward, touching her forehead to mine. I pushed her back using my head. The fight officials jumped between us.

Miesha looked shaken. She had a huge red mark on her forehead.

Get used to me owning you, bitch, I thought.

My mom met up with me after the weigh-ins for dinner.

"How are you feeling?" she asked, looking concerned.

"Better," I said, but she looked unconvinced.

I ate salted fish and vegetables for dinner, then we went back up to my room and lay on the bed.

"Can you tell me why I'm going to beat this girl?" I asked.

I felt like I was a little kid again on my way to a tournament.

"You want it more."

"Uh-huh."

"You've been training for this your entire life. You're an elite-level athlete. She's what, a high school wrestler? You have fought thousands of matches in the most high-pressure scenarios imaginable."

"More, more," I said.

"You know you can win if you're sick or injured. You're smarter than her."

"No shit," I said.

My mom made a cup of coffee and I posted a few more social media updates before turning my phone off until after the fight.

"That fucking bitch."

"What?" my mom asked.

I saw on social media that Miesha Tate had filed a complaint asking the athletic commission to fine me over the "head butt."

"One more reason to beat her," my mom said.

"Seriously, I'll just use the win money after I beat her ass to pay it off. I'll call it a 'fuck you' tax."

There was a knock at the door. Marina had come out to the fight from New York and had brought me spaghetti and meat-balls. I slept like a rock the night before the fight.

The next night, the referee stopped by the locker room to debrief me on the rules and walk me through what to expect him to do in the cage.

"I'm going to ask you guys to fight, you fight," he said, reciting his spiel. "You can touch gloves if you want..."

"Yeah, I don't want to," I interjected.

"OK, then," he said, a little caught off guard.

I looked down at the blue tape on my gloves. I was fighting out of the blue corner, meaning that when we started I would be on the right side of the cage. The blue corner is the challenger's corner. The red corner is reserved for the champion, the favorite.

I knew it was going to be the last time I ever wore blue gloves.

When we met in the cage, Miesha knew what was coming. She knew I was going to break her fucking arm. She knew it and there was nothing she could do to stop me.

Miesha's greatest asset as a fighter is that she can take a fan-tastic beating.

I expected Miesha to be smart and try to keep the fight at a distance. Emotion got the better of her. She ran out of her corner, head down, eyes closed, and swinging wildly. She fell into my clinch. I easily redirected her momentum and threw her to the ground. After a short scramble and an elbow to her face, I stood in her guard and spun backward around her legs to pass into a crucifix position, lying on top of her and pinning her arms down so I could elbow her face more.

Panicking, she gave me her arm when I wasn't even looking for it. I threw one leg over her head to go for the armbar. I could feel her elbow giving, but I could also feel her slipping out. I decided to start hammer-fisting her face instead. I rolled out of the position and stood up. She desperately held on to my back and we collapsed to the ground.

She was trying to hook her legs around me from behind. I grabbed her feet to unhook them, but realized my shorts were too short, and if I pulled too hard, I would flash my bojango to the world. I stood, picked her up, and slammed her on her head. I got on my knees to untangle her feet and slipped out and stood up. She tried to follow me up, but I punched her straight in the face and laid her ass back down. She stood up, trying to grab and push me against the cage. I reversed her and held her on the cage, kneeing her thighs to set up a beautiful *osoto* (backward throw), then cartwheeling over my head to improve my ground position. She grabbed the cage (a violation of the rules) to help herself up. The referee warned her of the infraction as we stood, and I hit her with a jab and a cross. She missed a kick from a mile away, throwing sloppy punches that I easily blocked. I hit her with a hard straight right and an even harder hip toss. I moved in to mount her. She turned and gave her back.

I knew the first round was winding down and figured a submission finish would be faster than a TKO. Zingano won by technical knockout. (A TKO, is where the fighter isn't actually knocked unconscious, but a referee, the fight doctor, the fighter's corner, even sometimes the fighter, makes the decision that the fighter will end up knocked out if the fight isn't called, so let's avoid that part in an effort to do less physical damage.) I purposely held my weight to the right side and hit her on the left side of the head to bait her to try to stand up. Pushing with her left hand, she moved to get up. It was exactly what I was looking for! I hooked her arm and spun into my favorite armbar.

Many people think that when you do an armbar, the arm breaks.

But it doesn't break. When you do an armbar, the aim is to put so much pressure on the person's arm that you pop the joint out of the socket. You can feel it when it pops. It's like ripping the leg off a Thanksgiving turkey. You hear it *pop-pop-pop,* then squish.

Pulling her arm straight, I arched back until I felt the squish, her ligaments snapping between my legs.

She was still trying to escape.

As soon as I felt the joint pop, my focus shifted to protecting myself and preventing her from escaping. I grabbed her hand and pushed it over the side of my hip, forcing her elbow to go more than ninety degrees in the wrong direction. I ripped off muscles from her bone and tendons.

With a vise grip on her injured arm, I sat up to punch her in the face with my other hand. With her elbow fully dislocated, there was nothing holding her in that position anymore except the pain and her fear of me.

She tapped.

Then, as far as I was concerned, she disappeared.

I felt relief, then I was overwhelmed by an indescribable joy.

I stood in the middle of the cage as the announcer called out, "Ladies and gentlemen, we have a time of four minutes and twenty-seven seconds in round number one. She is the winner by way of submission. She is still undefeated. She is the new, Strikeforce women's world bantamweight champion. Rowdy Ronda Rousey!"

The crowd roared.

Strikeforce CEO Scott Coker came up behind me and wrapped the championship belt around my waist, and I jumped. I had forgotten about that part.

I looked down at the black leather belt with its huge gold front, dozens of gems shimmering under the spotlights. It was much heavier than I expected it to be.

A calming peace swept over me. I had achieved what I had set out to do.

A microphone was thrust in front of me. I realized I was going to have to find words to say.

I thanked my coaches, my teammates, and my family. I was sincerely grateful for everything they had done to get me to this moment. I thought of my dad. I looked up into the stands almost expecting to see his flag waving there again. He had always known I was going to be the best in the world. I wanted him to hear that his sleeper had woken up.

"To my dad, wherever you are," I said. "I hope you see this. We all miss you, we love you, and this is for you. I hope you're proud of me."

I was rushed out of the cage to go straight for drug testing. A crush of officials accompanied by the television production crew tried to usher me backstage. I stopped, scanning the crowd for my mom.

"Come on," one of the officials urged.

"I have to look for her."

I spotted my mom, beaming and screaming in the crowd.

"There's my mom!" I shouted, and pointed.

"Come on," the official told me again.

"Let her go see her mom," Edmond told the guard. The entire line of us—me, my corner, security, the officials, the cameramen, and the event staffers—cut across the floor to where my mom was standing.

She wrapped her arms around me. I leaned in.

"I'm still proud of you," she said.

It was the first time I ever remembered her saying that to me about any competition. I felt like I had won all over again.

I'D RATHER EXPOSE MYSELF WILLINGLY THAN WAIT IN FEAR FOR IT TO HAPPEN AGAINST MY WILL

I have been asked if I have no fear. The truth is I fear a lot of things. I just don't let fear control me. I use it to motivate me. I confront things that scare me head-on, because fear is nothing more than a feeling. The girls I'm facing in the cage, they can hurt me. Fear can't actually hurt me. Acting without fear is called recklessness. Acting with fear is called courage.

I had been broken up with Dog Park Cute Guy for a few months and had gotten back into the dating game as I was rising up through Strikeforce. I met my new boyfriend at the club where I had been teaching judo. He was nice. He had a job. He had his own place. He didn't do heroin. Given my dating history, I was OK with kind of boring. Of course, people always later say serial killers were kind of boring neighbors.

I was at his house two weeks before the Tate fight and asked if

I could continue my social media hustle on his computer while he was out. He said sure. While trying to download a picture off Facebook so I could post it on Twitter, the "Save As" screen showed thumbnails of recent downloads. There among the images were naked photos of me. Naked photos of me taken *without* my knowledge. They were photos of me doing really mundane things like playing DragonVale on my phone or brushing my teeth. (Yes, I brush my teeth naked.)

Rage swept along my spine like ice as I scrolled through the pictures he'd taken over the last few months. What if he'd shared them? What if he had more hidden somewhere? What about the pictures on the phone? I deleted the photos. Then I erased the hard drive. Then I waited for Snappers McCreepy to come home from work. I stood frozen like a statue in his kitchen, getting angrier and angrier. I started cracking my knuckles and clenched my teeth. The longer I waited, the madder I got. Forty-five minutes later, he walked in the door.

He saw my face and froze. He asked what was wrong and when I didn't say anything, he started to cry.

I slapped him across the face so hard my hand hurt.

"I found all those naked pictures, you sick motherfucker!" I screamed.

"Let me explain," he pleaded.

But there was nothing to say. I moved to leave, but he was blocking the door.

"Let me out of here! I never want to fucking see you again. You will never fucking touch me again."

"You're not leaving," he told me.

"Fuck, yes, I am," I said.

He wouldn't move. I punched him in the face with a straight right, then a left hook. He staggered back and fell against the door.

Fuck, my hands, I thought. *I can't hurt them before a fight.*

I slapped him with my right hand. He still wouldn't move. Then I grabbed him by the neck of his hoodie, kneed him in the face, and tossed him aside on the kitchen floor.

As I ran out the door to my car, he ran after me.

"No, wait! Let me explain!" he cried.

"Fuck you, pervert!"

I got in my car. He jumped in the passenger's seat and grabbed the steering wheel. "You're not going anywhere until you hear me out." I walked around the car, pulled him by the neck of the hoodie again, dragged him out onto the sidewalk, and left him writhing there as I sped away.

After the Tate fight, I turned my attention to all the things I had put off dealing with. The situation with Snappers McCreepy was near the top of my list. I had deleted the photos I found, but I knew there could be more. The win had catapulted me into the spotlight. My stomach turned as I imagined him trying to sell the pictures. I worried that he'd post them on the Internet. I worried that someone else would take pictures down the road.

ESPN asked me to be part of their annual Body Issue, where they convince athletes to pose buck-naked. I figured if there was any possibility of naked pictures of me getting out, I wanted it to be on my terms, and being part of a spread of the world's best athletes seemed a tasteful way to do it. Fanboy bloggers, acting as if they were journalists, loved to ask if I would pose in a magazine like *Playboy* and I gave them all the same answer: "No one should be able to see my cash and prizes for five dollars. I don't care how much money they give me."

I plan to have children someday. I do not want my children or their friends or, God forbid, my grandchildren to search "Ronda

Rousey" and be able to find a picture of my vagina on whatever super-advanced version of the Internet we have in twenty years. Simple as that. So I only show in photos what would be revealed if I were in a bikini at the beach.

The morning of the ESPN shoot, I stepped on the scale and was 143. I stepped off. I studied my body in the full-length mirror on the back of my closet door. I wanted to look as fit and athletic as possible, every muscle cut and defined. I felt like the purpose of those photos was to capture the physical epitome of human potential, so that's what I was trying to look like. When I looked in the mirror, I felt pretty epitomized.

The day of the shoot, I drove to a studio in Culver City, California, not far from the house I moved into after signing my Strikeforce deal.

The studio was large and brightly lit with white walls. I was met by a friendly, perhaps-overly-caffeinated production assist-ant who led me to hair and makeup. I chatted with the hairstylist as he curled my hair into ringlets, which he then ran his fingers through, making them into loose waves.

A camera crew doing a behind-the-scenes video asked me questions.

I stripped down to my underwear and was handed a thick white robe bearing the ESPN logo. I slipped my underwear off underneath it. I danced around a little bit, loosening up. The smooth concrete floor was cold under my bare feet.

One of the assistants on set wrapped my hands in pink hand wraps. It was not the perfectly executed fight-ready wrap job that Edmond did, but it would work for some photographs.

When the time to take the pictures came, the person over-seeing the production walked me over to the closed portion of the set. I walked through the door into a small partitioned-off section. The walls and floor were black, lit only by the camera lights and two big pink spotlights. I squinted, my eyes adjusting to the stark contrast from the outer part of the studio.

"OK, close the set," someone called.

Anyone who was not necessary to the actual picture-taking process walked out. There were probably five people in the room, all women except for a single behind-the-scenes cameraman.

Enjoy yourself, buddy, I thought.

I was nervous, but excited. I felt comfortable in my skin and confident about my body. I believed what I told the ESPN interviewer: "Skinny girls look good in clothes. But fit chicks look good naked."

I took a deep breath and accepted that a small roomful of people was going to be seeing me naked. *I'm really going to do this,* I thought. Then I took off my robe.

"Are you ready?" the photographer, a woman, asked me.

"Well, I'm completely naked," I said. "It's not like I'm going to get any more naked." She laughed.

The pink lights shined behind me. Someone fired up a smoke machine and translucent white wisps curled around me in the air.

The shoot lasted for about an hour. Occasionally, we would take a break and the hair guy would come in and do a fix here or there. Or the makeup artist would apply a little powder.

In between those moments, the photographer snapped away, giving me commands.

"OK, now jump."

"Turn a little to the left."

"Move your hands just a bit."

"Perfect. Perfect."

The photographer showed me a few of the shots she had taken on a computer screen.

"Wow," I said, giggling. "I look good."

"Amazing," she said.

"You promise nothing will be shown that wouldn't be shown if I was wearing a swimsuit?" I asked.

The room full of people promised. (Of course, there was a shot or two where I'm pretty sure they interpreted that swimsuit to be a thong bikini.)

Then, one day, a couple of months later in July, ESPN had the issue delivered to my house. I was being followed around by a Showtime camera crew as part of a mini-docuseries to promote my next Strikeforce fight against Sarah Kaufman. The ESPN magazine people and the Showtime producers had coordinated so that the camera crew would be filming me when the magazine arrived.

I had expected I would have to flip through to find my picture, but there I was smiling coyly on the cover. I was speechless. I was surprised, not just by the cover, but by the version of myself staring back at me. I looked beautiful.

REFUSE TO ACCEPT ANY
OTHER REALITY

For a long time, people shot down my goals as impossible, but I knew it was only because I hadn't given them a reason to agree with me yet. They did not know what I was capable of.

JANUARY 19, 2011

TMZ CAMERAMAN: When are we going to see women in the UFC, dude?

DANA WHITE: Never. (*Laughing*) Never.

No one outside of my camp knew it, but I was having issues with my elbows during the lead-up to the Kaufman fight. I had been sparring one day when my left elbow hyperextended. I had never tapped in an armbar in judo competition and I had long ago lost track of how many times my elbows had been dislocated. The recurring joint trauma had loosened my ligaments on both arms.

I just need to pop it back in, I thought, but the pain persisted.

I can win this fight with one fucking arm, I told myself.

A few days later, my right elbow started bothering me. I could hardly move either of them. I couldn't even throw a jab.

Well, I guess I'll have to win this fight no-handed, I thought.

My fight against Sarah Kaufman was set for August 18, 2012. She was a good fighter, coming into our fight 15–1 at a point when I was 4–0. If I hadn't come along, she would have been next in line for Miesha and probably taken the belt.

I entered the fight against Kaufman with the same desire to win that I had carried into the cage against Miesha. But last time, I was a challenger with everything to gain. This fight, I stood to lose it all.

Knowing I was injured, the mood among my team was tenser than usual when we drove to San Diego for the fight. I reveled in the atmosphere. I thrive under pressure and tune out pain.

The night of the fight, Edmond warmed me up in the locker room. We usually hit the mitts just a little bit before going out in to the cage, but this night, we didn't.

"This girl is solid on her feet and she knows how to strike," Edmond said. "Do your judo. Move that head. Jab the shit out of her. Get that clinch, and that's it. Do this shit."

Wearing red gloves, I walked out as Joan Jett blasted over the speakers. There was nothing else on the planet at that moment but me and the girl standing across from me in the cage.

I opened with a triple jab, ignoring the pain. She backed up against the cage to defend my first throw attempt. I switched my grip, changed direction, and swept her back. I struck her on the ground to force the reaction I wanted and spun straight into my armbar. She fought hard to keep it, but her arm was mine.

Fifty-four seconds into the fight, she tapped out.

The crowd went wild. Sitting front row and center was Dana White.

He saw how it was in the stadium. He saw how crazy the fans were. He saw how great the fight was live. Then he saw the ratings. The fight drew a peak audience of 676,000 viewers, a twenty-three percent increase from the 431,000 people who tuned in to watch me beat Miesha Tate's ass.

The morning of September 8, 2012, my cell phone rang. The caller ID flashed a familiar name: Dana White.

The UFC president—and face of the UFC—had called me once before, to tell me to check out a commercial Showtime had produced promoting my fight with Tate. I had saved his number in my phone.

"Hey, I'm coming to town for the *Sons of Anarchy* premiere!" Dana said. Dana is the kind of guy who talks in all caps with exclamation points.

"It's a big thing," he said. "You should come to the premiere with me. It will be good visibility for you."

His enthusiasm was contagious. All I could think was, *Fuck yeah, I'm coming!* But I must've said something vaguely more becoming because we made plans to meet that night.

I dressed up the best I could and got in my car. The money I was making was enough to fix the windows, but no amount of money could eliminate the smell. I prayed it wouldn't rub off on me. I pulled up to the valet at Dana's hotel and the attendant walked up to my beat-up car, the backseat filled with dirty laundry, a stench emanating through the rolled-down windows. He looked horrified.

"It's better than it used to be," I wanted to say.

Instead, I gave him a $20 tip, the biggest tip I had ever given anyone, and an apologetic look as he slid into the driver's seat.

From the hotel, Dana's driver took us to Mr. Chow, a restaurant I'd never heard of, likely because it was way outside of my income bracket. It is one of those restaurants where celebrities are always being photographed.

It had been a year and a half since my pro MMA debut. Now

here I was, sitting, drinking wine with the president of the UFC.

Dana leaned in, his tone becoming serious.

"There is a specific reason why I brought you to this restaurant," Dana said. "About a year ago, right outside this restaurant, I told TMZ that women would *never* be in the UFC. I brought you here tonight to tell you that you're going to be the first woman in the UFC."

It took all of my self-control not to jump up and start dancing my happy dance on my chair. In my mind, there was confetti, a full marching band, and a choir from heaven singing. Still, I tried to play it cool.

"Oh my God, that's amazing," I said smoothly, though I couldn't shake the grin from my face.

Dana did not make me any grand promises. He told me that women in the Octagon would be an experiment; the success of my first fight would determine the future of the division.

"Thank you so much for taking the chance," I said. "I promise I will make you look like a genius."

My smile was so huge that it literally hurt my face.

We toasted, and his friends showed up and we headed over to the premiere in the chauffeured SUV. We were blasting Rage Against the Machine the whole way there, and I felt like I was on top of the world.

We pulled up to the Fox Theater in Westwood. There was a red carpet with a white step-and-repeat backdrop running along one side and a row of photographers on the other. Across the street, behind a metal barricade, fans lined the block, a couple rows deep. Cars were pulling up with celebrities getting out, and the fans were cheering. As I got out all the people started screaming my name. I had walked the red carpet before for events like the *ESPN Magazine* party and the World MMA Awards, but this was my first time getting recognized at a non-sports event. I was shocked by the crowd response. Five minutes later, I was still on the carpet posing for pictures with Dana, then pictures by myself, and waving to fans. I could hear people across the street yelling, "Ronda! Ronda!" I was getting more cheers than even the *Sons of Anarchy* cast. I suppose I should be more modest about it, but I was thinking, *Excellent* (with an evil villain finger tent). *Keep yelling. This is good for me. Yell in front of Dana all you want.*

"Have fun tonight," Dana told me. "Enjoy it. It's your night."

The after party for the event was held at Gladstones. I hadn't been to the restaurant since I had failed to return with a doctor's note.

As my buzz kicked in, I stood there for a moment, watching the bartenders in their red polo shirts with their forced smiles pouring drinks for the crowd.

That used to be me, I thought. *And now, I'm going to be in the motherfucking UFC.*

It was one of the greatest nights of my life. Good things were happening, but I knew the best was yet to come.

No one had believed the UFC would ever admit women. Not fans. Not other fighters. Not the media. Not my mom. Not the face of the UFC himself.

People told me it would never happen. They told me I was insane.

But you can't let other people affect your belief in yourself. People are going to tell you to be logical and to be reasonable. They're going to say that because no one else has ever done something, that it can't be done. You have to be crazy enough to believe that you are the one person in the history of the world who can create that change or accomplish that dream. Many people are going to doubt you and tell you reasons why you can't and why you shouldn't. You can choose to accept them or reject them.

I had ignored everyone who said it could never be done. Now I was going to be the first woman ever in the UFC.

THE BEST FIGHTERS ARE
PATIENT AT THE RIGHT TIMES

The night of a fight, I am impatient. As the hour of the fight grows nearer, my impatience intensifies. By the time they lead me into the Octagon, I am holding myself back, every muscle in my body yearning to unleash everything I have upon my opponent. The hardest moment comes when I am standing in my corner, staring down my challenger, just waiting for the referee to give us the signal to go. I hate those seconds, because for just a fraction of time, I have to accept that what is happening in the Octagon is not in my control.

But once I step into the Octagon, I am patient. I don't rush a submission. I take the time to set up. I'm not sitting there waiting for something to open up—that's passive. Active patience is taking the time to set something up correctly.

When Dana said he was bringing me into the UFC, he said they were going to hold a news conference, announce the addition of a women's division, and give me the UFC championship belt. I hated the idea of being "given" the belt. I wanted to earn it, not be handed it ceremoniously. I believe you shouldn't hold the belt until after you win it or after you defend it.

Dana wouldn't budge.

"When we brought José Aldo in from the WEC [another promotion the UFC purchased] and Dominick Cruz, they started with the belt," he said. "That's just the way we do it. We bring in the whole division with the champion."

"OK," I reluctantly agreed. "So when is the press conference?"

"Soon," Dana said. "We're still figuring it out."

In the meantime, I was under strict orders to tell no one. I told Edmond, but no one else. I didn't even tell Darin, who was still my fight manager.

Behind the scenes, the UFC was in negotiations with Showtime. The UFC's parent company, Zuffa, owned Strikeforce. However, Strikeforce had a TV deal with Showtime and the UFC fights are primarily aired on pay-per-view and through a deal with Fox.

The folks at the UFC thought they were on the verge of a deal. They were wrong.

In late September, two weeks after our drinks at Mr. Chow, Dana brought me up to Toronto for UFC 152. He planned to announce my signing there. I met up with him in Vegas and flew with him, his bodyguard, and a couple of his friends on the UFC's private plane.

It was my first time flying on a chartered jet. It was amazing. If I so much as glanced toward the rear of the airplane, a flight attendant would rush right over to ask me if I needed anything. I sat back in the leather chair and could hardly believe this was my life. I had started drifting off to sleep when someone mentioned to me there was a bed that I could sleep in.

Fifteen months earlier, I had been en route to Canada, hungry and exhausted, trying to find a comfortable position to sleep, crammed in a coach seat between Darin and an intoxicated Edmond. Now, I was being offered a bed. An actual bed, on an airplane. I felt like I had drifted off and awoken in an awesome alternate universe.

But when we got to Toronto, it turned out the negotiations with Showtime still were not resolved. I discovered it is easier to handle disappointment if you've had a good night's rest.

In early October, the UFC had fights in Minneapolis. They were going to give me the belt there. Again, I met up with Dana in Vegas and boarded the UFC plane. We got to the Twin Cities, but the negotiations still weren't done.

Once more I went home empty-handed, but not unnoticed. People started asking me what was going on. Fight fans wanted to know what brought me to town. Media wanted to know why I was traveling everywhere with Dana. Friends just wanted to know what the hell I was doing. And because I am a terrible liar, it was obvious I was hiding something. Before I knew it, rumors were flying that Dana and I were having an affair. I wanted so badly to explain, but I just laughed it off as ridiculous.

I went from being disappointed to growing frustrated over having to keep the secret. I couldn't wait to give everyone an explanation, to be able to hold up the belt and say, "See, this is why!"

We were traveling on a private plane, but I was on constant standby.

The news wasn't yet public, but I got permission to tell Darin and a lawyer whom he introduced me to because we had to start working out the terms of my UFC contract. Darin said we should formalize our agreement for him to serve as my fight manager. He "needed it for tax purposes."

"If you're ever the least bit unhappy with the job I'm doing, we'll just tear it up," he said of our contract.

It was early December when I flew out to upstate New York to help Marina drive her car out to L.A. I want to stop in North Dakota, I told her. So we planned a trip that would take us through the Midwest to Seattle, where we could catch our friend Nate Diaz headline a UFC bout on Fox, before driving down the Pacific coast.

We piled into Marina's 2007 Honda Accord, which was gold like mine, but smelled better. Fueled by coffee and beef jerky, we cruised the open road to the sounds of "Thunderstruck" by AC/DC, "Open Road Song" by Eve 6, "Midnight City" by M83, "Universally Speaking" by Red Hot Chili Peppers, and "Bohemian Rhapsody" by Queen.

It was evening when we arrived in Jamestown, North Dakota. I had not been back since we had moved away. We drove to the white house with green trim where my family had once lived. There was a FOR SALE sign in the front yard. I led Marina around back and discovered the back door was unlocked, just like we had always left it. I stood in the living room in the spot where our couch would have been and thought about the last time I saw my father alive.

"I want to see my dad," I told Marina.

"OK, let's go."

We walked back out to the car, and I called my mom, who told me to go to the funeral home and ask for directions to the cemetery. She told me she would call ahead. There was a man standing outside waiting for me when we arrived.

"I'll take you to the cemetery," he said.

We got back in our car and followed him. I had only been to the cemetery once, the day my dad was buried. When we pulled

up, he didn't even need to show me where Dad's grave was, I just knew. I had never even seen his grave after they put the headstone on it, but I knew exactly which one it was.

I got out of the car. It was dark and was kind of sprinkling. I walked over to where he was buried, and I stood there. Just me and my dad. I knelt down on the cold ground and talked to him for a while. I told him I missed him. I told him about the journey I was on. I begged forgiveness for my failures and asked for his guidance. I pressed my palms in the frozen grass and cried. I took my favorite ring—it was silver with a turquoise stone—off my right middle finger and pressed it into the soil next to his headstone. I promised to try to be a good person and do everything I could to make him proud to be my father.

I don't know how long I was there, but eventually I stood up and promised to come back someday.

Marina was at the car waiting for me. She had lost her father a few years before. She looked at me with the deepest understanding, and I knew from the way my best friend hugged me that we had felt the same pain.

Even with our stop in North Dakota, we made the entire trip from Albany to Seattle in fifty hours. We arrived in Seattle on December 5, the night before the fight press conference. The next morning, I got a call telling me that the UFC was giving me the belt at the pre-fight press conference in a few hours. When I told them I had nothing to wear, they told me to go shopping and they'd reimburse me.

All right, I thought. *I'm going to Barneys, bitches.*

I bought a dress and a pair of awesome shoes and got myself this big coat that I didn't even end up wearing.

Then before I knew it, I was standing backstage at Key Arena and Dana said, "Let's bring the champ out here." That was my cue.

I sauntered out in front of the room filled with media and up the stairs to the stage, in heels that were squeezing my toes. I was concentrating more on not falling than on basking in the moment.

"I'm going to make it official," Dana said. "The first-ever UFC women's champion, Ronda Rousey."

He presented me with the belt. It was big and gold and jewel-encrusted. It was heavier than I thought it would be. And it was mine.

He then announced I would be making my UFC debut less than three months later against Liz Carmouche and—in what I think came as a surprise to a lot of people who followed the UFC—our fight would be the main event for UFC 157.

It was only when I got back to the hotel room and threw the belt down on the bed that the weight of everything it signified hit me. I felt giddy and let myself revel in the excitement, but only for a moment. My showdown with Liz Carmouche was less than three months away.

THERE IS A MOMENT IN A MATCH WHERE IT'S THERE FOR THE TAKING AND IT COMES DOWN TO WHO WANTS IT MOST

In every match, there is a second when the win is up for grabs and one person reaches out and grabs it. It may happen at the very beginning of a match, when one fighter comes right out swinging and catches the opponent before she's ready. That opportunity to win might happen in the middle of the match, when your opponent lets up for just a second, to catch her breath or gather her thoughts. Sometimes, the fight is up for grabs at the very end, when you have both been trying your hardest. No matter how tired you are, you have to find a way to dig deep down and make it happen.

I don't care what you have thrown at me. I don't care if I'm tired or injured or trailing in the last second. I'm going to be the person who wants to win the most. I want it so badly that I am willing to die for it. I am going to be the one who summons my last ounce of strength and my last breath to do everything humanly possible to emerge victorious.

And when the fight is over, I am going to be the one who won.

The media circus surrounding my fight against Miesha was nothing compared to the frenzy surrounding the lead-up to my fight against Carmouche. No one associated with the UFC could recall a fight drawing more attention. It was, without being dramatic, historic.

She was not only an 8–2 fighter, but of all the girls I faced in my MMA career—before and since—Liz Carmouche would be the only opponent to break my focus. We were doing a promotional stare-down, where fighters literally adopt a fighting stance and stare into each other's eyes, a month before the fight. Whenever I do a stare-down, I look into the other person's eyes and think, *I'm going to rip your fucking arm off, and there's nothing you can fucking do about it.* I push out my thoughts through that stare. I want them to be able to read me through my eyes. So there I was face-to-face with Carmouche, channeling all my venom into my gaze, when she looked me straight in the eye and blew me a kiss.

I had been expecting anything but that. It rattled my brain for a moment.

Even before that day, I had a huge amount of respect for Liz. There were a lot of girls talking smack about me, but there weren't a lot of girls lining up to fight me. Carmouche wanted the fight bad. I knew Carmouche would be tough. She was not only a fighter, but she had been in the Marines and did three tours of duty in the Middle East. That takes a strength of character that no other fighter I had faced possessed. She had been in Iraq, where people shoot at you. It's not like she was going to be intimidated by trash talk. But in that stare-down moment, I knew that against Carmouche I had to be ready for anything.

Our fight on February 23, 2013, was at the Honda Center in Anaheim. Everything I had dreamed about and everything I had worked for was on the verge of coming true. But I also knew if I didn't win, it all would have been for nothing.

On fight night, I was lying on the floor in the locker room resting. One of the undercard fights was playing on the TV, and I happened to glance up just as Urijah Faber got Ivan Menjivar in a standing rear naked choke, which is basically a choke applied from behind.

I was watching the fight and thinking, *Menjivar shouldn't be leaning on the cage. He's holding Faber on his back (allowing him to keep choking him). He should stand in the middle of the cage and try to get Faber off. He should focus on untying his legs first, not the hands.* Then it fell out of my mind. I didn't even say it out loud.

When I exited the locker room, it was as if the rest of the world faded into the background. When I stepped into the cage, my entire world shrank down to 750 square feet.

We were less than a minute into the fight. Adrenaline was pumping. I was uncharacteristically in a rush, and I forced a throw before I should have. I didn't set it up. I just went for it. I tried to muscle it and I gave up my back. Carmouche capitalized on my mistake, literally jumping on it.

In that moment, I had a choice. I could either turn so we were both lying on the ground with her on top of me or I could try to stand up. I made a snap decision. I figured it would be better to stand up and give her my back than be on the bottom on the ground with her, because that's her best spot. But I knew that if I stood up, she'd go for the rear naked choke.

When I'm in a fight, I see things and analyze them and react to them. It's not like everything slows down because it's going fast, but time changes. It is like I am processing ten million pieces of information at once and making multiple decisions simultaneously based on that information.

I flashed to Menjivar holding Faber on his back, and I knew I needed to get away from the cage wall.

The easiest thing would have been to lean back and hold her on the cage. It takes a lot of effort to balance somebody in the middle of a cage while they're trying to rip your head off. Your body wants to do what's easiest. My body was telling me to lie down on the ground, or lean up against the cage. But my head was telling me to stand, balance, and untie her legs, while she was balancing on my back.

I tucked in my chin, cutting off her access to my neck, and defended the choke with my chin. I had to break the grip she had on me with both her hands and feet.

I was still trying to break the grip her legs had on me when she changed her hold on me from a choke into a neck crank. A neck crank is exactly what it sounds like: one person grabs the other and tries to pull the opponent's neck past the point where it's supposed to go. It's the closest you can come to ripping another person's head off with your bare hands.

They don't have neck cranks in judo. I'd never been in one before. I felt myself losing balance, as she was cranking. She was pulling my neck straight up, and the force was making me step back.

I had absolutely no emotion then. It was all one hundred percent making observations and decisions.

Pop. Pop. Pop. My sinuses popped. It felt like my face was imploding. I was getting closer to the cage.

My body, her body, and gravity were pushing me back. *No, I have to step forward,* I reminded myself. I moved forward toward the middle of the cage.

Her arms started slipping down over my mouthguard. My teeth cut halfway through my upper lip.

Carmouche's forearm was beginning to slip; but she's a badass. She cranked harder, forcing my mouth open. My top teeth were jammed against her arm as I felt my jaw dislocate. She didn't care if it forced my top row of teeth deep into her forearm, this was her chance. She cranked harder.

My jaw couldn't give any more. My neck was forced past its range of motion. I was literally on the verge of having my neck snapped in half.

I would rather die or be paralyzed than lose, I thought to myself.

Because not enough was going on, my sports bra started to shift and my boobs were now in danger of falling out in front of thirteen thousand people in the stands and everyone watching on pay-per-view.

But my mind was prioritizing. It was telling me, *Foot, foot, foot. I still have to balance and get her foot off.*

She was cranking my head to the left. I had to throw her off balance. I turned to my left and pushed her foot off to the left. She started to fall and there was a split second of relief where I thought, *Finally, she's off. I can fix my bra now.* I was certain my nipple was about to pop out. However, Carmouche missed the memo that this was a bra-fixing moment and kicked me right in the tit.

I heard the crowd going crazy. I was embarrassed that Carmouche made me look bad. Then I was pissed off that I was made to look bad and that the crowd was cheering about it. I resented them. I could feel my resolve growing with my rage. This girl was not getting off the ground again. I was standing in her guard (when you are on your back while grappling and your opponent is between your legs) and risked throwing a few punches to her face. She tried to catch me in a heel hook (leg lock). I backflipped out of it and started punching her repeatedly in the head. Forcing her to protect her face, I pushed her elbow to the other side of my head and moved to mount her. She reacted in a perfect way that allowed me to swing my legs over her torso and go for her right arm. She grabbed on to it with her left hand, and held on for dear life. I pulled, trying to break it free. She clung tighter.

I knew the first five-minute round had to be winding down; there could not be more than seconds until the bell. I took one leg off and reset my position, refusing to give up. I could feel her grip breaking. I tugged harder. Her arms slipped apart. There was no escape. With her arm between my legs, I leaned back and cranked. Realizing there was no escape, she tapped.

Carmouche had lasted four minutes and forty-nine seconds.

I was still—and now, in my mind, officially—the first women's champion in the history of the UFC.

After the fight I realized that I hadn't even entertained the thought of tapping, even though I could feel my jaw dislocating and knew that my neck could break. The thought of giving up never came into my head. When it comes to fighting, there is never anyone who wants to win more than I do.

FIGHT FOR
EVERY SINGLE SECOND

You will have times where you are behind. It does not matter if you are getting beat for four minutes and fifty-nine seconds of a five-minute round. You fight for that last single second in the round. You are not trying to win five rounds. You are trying to win fifteen hundred seconds.

It has to eat at your soul to know that anyone could best you for even the most infinitesimal fragment of time. It is not just about winning the match. It is about being so completely and thoroughly better than anyone else, that even the smallest error, the smallest fraction of time, the smallest thing that doesn't go your way needs to break your heart. It needs to matter that much to you.

People will mock you when they see that you are emotionally ravaged by caring so much. But it is exactly that passion that separates you from them; it is that passion that makes you the best.

To win, you have to be willing to die. If you are willing to die when you fight, if you are giving absolutely everything you have for every single second you are in there, you are going to separate yourself.

If you win the four minutes and fifty-nine seconds of the round, and at the very last second of the round, the other person just pops you one and the bell rings, you better be pissed that one second of that round escaped you.

It is not about just winning the round. It is not just about winning the fight. It is about winning every single second of your life.

The morning after every fight, I meet up with Dana for brunch. It's a thing we do. The very first time we did that, after my win at UFC 157, he floated the idea of me coaching against my next opponent on a co-ed version of *The Ultimate Fighter*, a reality TV show that's the *Real World* meets *Survivor*, if the contestants on *Survivor* beat each other into submission instead of voting each other off. Each season features two teams of aspiring fighters coached by current UFC fighters. A fighter is eliminated each episode, with the final two facing off in a live event. The winner of the show gets a UFC contract.

The goal for the season Dana was proposing was to basically create an entire women's division from scratch, using the show to familiarize fans with up-and-coming female fighters.

After signing me and Carmouche, the UFC had added Miesha Tate and Cat Zingano. Miesha and Cat were scheduled to face off six weeks later, with the winner of that fight being next in line to fight me. As part of the lead-up to that fight, I and the winner of Tate-Zingano would coach on TUF.

Zingano won by technical knockout. Manny, who had gotten me into MMA in the first place, was a finalist on the show early on. His fight in the finale was the first MMA match I made a point to sit down and watch. I had been living in Boston and was so excited and nervous for my friend that I spent the entire fight running back and forth on the sectional couch. Manny had lost to Nate Diaz, but Manny's performance impressed Dana so much that Manny was also given a UFC contract. I had seen how much impact TUF could have on a fighter's career and understood what a launching point the show could serve as for an entire women's division.

I wanted to leave a bigger mark on the sport than just my name first in the record books. I wanted to build a division that would be able to survive after I leave the sport.

With that goal in mind, I recruited a team of assistant coaches to accompany me, including Edmond, Manny, and Marina, and in July 2013, we were headed to Las Vegas for six weeks to film the show. The pay was not great. We would film thirteen total episodes over six weeks and receive $1,500 a week. My only question about the compensation was: "Are we getting paid the same as the male fighters who have done the show?" I made it very clear: If they're paying me less than the guys, that's messed up. But if this is what everybody gets paid, then this deal just needs to get done. I thought everyone was on the same page.

Three days before filming was scheduled to begin, unbeknownst to me, Darin and my lawyer called the UFC and said, "If Ronda doesn't get twenty thousand dollars an episode, she's not doing the show."

Dana White does not play these kinds of games.

I had spent the morning running errands in preparation for spending the next month and a half living in Las Vegas. I was just pulling into my garage at the house on Venice Beach that I had just rented when Dana White called. I put the brand-new black BMW X6 M that the UFC had recently gifted me into park. ("I can't have one of my champions driving around in a busted-ass Honda," Dana had said.)

"Hey, Dana, what's u—"

"What the fuck?" Dana roared. "What the fuck" is how he starts conversations when he's upset. "Twenty thousand dollars a week? Are you fucking serious? I mean you must have lost your goddamn mind."

I racked my "goddamn mind" trying to figure out what he was referring to. I had absolutely no idea. I was caught totally off guard.

"Your fucking lawyer and your fucking fight manager call me up, telling me twenty thousand a week or Ronda's not doing the show!" Dana laughed in disgust.

"Whoa, whoa, whoa," I said. "Hold on."

Dana was too angry to stop.

"Seriously, three fucking days before filming starts?"

"What I told them—" I started, but Dana cut me off.

"No one gets twenty thousand a week!"

"But," I tried to interject.

"I'll kick you off the fucking show before I pay twenty thousand a week. I should kick you off the show just for asking for twenty thousand a week!"

"I would do this for free," I said. "I just want to know if the men get paid the same. That is all I asked."

"If you have questions, you and me should communicate directly," he said. "You shouldn't send these ass-clowns to go do this kind of stuff."

"Dana, I'm sorry," I said.

"I mean what the fuck?" He was still angry.

"Look, I'll get it figured out," I said. "Please don't kick me off the show."

"I don't know what I'm going to do," Dana said. Then he hung up.

A knot twisted in my stomach. I didn't like the uncertainty. It made me anxious. But then my anxiety gave wave to anger. Why would they call Dana and make outrageous financial demands without my permission? What the fuck?

For me, it was never about money. I knew if I followed my passion and did it better than anyone the world had ever seen, the money would come.

Still flustered from my conversation with Dana, I called Darin, and he told me I deserved to make more, that other stars on reality TV made more. I told him I didn't care, that I wasn't a reality TV star and to never pull that shit again.

As he spoke a familiar feeling of betrayal swept over me. Four months before, just two days after I signed a contract with Darin, I learned that, at a restaurant in Vegas, Strikeforce CEO Scott Coker had asked Darin if the rumors circulating about me and Dana were true. Darin laughed. "You know crazy things happen on that plane," he said. Hearing that my own fight manager had not defended me against such blatantly false and sexist speculation made me feel sick to my stomach. To me, it wasn't a laughing matter. My relationship with Darin had never been the same.

Three days later, I left Mochi with a friend in L.A. and headed to Las Vegas to shoot the show. I had not talked to Dana since that day in the car.

When I got to the gym, a guy from the film crew said, "Just walk around the gym. We're going to get some shots of you checking the place out."

I walked into the gym, looking around. I looked around the huge open space filled with everything an MMA fighter could ever want for training, a full-sized Octagon in the center of the room.

There were two huge photos of me and Cat on the wall. The doors opened, and I expected Cat to come walking through them. Instead, it was Miesha Tate. She was smiling. I was caught off guard, but I had to laugh.

Cat must have brought Miesha in as one of her assistant coaches, I thought. *Cat knows our backstory and wanted to fuck with me. Touché.*

"I knew they were going to set me up with something," I blurted out.

I didn't like Miesha, but I respected her for providing me a rivalry and a good fight when I had needed one. "Nice to see you again."

"Nice to see you too," she said.

The last time we had been this physically close together, the referee was raising my arm in victory.

"What are you doing here?" I asked.

"I'm here to coach," Miesha said.

"Coach what?" I asked.

"That's what you're here to do, right?"

The confusion set in.

"Are you helping Cat's team out?" I asked.

"I'll leave the explaining to Dana, but..." Miesha trailed off and just stood there smirking.

Understanding crashed down on me as if one of the lights from the gym ceiling had fallen on my head: Dana was making an example of me. He was showing me what happened when you messed with the UFC. He was replacing me with my worst enemy.

Panic set in. I thought about how much my team of coaches had already put into the show, how they had put their lives on hold in order to help me. How was I going to tell my team? Where was Dana? How could he betray me like this? I was furious. I was hurt. I could feel the emotion washing over my face.

It's strange the things that push a person over the edge. Miesha Tate could try to punch me in the face. She could belittle my fighting ability. She could disregard everything I had accomplished. None of that had fazed me. But the way she was smirking at me, savoring my anguish, set something off. I went from disliking her to having never loathed someone so much in my entire life. What had started as a promotional rivalry became real animosity.

It is one thing to be against someone while you're fighting in the Octagon. That's business. It is another thing to take pleasure in someone else's unhappiness outside of it. That is just fucked up. Seeing the pleasure and satisfaction she got from my distress was too much. I never like anyone when she is standing across from me in the cage. But if I saw that same girl outside that setting, in a complete panic, I wouldn't laugh at her. I would say, "Hey, it's cool. Chill out."

That is the difference between me and Miesha Tate.

I pushed through the doors Miesha had just walked through.

"Where's Dana?" I started asking everyone in the halls. No one would tell me; it would have ruined the opportunity to turn my panic and embarrassment into reality TV gold. I walked to the locker room area.

When Dana arrived, I was flipping out.

"Let me explain," he said.

Days earlier, Cat Zingano had injured her knee. She needed major knee surgery and was going to be out for months. The morning we were supposed to start filming, Cat was in an operating room. The UFC called Miesha. She and I would coach opposite each other on the show, then fight at the conclusion of the season.

It was all a misunderstanding, Dana said.

I looked around at the camera crew filming the entire scene. The cameraman was smiling.

This wasn't a misunderstanding, I thought. *This was an ambush.*

I had been naïve enough to believe that because the show was affiliated with the UFC, the producers would be respectful of the fighters. The UFC bankrolls the show, but the production company, Pilgrim, treats you like a reality TV show personality. They don't see you as a world-class, elite-level fighter who deserves respect and who fights for her life for a living.

It was a rough first day. Things would only get worse.

Following the show's formulaic format, we selected our teams, but this season we selected four girls and four guys each, and two winners—a man and a woman—would be crowned at the end of season.

I selected: Shayna Baszler, Jessamyn Duke, Peggy Morgan, Jessica Rakoczy, Chris Beal, Davey Grant, Anthony Gutierrez, and Michael Wootten. Miesha picked: Julianna Peña, Sarah Moras, Raquel Pennington, Roxanne Modafferi, Cody Bollinger, Chris Holdsworth, Josh Hill, and Tim Gorman (who was hurt and replaced by Louis Fisette).

Based off a coin flip, I got to pick the first matchup of the season. I put my first women's pick, Shayna, up against hers, Julianna. One of the most experienced women's MMA fighters and in many ways an unsung pioneer in the sport, there was no fucking way Shayna was going to lose.

But Shayna lost, getting caught in a rear naked choke in the second round. During the fight, I could tell Shayna felt like she was losing the round. I saw her focus shift away from what she was doing in the cage at that second to what she was going to do in the next round. That's when she got caught.

It was a gut-wrenching defeat for Shayna and our entire team. I did not want the defeat to set the tone for the next six weeks. The entire ride back to my temporary apartment, I thought about the fight. I thought about it that evening. I thought about it on the way to the gym the next morning. I thought about how Miesha had celebrated the fact that Shayna—whom Miesha claimed was her friend—was being crushed under the pieces of her shattered dream. As the coach, I was responsible for the team's morale.

When I thought about what I could say, I thought about what my mom used to tell me: "In every match, there is a second when the gold medal is up for grabs. The only way to make sure that you are the one who grabs it is to make sure that you fight every single second of that match."

My mom's words echoing in my head, I called my team together.

"You will have times where you are behind," I began. "Frontrunners are a dime a dozen. It's easy to stay in the game when you're winning. What sets the special fighters apart is the ability to battle beyond your greatest losses and adversities."

By the time I got to "... It is about winning every single second of your life," there wasn't a person on my team who wasn't ready go out and beat someone up. I saw a light in their eyes, a fire that hadn't been there before. We trained right after I spoke, and everyone was focused. The team's spirit was high, but it was also serious. No one was joking and smiling. They were going at it twice as hard as they had been the day before.

I put so much thought into those words. The kids were so into it. Several of us got the words tattooed onto ourselves after the season ended. If viewers had seen the speech, they would have been thunderstruck. Instead the producers put in a hot tub scene.

Since her fighter won, Miesha got to pick the next fight. She pitted Chris Holdsworth against my guy Chris Beal. Chris Beal's hand was broken in his initial fight to get into the house and Miesha openly acknowledged that she wanted to exploit that.

What was not shown was what happened in the moments leading up to his fight. Chris Beal was warming up, when Dana came into the locker room, upset because he had just received a call from another fight promoter who said Chris was still under contract with him. Chris wasn't yet in the cage, and he was already being forced to defend himself.

When we were filming, no one aside from us knew the cast. How would anyone even know Chris was on the show? What are the odds that this promoter would call at the most inopportune time, moments before the biggest fight of his life? Who would stand to benefit the most? What is the probability of all these factors colliding at the exact moment when it would most negatively impact a member of my team? My mom, who is a statistician, always says, "If something is highly, highly improbable, it is probably not a coincidence."

We hadn't even been filming a week, but it was crystal clear that producers were more interested in making a show about catfighing than cagefighting. Whenever Miesha walked by me, she would sneer or blow me a kiss. She made snarky comments about my coaches and played juvenile pranks. The producers gobbled it up.

"Just take her outside and kick her fucking ass," my mom said when I flew her in to serve as a guest coach.

Everyone involved with the show saw the situation

spiraling out of control. Dana called me and Miesha in to talk and demanded both sides cut the bullshit. But Miesha kept blowing me kisses and looking to start problems with my team. They especially targeted Edmond, who as our only striking coach, was absolutely essential to the team. Miesha and her troll of a boyfriend purposely agitated Edmond, trying to instigate fights and get him kicked off the show. I held myself and my team back from engaging in any further confrontations, but kept flipping her the bird.

It was only July, but I was counting down the days until December 28, when I could take it all out on her in the cage. I just hoped I could hold myself back until then.

My only goal on the show was to take my team of aspiring fighters and put all of my efforts into mentoring them. I know how hard it is to scratch and claw your way up through the sport. I know how hard it is to juggle multiple jobs while training so you can make ends meet. I understood that succeeding on *The Ultimate Fighter* could change the trajectory of a fighter's career. The kids on my team needed this chance. They deserved every piece of my being that I could give to them. If I was made to look like a crazy bitch as a result, I accepted that.

I decided long ago that I'm going to say whatever I'm going to say, and people are just going to take it however they want. I wasn't going to waste a single second caring about what anyone else thought.

YOU HAVE TO BE WILLING
TO EMBARRASS YOURSELF

You have to ask yourself, "What is the worst thing that could happen? What is the worst possible outcome?" When I'm fighting, the worst that could happen is that I'll die or be permanently maimed. For pretty much everything else, the answer is the worst that could happen is I'll suck or make myself look like an idiot. Compared to dying, that's pretty low on the scale of bad things that could happen. Fighting really puts everything in perspective and keeps me from being afraid.

I had always known fighting wouldn't last forever. I was achieving my goals at a faster pace than even I had expected. And now I was looking ahead to the future. I wanted to parlay my fighting success into a next step, just as Gina Carano had done when she made the move from fighting to film. This seemed like a nearly impossible challenge; those were my favorite kind, but first I wanted to talk to Edmond.

One morning at GFC, I was sitting next to Edmond on the edge of the ring during a break in my workout when I told him about a meeting I had recently had with an entertainment agent who thought I could be a Hollywood star. I asked him what he thought about me trying to do movies. By now, I could usually gauge how Edmond would respond to an idea, but this time, I didn't know what to expect.

The sole purpose of a trainer is to get fighters ready for a fight. Coaches are not fans of "outside distractions." He paused, thinking about everything I had told him.

"Is it because you really want to act? Like you are passionate about acting?" he asked. "Or is it you just want the status of being famous in your movies?"

"I really do want to act and I really want to be good at it," I said. "For some reason, I feel compelled to entertain."

Edmond paused again.

"You can't carry two watermelons together in your hands," he said, holding out his hands as if to show me. "It doesn't work that way."

I couldn't help but smile at the analogy. Armenians have a big thing about watermelons.

"But you know what you are doing," he continued. "Most fighters, I would say, 'No, focus on fighting.' But if you can keep it serious and do both, do both. Just remember, it is because of fighting you have these movies."

He was saying aloud what I already knew. I was under no illusions that Hollywood would care about me if I was not the UFC champion. If I were to lose a fight, I would just be one more blonde aspiring actress in a city of blonde aspiring actresses.

"But I will tell you one thing," Edmond said. "This is a gym. You walk into this gym and I don't want to hear about no movies. When we do training camps, you focus on nothing else. When you're out there, you do what you want to do, but in here, all we do is fight.

"Now, back in the ring," he said.

I jumped up, determined to prove to him that I was more dedicated to fighting than ever.

Before I became ensnared in *The Ultimate Fighter*, I'd been laying groundwork for an acting career. I'd signed with the entertainment agent, Brad Slater from the William Morris Endeavor agency, and was going to meetings with producers, studio executives, and casting people. I got an acting coach. I had even been up for the role of Atalanta in *Hercules*. I tried so hard to get that role, and when they didn't pick me I was really disappointed. It was a loss and it bothered me. Whenever I had a hard time on TUF, I'd think, *Fuck, I want to be in Hercules.*

Then, Brad called to tell me that Sylvester Stallone wanted to meet me. I was an unknown in Hollywood, and he was Rocky and Rambo and Barney from *The Expendables*.

We went to lunch with Kevin King, Stallone's producing partner, and the man himself. They were doing a third *Expendables* movie, and Stallone thought maybe I would be a good fit for the part.

I was flattered. Stallone asked me what I thought of acting, and I said I was working hard to get better at it.

"I always felt like you had to be a good liar to be a good actor," I admitted. "But I've started realizing it's not so much telling a lie as it's convincing yourself that you are in this situation, then doing whatever you would do in that situation."

"The greatest actors aren't the biggest stars," he told me. "A great actor can play anyone in any situation, but you don't see people lining up around the block to see most critically adored actors. You see people lining up around the block to see stars like Al Pacino, who in every role is himself. He doesn't play different people. He's Al Pacino as the cop. Al Pacino as the lawyer. Al Pacino as the gangster. Al Pacino as the blind retired Marine or whatever. He always plays himself, and people just fall in love with that character of *you*. That's what makes you a star. That's what makes people line up around the block.

"That is all you need to do," he said. "Just relax and be yourself. That's what stars are. They are just themselves in every situation you put them in.

"Let's talk again soon," Stallone said when lunch was over.

When I got back from Vegas, I was lower than I had been in a long time. I knew that when *The Ultimate Fighter* aired, I was going to look like a reality TV show nutcase. I felt like I had to rush. I needed to get accepted for roles and already be filming a movie when the show started airing or else Hollywood might not want me.

Then, Stallone wanted a second meeting. This time, just the two of us. I met him at Roni's Diner, a diner and pizzeria across the street from his office. It had dark wood tables and rows of black-and-white photos of celebrities on the walls. The meeting was casual, but it felt more businesslike this time. As Stallone launched into telling me why he thought I was right for the part, it was obvious he did this kind of thing all the time. I tried to pretend that I did too. I shifted into sales mode, trying to emphasize why I thought I would be good for this role. It was a strong female character. *Check.* It involved fighting. *Check.* I really respected his work. *Check.* By the time the actual check came, I felt like we were in a pretty good place. We stood up to leave, and he walked me to my car.

"You think you could fight with the curse? You think you could handle this?" he asked me, referring to the belief that acting is the kiss of death for an athlete's career.

"One hundred percent. I promise I'll make you look like a genius," I said, thinking back to when Dana told me he was bringing me into the UFC.

"All right, then. Let's do this," he said, and he shook my hand.

I broke out into a huge smile. I wanted to hug him. I wanted to do a happy dance. It was only in that moment that I allowed myself to accept how badly I had wanted the part.

The next week, I met Stallone again at the diner where he was finishing up lunch, and we walked over to his office. It was hot out, and I was wearing a t-shirt dress.

"Look at the size of your arms," he said.

I tensed up for a second. It was the kind of comment that had made me so self-conscious in high school. But I wasn't in high school anymore, I reminded myself. All those people who had made fun of me had been idiots, I realized. I'm fabulous.

Stallone was still checking out my biceps.

"Man, those are awesome," he marveled.

Back at the office, we read through the script. It was a work-in-progress Stallone told me. They were going to be making a few changes to it. Then we switched from reading lines to talking about acting.

"Always start out being over the top in the first take," he said. "That way you keep yourself from feeling ridiculous the rest of the time. It's so much easier to tone it down than to rev it up.

"Acting is just playing," he added. "You're having fun. A lot of people take this too seriously. Never be afraid to embarrass yourself."

I arrived in Bulgaria to begin filming in early August. When I got there, they showed me the outfit I was going to be wearing. I mentioned that it was different than what I had originally been shown.

"I know," the wardrobe person said. "Stallone said that your arms were so awesome that he had us do a cutout so we could show them off."

I felt my cheeks flush, but it wasn't from embarrassment. It was with pride.

SUCCESS IS
THE BEST REVENGE

When something bad happens to me, I get mad and then I get motivated.

In the moments that you fall hardest—when you lose a job, or find out a boyfriend is cheating on you, or realize that you made a bad financial decision—you can channel your shame, your anger, your desire, your loss. You can learn, take chances, change course. You can choose to become so successful that no one can ever put you in a situation like that again.

My mom's old judo coach put it bluntly: Winning is a bitch, but revenge is a motherfucker.

Spite can be a powerful motivator if harnessed in the right way.

I spent eight weeks in Bulgaria shooting *Expendables 3*. On set, I threw punches and traded scripted verbal jabs. I ran up stairwells and fired blanks-filled guns. I was starstruck by Harrison Ford. I would see him on set and think, "Oh my God, it's Han Solo. Be cool. Be cool." And then I would be so not cool.

Professional boxer Victor Ortiz was also in the movie and

his coach found a gym in Sofia where we would go to work out. I was convinced it was a front for some kind of mafia money-laundering operation, because it was a state-of-the-art gym with top-of-the-line equipment, but hardly anyone was ever there.

Wrestling is big in Bulgaria, and I found some guys to grapple with, but it wasn't the same the level of training I was used to doing back home. One day, my costar Jason Statham asked if he could come watch me train. I started out just hitting the heavy bag, but it was miserable without Edmond to wrap my hands before I trained, to correct me if I make a mistake.

Still I was glad to have Statham there. Talking to him while I hit the bag made me feel cool and reminded me of the familiar comfort I had back home at GFC, where Edmond would stand and watch me hit the bag.

Then a couple of Bulgarian wrestlers whom I had worked out with before came into the gym.

"Ronda, do you want to wrestle?" one of them asked me. This was my chance to look like a badass. I looked at Statham and winked.

And that day, I just wiped the floor with them. I was doing all this crazy ninja shit, flips and every showboating acrobatic move I could think of. The guys I was wrestling with were really cool about it. Statham was awestruck.

"Proper blown away! I've never seen anything like that in my life," he said.

I missed Edmond. Initially, he wanted to come out and train in Bulgaria with me, but Armenian boxing legend and three-division world champion Vic Darchinyan asked Edmond to train him for an upcoming fight. That camp coincided exactly with the film shoot.

I called him every day.

"Did you train?" he asked.

"Yeah," I said, then told him what I did.

I would wrestle, grapple, run up stairs, run up mountains, run on the ellipticals, swim, shadowbox, but I wasn't able to do real training like I did at home because most of the time I had to do it alone. I was also putting in almost sixteen hours on set a day, and my schedule varied daily.

There was a day when we shot a scene where we had to run up an inclined roof to a helicopter. Call time was five a.m. I wanted to work out first, so I woke up at four a.m. The hotel gym didn't open until eight a.m., so I ran stairs in the hotel—eleven flights, eight times—before rushing back to my room to shower. Then I had to run up on the roof, a fifty-yard sprint at a forty-five degree angle, and I had to do that probably thirty times. When we finished shooting, it was afternoon, so I jumped in the car and had my driver, Alex, take me straight to a gym where I could wrestle with a bunch of guys there.

There wasn't one second I was there that I forgot about Miesha Tate.

When I got done filming *Expendables*, I flew to Atlanta for ten days to film a part in the seventh installment of the *Fast & Furious* franchise. I returned to L.A. forty-seven days before my fight with Miesha and headed straight into camp.

Everything we did in the lead-up to the rematch with Miesha was about ensuring that I would be able to handle anything. It wasn't so much about being ready for what she might do in the cage as it was about being able to control my emotions and getting back into fighting form after such a long layoff.

Edmond is really good about pushing me to use my anger as a tool. In training, he will purposely ignore me or make comments to try to make me emotional and put me in the situation where I have to suppress it.

He refuses to allow me to kick. Throwing kicks isn't part of the way I fight. But I would occasionally throw a kick in practice out of frustration or rage.

"Don't do that," Edmond said one day. "When you kick, I know it means you're angry."

He was right.

Ahead of the fight, Edmond brought in sparring partners who would go nuts, throwing crazy hooks and taking cheap shots. He had me go long rounds, trying to test my patience.

He would intentionally do things to try to get me aggravated before I sparred. He would ignore or snap at me, and I would get upset because I didn't understand why he was acting that way.

One day during camp, I asked him if he was going to hold mitts. After all the effort it took to get him to hold mitts for me, it's still a big deal for me, a ritual.

"No," he told me. "Go hit the bag."

As I was hitting the bag, he came up to me and looked over my shoulder.

"Why are you doing it like that?" he asked, then walked away.

That was the only thing he said to me that day. I spent the next few hours going back and forth between confused and upset.

I was asking myself, *What's wrong? What's the problem? Am I sucking? Does he want me to give an excuse for why I'm sucking?* I was already emotional, because I always get emotional during camp, and I started crying. And the whole time, he was looking at me. Then I realized I was letting him get in my head. He wanted to get in my head and make me emotional so that if I got emotional in the fight, I would be able to handle myself.

But there were also things that weren't getting handled in camp. Darin was responsible for making sure my training partners got paid. I had learned shortly after the camp for UFC

157 that—even though I had formalized my agreement with Darin—they hadn't been getting their checks.

That was a real concern. If you're not paying your sparring partners, they could just decide not to come to practice one day, and it would be just like I was back in Bulgaria with no one to train with.

One afternoon, Edmond and I were sitting on the edge of the ring as I unwrapped my hands when he said, "Ronda, fight managers are fine, but as long as they do the job right."

I could tell he was trying to tell me something without over-stepping his bounds, and I knew he was right.

"I know," I sighed. "I'll deal with this shit after the fight."

The day of the fight against Miesha, I was lying on the bed in the bedroom of my suite trying to rest when I heard an altercation between some of the people in the other room. I blocked it out, rolled over, and forced myself back to sleep, but I was angry. I don't like drama before I fight. I don't like distractions before I fight. I would deal with whatever was going on there after the fight.

I thought about the fight that was mere hours away. I thought about the first time I fought Miesha. I thought about TUF. I thought about the situation that had just gone down in my suite.

Somebody was going to have to pay. And that person was going to be standing across the cage from me very, very soon.

For me, anger is motivating. But I can't allow anger to consume me to the point where it impacts my judgment. When you're angry and trying to solve a problem or deal with a situation, you're not going to solve it wisely. In a relationship with somebody, if you're angry, you're not going to say the perfect words. When you're relaxed, then you calm down. You can think logically and rationally to solve the problem more efficiently. It's the same thing when you're fighting.

LEARN TO READ
THE REST BEATS

A big concept of fighting that many people don't get is one I call reading the rest beats, like when you're reading music. One reason why many people get tired in a fight has nothing to do with them being in bad shape. It's about knowing how to find those tiny split seconds of rest; they can make all the difference in a fight. It is the moments where I'm resting while still putting pressure on my opponent that allows me to maintain such a high pace throughout the fight.

For example, if I'm holding someone against the cage, I'm not using my muscle to press against the cage. If I lean on my forward foot and adjust my shoulder, all my weight is going on the person. I'm using gravity against and pressuring my opponent, all the while my muscles are resting.

Know when to explode and know when to relax—that's the only way to survive.

Time does not always heal all. Sometimes, it just gives you more time to get pissed off. I had been waiting almost six months from the end of filming *The Ultimate Fighter* to get to this fight.

My rematch against Miesha was the co-main event for UFC 168.

She walked into the arena to Katy Perry's "Eye of the Tiger." I have my game face on from the minute I leave my hotel room on Fight Night, but I rolled my eyes that night.

A few minutes later, I was stomping toward the cage in my battle boots to the sounds of Joan Jett. I have never wanted to destroy someone so badly. I did not so much want to break her arm again as I wanted to rip it off. I glared at her across the cage, feeling nothing but cold, calculated wrath.

"Touch gloves and let's do this," the referee said, giving the standard pre-fight spiel.

I stepped back without raising a hand.

The referee said start. I was going to be in control every second of the fight. To me, it wasn't just about winning. I wanted to hurt her. I wanted to show her just how dominant over her I was. I wanted her to never again think that she could step into the cage and face off against me. I wasn't going to rush for a finish. I was going to pick her apart in every aspect of her game.

We met in the middle and traded boxing blows. I landed everything. She never got off a clean shot. I dragged her to the ground, but she popped up. I shoved her against the cage and started throwing knees to the body. I manhandled her to the other side of the cage. She pushed me off, and for the first time in my MMA career, I threw a kick.

She kicked back at me, but I caught her leg, threw it skyward, and she landed hard on her ass. I went in to punch her and she desperately grabbed for my legs. I tripped and pulled her into my guard. As she tried to defend against my armbar, I threw punches at her face and elbows to her head. I simultaneously worked to set up a choke with my legs as I struggled with her for her arm.

Pushing up with her legs, Miesha stood up and we were

back on our feet. Miesha's nose was bleeding. We again traded punches in the middle of the cage. Sick of that shit, I threw her back on the mat. Miesha tried to get on top of me, and I pushed her off with my legs. She bent toward me, and I somersaulted backward over my shoulder and onto my feet, jabbing her face on the way up. She dived at my legs, and I easily reversed attack, throwing her over my hip. We grappled a few more seconds, then were on our feet again. She came in to throw me, and I stepped out of it. I pushed her against the cage. Then I heard the wood clapper signal ten seconds left. I threw a few final punches until the air horn blew.

I won the first round decisively. There wasn't a single second of that round where I wasn't in complete control. She walked back to her corner bloodied.

Edmond came in with the stool and a bottle of water. I sat on my stool, for the first time ever, hardly breaking a sweat and took a sip of water.

"You're doing great," Edmond said. "Just keep it up."

I nodded.

"Oh, and Ronda," he said, as he picked up the stool to exit the cage. "Don't throw any kicks."

The beginning of the second round was a big, new experience because I had never been in the second round in an MMA fight. I looked across the cage and I could see Miesha's satisfaction with getting to the second round. It was oozing off of her. I was pissed off that that girl was fucking happy. She came into the second round smirking. And I swore to myself that this fucking bitch would not come into the next round smiling. I was going to take that fucking big smile off her face.

I tossed her to the ground at the beginning of the round, and she lay on her back like an overturned turtle, kicking her legs in the air in an attempt to keep me away. *Oh you wanna kick?* I thought. *Fuck you, bitch.* I threw the last kick of my entire MMA career right back at her.

She got up and I threw her hard, slamming her flat on her back for what would have been a judo ippon and let her up. This ass-whupping was not yet over. A few seconds later, I had her up against the cage. She could do nothing against me. I kept throwing blows, then pulled her away from the chain link of the cage. I threw her to the ground with another hip throw. I wrapped my left arm around hers, using my shoulder to block her from clasping her hands together. With my right hand, I punched her in the face. She arched her back and kicked her legs up, wrapping them around my neck. Pushing with all her strength, she slipped her arm away, trying to roll me in the process. But I had her on her back and moved over to a mount (when you are sitting on top of your opponent while grappling), fully on top of her while she lay on the ground. She wriggled underneath me while I punched her over and over in the head. All she could do was hold on to her arm. I had her flat on her back and was sitting on her stomach. *Bam. Bam. Bam. Bam.* I threw a flurry of punches straight to her face. All of the rage I had built up was being unleashed. I got her in an armbar, but I didn't have it quite right. She escaped the armbar, but there was no escape from me. I locked her head with my legs and punched her ribs. I kept pounding her until the horn sounded at the end of the round. When we broke to return to our corners, her face was swollen and dripping blood.

She lasted through the second round, but the smile was gone. I had dominated her for another five minutes. Edmond and Rener Gracie walked into the ring. Edmond set down my stool and gave me a drink of water. Rener put a bag of ice on the back of my neck to help cool me down.

Coming out of the second round and heading into the third, I felt different. After the second round, I was confident but in unfamiliar territory. By the third round, I was settled in. I felt like I could fight a hundred rounds. I knew I had won the first two overwhelmingly. And I wasn't feeling tired. I was certain I could go the distance with maximum intensity and focus if the fight lasted all five rounds.

I'm here for five, I told myself.

But we were never going to get that far.

Miesha was getting tired. I had been beating the shit out of her. She was going to revert to what was comfortable for her, which was to come out swinging wide or try to shoot for my legs and the takedown.

"She's going to come in, put her head down, and swing wide," Edmond said. "Come in tight and narrow and throw straight."

I repeated his instructions in my head, anticipating her next moves and planning my own.

We stood up for the third. She looked bloodied, battered, and beaten.

I came out with a straight 1–2 (a jab followed by a cross, or a bigger power punch that can inflict damage) and knocked her out on her feet. She didn't fall but staggered backward. I came in with another jab and kept coming in after that. She fell against the cage.

I pressed her on the fence and heard her breathing. It was wheezing and rattled. She was breathing out like she was deflating with her breaths.

I knew that she wasn't there. She was out on her feet. She never knew what happened to her in the third round. She was broken down, and it was time to go in and finish. I wanted to break her standing, so she'd be easier to submit on the ground. I went in for one last throw and we tumbled to the mat. Less than a minute into the round, I flipped her onto her back and grabbed her left arm. She had no strength left to fight. I took her arm, and with one leg across her chest and the other behind her neck, I leaned back and arched my hips. She didn't know exactly where she was. She didn't know exactly what was happening, but she knew that she was in an armbar, and it was time to give up.

People learn to tap quickly after you've destroyed one of their arms before.

Afterward, there were people who thought she challenged me in that fight, because it went into the third round. But I had dragged that fight out intentionally, wanting to punish Miesha for as long as I possibly could. When I had thoroughly defeated her, when I had crushed her all the way down to the bottom of her soul, then I went for the armbar.

Miesha was beat and exhausted. I had never felt better in my life.

After all that had gone down between us, after all the shit she instigated on TUF, Miesha got to her feet and extended her hand. I viewed her gesture as merely an effort to save face in front of the crowd. Taking her hand before receiving an apology for everything she had done would disrespect everyone I cared about whom she had wronged. I stared at her blue glove for a second.

My handshake is more than just for show, I thought. It was not an issue of sportsmanship. It was an issue of principle.

I turned away, relishing the win. As boos rained down, I walked toward the only thing that mattered: the embrace of my family.

Ahead of the fight, the UFC had approached me about taking another fight less than two months later—assuming, as we all did, that I would beat Miesha. It would mark the quickest turnaround for a champion to successfully defend the title in the organization's history.

I had agreed.

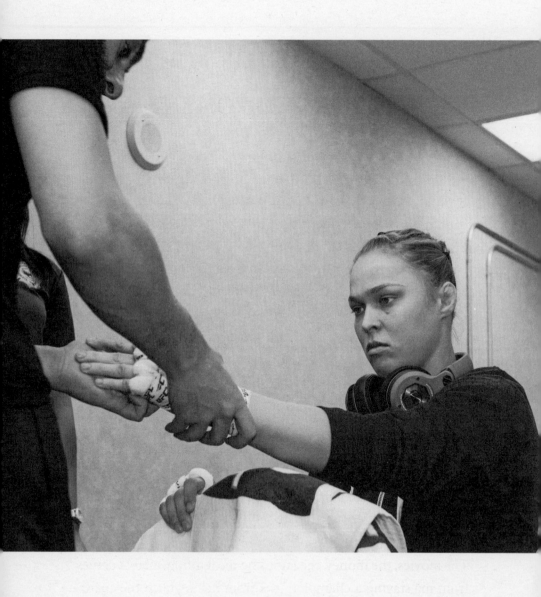

PREPARE FOR THE
PERFECT OPPONENT

Never hope for mistakes from your opponents. Assume they are perfectly prepared. Assume they make weight. Assume they never get tired. Assume all their reactions will be the correct ones. Expect that they will have their eyes open, ready to take advantage of any mistakes that you make.

All of my opponents hope that when we face each other, I will do something wrong that they will be able to capitalize on. I assume that the most perfect version of my opponent that has ever existed is going to be in front of me when we meet. I expect that she will not make a single error, and so I will have to lead her into a trap, where the correct reaction is exactly what I am waiting to capitalize on.

I never allow any opponent to come out better than I expect her to. That's why my fights end so dominantly.

The movies, the money, the fame, the recognition, all of it comes from me staying a champion, not from having been the champion. I could lose every single thing that I have worked for every single time that I get in the Octagon. That's why I train harder every time. Every fight, I have even more on the line. Every fight, I seek to challenge myself a little more. That's why I accepted the fight against Sara McMann.

I had been out of the cage for ten months between my fight with Carmouche and my fight with Tate, and the time away took its toll. I felt just a little bit slower, my timing not as sharp, the cage a tiny bit more unfamiliar. I didn't need to be perfect to beat Miesha Tate, but I expect perfection of myself.

Like everything else that comes with fighting, or success in general, most people have no idea what goes into getting to that moment in the spotlight. For me, it starts six weeks out. Fight Night comes after the preparations are done. The moment that everyone sees is merely the finale of the six-week camp that ensures I am at my absolute peak when I walk into the cage.

The day after my fight with Tate, I asked Marina about the commotion in my suite before the fight. She recounted what she had seen: Darin had come into the room, reeking of booze, wearing the same clothes as the previous night, and tried to start a fistfight. That was the final straw. A few days later, I texted Darin. *We have a lot of things to discuss*, I wrote. Darin replied that he was out of town. Edmond said he would handle the situation, and I turned my attention back to what really mattered.

With the McMann fight only weeks away, we went straight into camp. I loved it. I felt like we hadn't had our best camp possible ahead of UFC 168 and now we had an opportunity to do it all over.

Camp is a countdown, a doomsday clock for my opponent. From the first day of camp until the announcer declares "And still champion, Rowdy Ronda Rousey," every second of my life is focused on fighting. I pick up my training. I follow my diet.

I approach each camp the exact same way, no matter who my opponent is. If I'm at my best, it doesn't matter who is across the cage from me on fight night.

Week 6

Starting in Week 6, I start imagining every imaginable way I will win the fight. By the time it gets to Fight Night, I have played out thousands of ways I could win in my head.

The first week of camp I get my heaviest. I try to put on weight in the form of muscle. Even when I'm training, I don't lift weights or do a bunch of bench presses. But during the first week of camp, I shadowbox with one or two pound weights. My body is really well conditioned, and I put on muscle so fast that by the end of the week, I look jacked.

On Monday evenings, now through the end of camp, I swim. It brings me back to the youth club swimming I did as a kid, when my dad declared I'd be a champion. The quiet time in the pool gives me time to think by myself and keeps my shoulders loose and flexible for boxing.

Week 6 is the only week of camp where I don't strictly follow a diet. I still eat healthy stuff, but I eat a lot of food. In the morning, I have a breakfast bowl.

BREAKFAST BOWL (FROM MY MIKE DOLCE MEAL PLAN)

2 tbsp oat bran (dry measure)
2 tbsp chia seeds
2 tbsp hemp seeds
½ cup blueberries
4 chopped strawberries
¼ cup raisins

1 tbsp almond butter
1 tbsp agave
Cinnamon (to taste)

> Boil one cup of water and combine with bran, berries, and raisins. Mix in seeds and cinnamon. Add agave and almond butter. (You can add a little more water if it seems too thick.)

> If I'm in camp, I might sub the agave for Stevia or I might take the almond butter out.

Even when I'm not in camp, I crave that bowl every morning. It is part of my daily process. On the rare occasion when I'm out of an ingredient and I can't make one exactly right, it feels like my universe is wrong.

Aside from breakfast, it's pretty much my Armenian barbecue week. Armenian barbecue is basically beef, chicken, rice, and vegetables, but mostly meat. It's heavy, hearty, healthy stuff. And there's borsch. Lots of borsch, which is cabbage beet soup that tastes like angel bathwater.

We had decided to train at home the entire camp as we prepared for McMann. I had been on the road so much that year that all I wanted was to be home. But there have been times when I felt I needed to change my environment. Ahead of the Carmouche fight, we headed up to train in the altitude and the quiet of Big Bear. It's easier to change your mindset if you change your environment. It's hard to sit on the couch and then suddenly be like, "Oh I'm in camp now."

No matter where I am, I end that first week of camp feeling strong and energized.

Week 5

During Week 5, I start my diet. Right before my fight with Tate, I realized I needed to find a better way to make weight. After a decade, deprivation dieting was taking its toll. Not only was it a super-unhealthy approach, but it didn't work. I reached out to Mike Dolce, who serves as a nutritionist for a number of fighters in the UFC. It was worth it. For the first time in a camp, I never felt weak. (While Dolce works with fighters, his diet is really for anyone. He has written several Dolce Diet cookbooks, and I highly recommend them.) I worked with him for the month before UFC 168, and I have used him for every camp since.

Starting in Week 5, Dolce sends me a new diet every week. But the plan is flexible. Every morning, I weigh in. I'll text my weight to him and then he'll text me back, *OK, change this meal today* or *You're doing great*. He changes things up according to what he thinks I need nutritionally as well as to get my weight where it needs to be.

When I started working with Dolce, my entire relationship with food changed. I no longer had to figure out what the right thing to eat was. I no longer doubted myself and the decisions that I was making. When I started working with Dolce, I felt guilty for being so full all the time. Then one day during the McMann camp, it clicked: *Oh, I'm supposed to be full.* For a long time, the feeling of being full and the feeling of guilt were synonymous to me. But now, I've stopped feeling bad about it.

Communication is the key with Dolce. I keep in constant contact to let him know how my body is responding to the diet, how I am feeling, and he makes the necessary tweaks. Dinners involve things like chili or scrambles. If I say "I ate so much that I'm so full after dinner," he might tell me that I can skip my before-bed snack. In between meals, I get things like fruit, nuts, or yogurt with chia seeds. I rarely cook, but Marina is my roommate and helps make my food or cuts the ingredients up and puts them in Ziploc bags so even my culinarily-challenged ass can whip something up.

I box with Edmond. I grapple by doing either judo with my longtime training partner Justin Flores or wrestling with Martin Berberyan or by doing Brazilian Jiujitsu with brothers Ryron and Rener Gracie. Each partner is different. I have known Justin since I was an eleven-year-old kid doing judo and he used to babysit me and try to sit and fart on me. Martin ran wrestling at SK Golden Boys and is a three-time Olympian and a world medalist. He is quiet and calm. Rener and Ryron are outgoing and fun. They have a very different ground game from me, and I love to trade ideas with them. The varying personalities and styles balance each other out.

Depending on my opponent, Edmond brings in outside sparring partners. If I'm going up against a striker, he'll bring in girls who are world champions in boxing or kickboxing.

He starts calling other coaches and asking, "Hey, do you have anyone around this size and skill level?"

But if my challenger is a grappler, he mostly only has me go up against guys. McMann had won an Olympic silver medal in wrestling, so in preparation for her, I grappled and wrestled a lot. But it's also a matter of excelling where your opponent is weakest so you can capitalize on those vulnerabilities.

Monday to Friday, I work out twice a day. I leave my house at nine in the morning to be at practice by ten, work out for an hour and a half, shower, sleep, and repeat. I basically do whatever Edmond thinks I should be doing. I really leave a lot of planning up to him and just do what he tells me. Saturdays, I only have MMA sparring. Then on Sundays, I rest. Outside of camp, I'll train every single day, but in camp, I really rest. I get home exhausted at around eight p.m. I make my food, hang out with Mochi, and then read before bed.

I used to think I had to be miserable to earn success. But I've lost that need and realized that it's very old-fashioned. Boxing great Mike Tyson said "a happy fighter is a dangerous fighter." I think he's right. I'm happier—and more dangerous—now than I've ever been.

Week 4

In Week 4, we start to pick it up. Between practices, I like to nap. I used to get a temporary apartment during camp, but then I just started blocking off a room at a nearby hotel three days a week for the last month of camp. I rest at the hotel between workouts, but go home to sleep in my own bed at night.

I am almost totally isolated from the outside world during camp, emerging only to do media. I have no energy to see family or friends. I don't dread any part of the process, even the hardest parts. I just take a deep breath and focus on performing the best I can. I've grown to embrace delayed gratification so much that I even appreciate going through the most challenging parts. I collapse in bed every night, proud of the work I've done and savoring the hours of rest I've earned.

During camp, Edmond is the boss. It's my coach's job to make me do things I don't want to do, especially when it comes to preparing me for a fight. I don't argue with him, because if I get to a point where I get an attitude that "I don't feel like doing this" or "I'm not going to do it because I'm badass," then the whole machine falls apart.

This is also when we begin getting into the mental aspect of the fight and the game plan against my opponent. We look at her tendencies, anticipating how she might try to approach me and what I can do to throw her off her game. We analyze her strengths and weaknesses and look at ways to exploit any holes. The goal is to create a situation where I feel completely in control and she feels completely overwhelmed.

It was during Week 4 of the McMann camp that I started dropping everybody in the gym with a liver shot, a knee or punch directly to the liver. The danger of a liver shot is the pain is so intense it incapacitates a person temporarily. One clean liver shot, and you're done.

Weeks 5 and 4 are hard, but Week 3 is the hardest.

Week 3
Week 3 is "Hard Week." Week 3 is the peak of the training camp. It's the week where I do the most of everything. It's the week where I hit the bag more. It's the week where I hit the mitts more. It's the week where I have the most sparring. It's the week where I go the most rounds in practice, where I fight the most minutes. Sparring is the most important part, because it's the closest thing to an actual fight. The mitt work is tactical, but when you're sparring, you're fighting. A full-length championship fight can go five five-minute rounds, so Edmond has me do six rounds. That way, I know, if it ever came down to it, I could go five rounds in the Octagon and keep firing.

We don't have a set schedule to watch video of my opponent's past fights, but we are definitely watching film three weeks out. We're analyzing what she does, breaking her down, looking for patterns, and identifying opportunities.

By the end of Week 3, I feel completely torn down. Literally, when I'm not training during Week 3, I just lie on the mat or floor or bed or anywhere flat, exhausted and think, *Fuck*. Week 3 pushes me mentally to the edge, which spills over into Week 2.

Week 2

In Week 2, two-week-itis hits. It's when I get my most nervous. Before Week 2, the fight seems like it's far off. Three weeks is close to a month, and a month is a long time. But two weeks out, it starts getting real. The fight is about to happen. Two weeks out is when I'm at my most emotional. I cry over everything, even more than I usually cry over everything.

My body is the most torn down, because I just finished "Hard Week," and I'm entering "Speed Week."

Week 2 is Speed Week, because it's all about short rounds, just being fast, working on footwork, bringing my speed and explosiveness back, things like that. Week 2 is where I'm getting very, very light. We cut down on the sparring and make the rounds very short. It's all about being quick the whole week.

By the end of the week, we do a lot of the playful stuff. Edmond starts bringing out things that are like games, throwing and catching the balls to keep my eyes sharp. He cuts pool noodles in half and whacks me with them. He flicks towels at my head and makes me dodge them. Week 2 is when he gets really creative. He tries to make me really happy during that week. He even asks me to wear bright colors, because he thinks it lightens the mood. Once I get over crying for the first few days, Week 2 is actually the most fun week.

As the fight gets closer, I get tired of being nervous. By the time I'm actually leaving for the fight, I'm just so excited to do what I am the best in the world at that I'm not even nervous anymore. Now, I'm just impatient, eager to enter the Octagon and handle business.

Fight Week

Fight Week is the final week of camp, the countdown to Fight Night. I fight on Saturdays.

On Monday night, I pack all my stuff, which is more throwing everything I can possibly think I will need in my bags and inevitably forgetting something.

On Tuesday morning, we all meet at the gym. If my fight is in Vegas, we drive. We meet at the gym and leave late morning in an automotive caravan. It's Edmond, Martin, Marina, Justin, me, and a few other people from the gym. I like the road trip, but when I'm going to Vegas for a fight, I don't want to drive. I slip into the passenger seat and someone else takes the wheel.

In the days ahead of the fight, I get artificially heavy. A week out, I'll start eating a bunch of salt and drinking two gallons of water a day. When you water load, you put as much water in your body as possible, and get super, super-duper hydrated. Your body gets used to putting out so much water, that even after you cut the salt, your body keeps flushing the water out for a few more days. I bloat up from the water. My weight is usually 146 when I leave in the morning. By the time I get to Vegas, I'm usually five pounds heavier, because I'm so full of water. As we drive, I'm drinking constantly. At every exit, I'm like, "I gotta pee. I gotta pee. I gotta pee."

We listen to music the whole way there, and as we pull into Vegas, I blast Joan Jett's "Bad Reputation" as a prelude of what's to come.

When we get into Vegas, the first stop is the UFC offices. I check in with them, usually sign some posters or something.

Dolce meets me and checks my weight. From there, I check into the hotel. Dolce has me eat. I chill out for a bit. I'll do one workout in the evening just to sweat and lose weight, then eat whatever Dolce tells me to eat. Then go to bed.

Fight Week Wednesday, I have a lot of media. It's when they do all the little media snippets. We film the prefight interviews that people see coming up on the big screen before we walk out. It's my least favorite interview to do ever, because they try to feed you things to say and it pisses me off.

After that, I do a photo shoot where they take pictures of me holding the belt for posters for the next fight. It's taken assuming that I'm going to win, which I always do. This way, when the next fight comes up, they already have the promotional pictures.

Wednesday is the last day I really get to eat meals. Dolce drops off a cooler of food for me with salad, chia bowls, vegetable stir-fry, maybe an egg omelet, fruit, and little trail mix snacks. It has all my waters and everything I could possibly need to eat that day.

Thursday is press conference day. In addition to the press conference, that's when I do individual interviews for a few hours. After that's done, I'm pretty much left alone as far as obligations until the next day's weigh-in. The media circus over, my focus shifts to making weight. I cannot weigh even a fraction of an ounce over 135 pounds at the weigh-in.

I'll go train again, just to get a sweat on. This is when I really start my weight cut. In the days ahead of a fight, my weight generally looks like this: Tuesday, I'm 151. By Wednesday, I'm already 148. Thursday, before I even start the cut, I'm usually around 146. Then I'll start taking the baths to lose water and usually get down from 146 to 138.

Thursday morning, I stop chugging water and start sipping

it. By afternoon, I really start cutting my water. One mistake many people make is that they cut out the water way too soon. They'll be cutting water out all week. I only cut water for the last twenty-four hours. Thursday evening, I'll check my weight, train, check it again, and then take a couple of baths to work up a sweat before bed. Thursday nights, I am hungry and dehydrated and I don't sleep that well.

Then I'll wake up between 138 and 137 on Friday morning, take a couple more baths to lose the last two pounds before the weigh-in and hit 135. I no longer feel the stress I used to feel when I was cutting weight for judo.

Friday is when we have the weigh-in and the stare-down. I head down to the weigh-in ready to fight. During weigh-ins, some chicks come in and they try to act tough while others come in dresses or bikinis, trying to look hot. I want to be ready to throw down right there if need be. If my opponent tries to get rowdy onstage and I have to show her what rowdy really is, I want to be the one that could hold it down right there.

Once we've both weighed in, the two fighters face off for the staredown. Looking into McMann's eyes, I thought, *I'm going to fucking destroy you tomorrow.*

After weigh-ins, Edmond disappears. He checks in on me, but he lets me be. I go backstage with my family—my mom, usually my sister Maria, her husband, my nieces, on rare occasions, my sisters Jennifer or Julia— and security leads us through the hidden tunnels back to my room. I drink water to rehydrate and eat whatever Dolce has put together for me.

We lie on my bed and my mom tells me all the reasons why I'm going to destroy the other girl in less than twenty-four hours. It is a ritual we have had since I was a little kid. She lists every reason why I'm the best in the world like it's a bedtime story.

Friday night, I try to stay up as late as possible. Closing my eyes in bed, I know I have prepared and that I am at my best. I reflect on all my hard work that led up to this moment, not only in camp, but in the days, weeks, months, years, decades that preceded it. I open my eyes one last time, and staring into the darkness, I know that even if I'm at my worst, no one will beat me.

When I fall asleep, I sleep well.

DON'T LET ANYONE
FORCE YOU TO TAKE A
STEP BACKWARD

Sometimes you get overwhelmed and you take steps back, often without even realizing it. We were striking in the gym when my coach Edmond stopped practice.

"When you were doing judo, if you put your mind to it, could anyone make you take a step backwards in your whole life?" he asked me.

"No, of course not."

"If you put your mind to it in judo, would anyone be able to make you take a step back even once?" Edmond pressed.

"No."

"So why am I able to make you take a step back when striking? You shouldn't take a single step backwards in your entire fucking career."

Edmond was right, of course. I had been allowing myself to be pushed back toward the ropes in the gym without even noticing it. A fighter never wants to get backed up against the cage. Once he'd pointed out my weakness, I corrected it. No one has a right to make me step backward. Even if that person is physically stronger than I am, I should be smart enough not to take that step back.

I haven't stepped back since that day.

A minute into my fight at UFC 170 on February 22, 2014, I grabbed Sara McMann by the arm, thrusting my knee into her side and nailing her right in the liver. She buckled, defenseless, and I knew that the fight was over. The referee jumped in between us, calling it a TKO. It was my first MMA win that did not come by armbar. I caught Edmond's eye in my corner, and I could tell it was the happiest with me he had ever been.

Coming out of that fight, I was feeling pretty happy too. I had given this girl an impressive beat-down, and my love life was looking up.

I had always had a strict policy against dating fighters. I'm a big believer in keeping your business and personal lives separate. Plus, being around fighters all day in the gym, I hear the way they talk about girls.

I started hanging out with "Norm" before I had even been signed to the UFC. In the beginning, we were just friends. The main reason that I even hung out with him had more to do with physical proximity than physical chemistry; he lived in my neighborhood.

"You want to hang out?" he asked.

"Listen, the only time I've got to hang out is, if you can stop by my house at six a.m. and take me skimboarding, then we can hang out."

He would wake up before the sun came up, just to have the chance to hang out with me. He was the exact opposite of Dog Park Cute Guy in that regard, and considering DPCG had stolen my car to go on a drug bender, the difference between the two guys seemed like a good sign.

Norm made me laugh. He called me "Wonder Woman." Then one day, we were at the beach skimboarding, and he started making these really goofy jokes. He pretended to make these not-so-stealth stealth moves, and I busted up laughing and that was the start of that.

That time in my life marked the start of a lot of things. I got my shot in the UFC. I moved to my new house. I filmed my first movie. Being with Norm was a casual, easy thing in my very chaotic life.

Norm had no family in L.A., so I brought him home for Easter.

"What did you think?" I asked my family afterward.

"He seemed like a douche," Jennifer said.

"I don't know," my mom said. "He seemed OK. A little too impressed with himself."

"OK?" I asked. My mom was hard to read. "Like douchey OK or nice OK?"

My mom pursed her lips and thought.

"Well, the problem is you set the bar with your first boyfriend," my mom said. "Honestly, after Dick, you could bring home a gorilla and we would be like, 'Oh, hello, fine sir. So nice to meet you. Can I offer you a banana?'"

It was not a ringing endorsement for Norm.

When I got back from Bulgaria and was training for my fight against Tate, Norm told me I was fortunate, that it was "much easier to succeed in the women's division" than it was in the men's. Then, right before my fight with Tate, he told me things weren't working out.

"I don't want to have to answer to anyone," he said.

But after I won, he said he had made a huge mistake and asked me to take him back.

A few weeks before my fight with McMann, he said, "I'm just not ready for commitment." Three weeks later, just days before my fight, he showed up at my door on Valentine's Day, apologizing and offering to whisk me off on an exotic vacation. I was reluctant to go another round. But we headed to the rainforest the week after my win.

We had just gotten back from our trip and I was standing in his kitchen when he pulled out the little box. Inside was a white gold necklace with a diamond pendant. "Wonder Woman" was inscribed on the back. I was ecstatic to see him make such an effort.

"I want to date you for real this time," he said.

I wanted that too.

"Don't lose this," he said, referring to the necklace. "I spent a lot of money on it."

He wanted to be with me, he said. But he also wanted me to be things I wasn't. He wanted me to do the dishes. He wanted me to do his laundry. He wanted me to clean up shit in the morning. He wanted me to pretty up more and dress up more, and do my nails and my makeup and things like that. He just wanted me to be this chick I wasn't. He always made me feel like I was too messy, that I was not domestic enough, that I wasn't girly enough.

The truth is, some days, I get made up into this red-carpet-walking cover model. A team of makeup, hair, and stylist people go to work on me like a NASCAR pit crew. After they're done, I look in the mirror and think, *Damn, I look good.*

But most days, I get in my car after a two-workout day after my coaches and training partners jab, drill, and wrestle me until my body aches. I walk out bruised and sore in loose clothes. I am still sweating, even after taking a shower, because I worked out so hard. Afterward, I sit in the car and think, *Damn, I look like a yeti.* That's more who I really am.

With a couple of movie roles in the works and a couple of UFC championship fights under my belt, I thought, *Maybe I have too many people telling me how awesome I am all the time.* Maybe Norm served as a kind of ego checks-and-balances system. But he never called me beautiful. He was never complimentary.

"That was a great investment," he said one night about a chick in my division who allegedly got a boob job.

I tried to conceal my disappointment. He never complimented me on my body. To have him ogling another girl's chest hit both at my heart and my pride. It was an all-too-familiar feeling. *That was a Dick thing to say,* I thought to myself, thinking of IttyBitty.

But I was trying to justify staying with someone who was making me feel bad about myself. He became cold. He never kissed me out of nowhere. He never once brushed my hair behind my ear. He never wanted to hang out with my friends.

Then one day, I accidentally left my necklace in the bathroom at a gym. I went back after I'd trained, and someone had scooped it out of there. I didn't want to say anything about it. My heart ached over losing it. The idea of having to tell him his gift was gone made my stomach hurt.

One day, he mentioned that he hadn't seen me wearing it. I burst into tears.

"Listen, I lost it," I said. "I don't know how, but I've been looking for it."

"Well, I'm never going to make the mistake of buying you something expensive again," he said.

I thought of my dad. When my parents had gotten engaged, my dad gave Mom a ring. She lost it. Upset, she broke the news to my dad. And he was happy.

"That's OK," he said. "You deserve a better ring anyway."

He bought her a nicer ring.

I knew Norm would never be anything like my dad.

I had already gone through an entire relationship where someone tried to break me down and change me, and here I was letting someone else treat me the same way. I wanted to break up with him in that moment, but we both had fights coming up. You never mess with a fighter ahead of a fight. Well, I never do.

He returned from his fight, which he lost, and two weeks before my fight with Alexis Davis, Norm broke up with me for the final time. It was right in the middle of two-week-itis, when I'm at my most emotional.

My dad wasn't a fighter, but he had learned this when he proposed to my mom when she was training for the world championships. He flew out to New York and asked her to marry him.

"I'll get back to you," my mom said. "Right now, I'm busy."

And, at that moment, as I was preparing for Alexis Davis, I was busy. Something inside me snapped. Norm had no respect for me, but I needed some self-respect.

"You know what? This is the third fight in a row, where you fucked with me right before the fight," I said. "Fool me once, shame on you. Fool me twice, shame on me. Fool me three times, I'm a fucking idiot. Do I look like a fucking idiot to you? I'm never coming back again."

I wasn't even sad over the breakup. I had come to the realization that "Norm" was merely average when it came to everything:

average looks, average intelligence, average fighter. There's nothing really exceptional about him, except for the fact that he was an exceptionally shitty boyfriend.

I didn't cry. Every other time that we had trouble and every other time he fucked with me before the other fights, every other time that we broke up, I cried. Now, not a single tear came out of my eyes.

I was pissed that I had let myself make so many of the same mistakes I had made years before. But I was never going to let someone make me feel that way ever again.

Like clockwork, he soon started sending me texts saying, *I made a mistake.* Reflecting on our relationship, all I could think was, *Yeah, so did I.* We never spoke again.

I wasn't going to sit around and feel bad about myself because of this asshole. I had a fight coming up. Every single time that he fucked with me before a fight, the other girl got it.

I thought to myself as I walked to my car, *If that is any foretelling of how this fight's going to go, this chick's getting fucking murdered.*

My showdown with Alexis Davis was two weeks away, and I was very much looking forward to that fight.

THE ANSWER IS:

THERE IS NO RIGHT ANSWER

People always ask, "What if someone has the answer to your armbar?"

I always tell them that no matter what my opponent tries to do, I will have a response. Then there is a response to my response, and there's a response to that response. I memorize all the possible responses, so I go down the chain a lot quicker than the other person can.

Some of my critics say that I just do the same move over and over again. They don't realize that every single person that I fought studied all of my armbars, and they tried a different kind of correct reaction every time, but there is no right answer.

Depending on what my opponent does, there is a different reaction for everything. Every armbar I've done is entirely different to me. Just because it ends up looking the same doesn't mean that I got there the same way.

There are over 100,000 ways to get the same result.

After the McMann fight, I was cast in the *Entourage* movie. Filming was a blast, but made me miss fighting. I knew my knee needed some maintenance surgery, but wanted to fight one more time before spending months recovering.

I fought Alexis Davis in UFC 175 over Fourth of July weekend of 2014 in Las Vegas. It was my tenth professional fight. There was talk about her being one of my toughest matchups because, similar to my judo and boxing training, she had a black belt in Brazilian Jiujitsu and was noted for her Muay Thai striking. She had never been submitted. What people trying to draw parallels between our stylistic similarities did not understand was that no woman on the planet is capable of matching up with me stylistically.

The entire time I was coming up through MMA, Edmond used to tell me that styles make fights. The styles of two people in a fight could bring out the best in each fighter, and the fight itself could be better. Or the styles could be so mismatched, where my style is so good at beating yours, that even though we're at an equal skill level, it'll seem like an extremely lopsided fight.

No matter who fought me, no matter her skill level or her style, I wanted every fight to look like an extremely lopsided fight.

When I set out to do MMA, I wanted to create a style that could never be beaten. It wasn't about being good at judo or boxing, it was about creating the perfect MMA style; it would be one that had no weakness. I spent years building that style. It's something I will continue to work on my entire career, but by the time I faced Davis, I knew that no one could match up with me in the Octagon.

During the lead-up to the fight, Davis was asked again and again about my armbar. "I definitely think I am going to be able to stop the armbar," Davis said. "This is something I train for constantly every day…It's not a problem for me. Black belts armbar me every day. I am not afraid to say that, but you know what? I defend armbars more often than I get them."

What no one seems to realize is that I try to come out different for every single fight, so whatever footage my opponent was studying before is obsolete when she comes out to fight me.

Despite the fact that I had kept the fight standing against McMann, I think Davis was also expecting me to rush for the takedown because she's a striker. But this time, instead of charging in right away, for the first time in a fight I feinted, or faked like I was going to throw a punch and then didn't. The goal was to throw her off her game.

I feinted at the beginning, and she reacted. I jabbed twice. She tried to come over and hit me with her right, but she was totally off balance. If she had thrown a pillow at me, it would have had more impact than her punch.

I threw a 1–2 and hopped out of the way. I jabbed again, then got out of the way. I was measuring the distance between her and me. I knew exactly where she was going to be on the receiving end of my punches.

This time, I showed the jab, then came in with an overhand right.

When you hit someone with a knockout punch, it's like you can feel the connection from your knuckle all the way to the ground. With that punch to Davis's face, I was certain my fist had hit the earth. I punched her so hard I broke my hand.

Boom. That was it. Or at least it could have been.

After I hit her with the overhand right, I already knew she was out. She was asleep. I could have walked away right then.

But the boos from the McMann fight still echoed in ears.

When I beat McMann, fight fans had been critical of the TKO call, debating if the referee had called it too fast. This time the referee didn't say anything. The fight was still going.

I clinched Davis and threw a knee, then threw her to the ground. We hit the ground, and I kept throwing punches in rapid-fire succession.

One, two, three, four, five, six, seven, eight, nine.

The referee jumped in. Davis didn't even know where she was.

The entire fight lasted sixteen seconds. It was the second-fastest title fight win in UFC history.

I will never know if Alexis Davis had an answer to my armbar, but she had absolutely no answer when it came to stopping me.

I HAVE BEEN THERE

Some lessons have to be experienced to be understood.

After the Davis fight, I had two-for-one surgery, where doctors cleaned up my knee and inserted a pin into my broken right hand. Seven months later, my knee felt better than it ever had and I had developed a badass left hook. I was ready for another fight.

I had been preparing nearly two years to face Cat Zingano.

Our *Ultimate Fighter* fight had fallen through when she injured her knee, but I knew we would face each other one day.

During her recovery, her husband committed suicide, leaving behind Cat and their young son. I knew she was going through the toughest fight in her life. But Dana never wavered in his belief that she deserved a title shot. She was still the No. 1 contender to challenge me for my belt. After a year and a half, Cat returned to the Octagon in late September 2014. Following her comeback win, our fight was slated as the co-main event for UFC 182. We would face each other right after the New Year. But Cat was dealing with a back injury, and a week after the fight announcement, her camp asked for the fight to be moved back. The UFC agreed, rescheduling our bout for February 27, 2015, where I would fight in front of my hometown crowd at L.A.'s Staples Center.

After Cat requested the later date, Dana informed me they had another fighter quietly preparing to face me in case Zingano backed out. I always prepared myself for the fight and not the opponent, but that approach took on an entirely new meaning this time around. Zingano is a left-handed fighter like me. The other girl fights from a right-handed stance.

But Cat came through.

That night in the locker room, Edmond warmed me up.

"This is a historic fight," he said. He had never said that before, not when I faced Miesha for the Strikeforce title, not when I faced Carmouche for the UFC women's debut. But he was right, something about this night felt different.

Minutes later, I was pounding through the hallway, battle boots on, hoodie up, game face on, born ready. I glared across the cage at Zingano, watching her pace back and forth. The referee called us to the middle.

We touched gloves.

The fight began.

Cat came with a flying knee. I angled left. She missed, grabbing me and trying to throw me. I did a backward cartwheel off my head and spun out. When we landed, I turned Cat, getting on top of her. She sling-shotted her legs away from me and got on all fours, trying to escape. I kept a grip on her left elbow, trying to pull her onto her back so I could mount. I threw one leg over her back and knew the grip on her elbow was slipping. I timed the right moment to let go and pinned her other hand behind my arm instead. Something just felt right. I spun to my left side and threw my other leg across her neck. I pulled her arm straight, then arched my hips. She tapped.

When I'm in the cage, my perception of time shifts. I am processing so many pieces of information it is as if the world around me slows down. But my synapses are firing so rapidly and my muscles are moving so quickly it is as if the world is in hyperspeed. Every second is individual on its own.

In terms of seconds on a clock, my entire fight against Cat Zingano lasted fourteen.

It was the fastest submission in UFC history and the fastest win ever in a UFC title fight.

I jumped up, victoriously. Cat stayed crumpled on the mat.

For the first time in my life, I saw a person on the ground. I recognized the disappointment on her face. It was the same as having-your-heart-pulled-out-of-your-chest-and-crushed-in-front-of-you pain I felt when I lost the Olympics.

For the first time in my career, I knelt down and embraced my opponent.

I felt empathy. The knee injury. The death of someone you love to suicide. Building something up so much, believing that it will solve all of your problems and take away all of your pain. Losing.

I had been there, experiencing that same kind of devastation. The overwhelming numbness. The disbelief.

It felt weird for me to give a shit. Every single fight, I look at that person who lost, I see her devastation, and I think, *She was trying to do the same thing to me,* and I don't really feel that bad.

I felt like I had known from the moment I was born, it wasn't going to go Cat's way. That belt wasn't meant for her, just like an Olympic gold medal wasn't meant for me. But I also knew that the worst moments of my life brought me to the best times. Loss. Heartbreak. Injury. I had come to understand every event was necessary to guide me to where I am today. I hoped the same would be true for Cat.

THE HARDEST PART IS KNOWING WHEN TO WALK AWAY

There is always going to be one more fight where people will say, "You can't walk away. You haven't fought this person." There is always going to be somebody else. There's no situation that exists where, when the day comes that I want to retire, people aren't going to think that I was a coward for not taking that one last fight.

I'm just going to have to find a way to accept that fact and recognize when it really is time for me to walk away.

After my win over Cat, I sat in the media conference backstage and everyone wanted to know what I was going to do next. I have dominated for so long, and I know no one will ever beat me in the cage. No girl will ever look into my eyes and see the fear I see when I stare across the Octagon at the beginning of a fight. I will never be scared of anyone.

But one thing I am scared of is retirement.

Winning is addictive. The highs are super-high. There's a lot of risk. There's more at stake each time I fight. I get a new fix every time I defend my belt. But, winning will only last for so long.

When I'm finally done fighting, when I walk away from MMA and I don't get that rush anymore, how am I going to deal with it?

My mom always says that when you're younger you love the roller coaster, and when you're older, the merry-go-round starts to seem a little bit nicer. Someday soon, I wouldn't mind a couple of less-risky, slow-burning victories over flaming, white-hot ones. At some point, I'm just going to get too old for the thrill rides.

I'm thinking about what's next. I worry about it a lot. I'm scared of ending up in the same mess I was in after the 2008 Olympics. I'm trying to identify all the mistakes that I made back then, so I don't make them again. Back then, I never even had a Plan B. That's why I'm so into making sure that I have other options, like acting, lined up. Now, I'm thinking about Plan B and C and D.

I also worry that I won't be able to stay away. I will always be a fighter, but I never want to be that person who retires, then comes back because they can't handle retirement. I want my retirement to be fucking final.

My life turned into something much bigger than I thought. While I chased this dream, I was broke. I worried about whether my next parking ticket would leave me short on rent. I worried about filling my gas tank so I could get to my third job. When I finally got into Strikeforce and then the UFC, for the first time, I started thinking about more than just myself. I had created the job I wanted, and I inadvertently created something not just for myself, but for all the other women too.

When I started out in MMA, I wasn't trying to change the world. I was trying to change my life. But, once my life changed, I realized that wasn't enough. Then it became about changing the world.

Once I became the champion, I realized that that is not all there is. I have to think about what's going to satisfy me for my whole life, what's going to sustain me. Even more meaningful than having the title is having a legacy.

I think about Royce Gracie, who was the first UFC champion. The very first time I had ever been to the Staples Center was to attend a UFC on Fox fight. He walked into the arena and sat down in the front row, and there was something about the look of satisfaction he had on his face as he looked around at something he had created.

That's what I want.

Fighting takes a toll. Physically, you can only take so much. Mentally, you can only take so much. I look forward to the day where I can give up my belt, and let two other girls fight for it. Even though I will know that I could beat those girls and take that belt back, I will accept that it's their turn to carry the belt and the title and everything it represents. When that day comes, it will no longer be only my responsibility anymore. When that happens, women's MMA will be self-sustaining. When that happens, I want to be like Royce Gracie, watching the next generation of fighters with a sense of satisfaction. I want to be that dude, front row, introducing my kids to everyone.

That day is somewhere on the horizon, but it's not here yet. I don't feel like women's MMA is ready for me to walk away. I'm not ready either.

Right now, I'm still living from hit to hit.

WINNING

The fight is over.

I keep going until the referee literally touches me, shakes me, and grabs me to let me know I have won.

I can feel my opponent go limp, whether conscious or not. Every muscle in her body admitting defeat. I don't think she ever believed she could beat me, but she had hope. Now she is left with nothing but throbbing pain and her attempts to comprehend how it all went so wrong for her so fast.

I blink. I always blink.

The experience is not quite like coming up from underwater, although the sound of the crowd seems like that. It is not like emerging from a dark room, but the lights of the arena feel like that.

You go from having on super blinders with no peripheral vision and earplugs into seeing and hearing everything all at once. It is as overstimulating as an experience can be.

I am flooded with relief. Then joy. It is hard to digest it all at once.

Relieved and happy, the crowd is at full volume, and the lights are at full brightness with the spotlight shining in my face. Every muscle in my body—which seconds ago had been engaged, ready to act at any second in hand-to-hand combat—is relaxed. All of these emotions I've been blocking out are rushing in, and so many things are going on in my head all at once.

It's hard to snap back, to return to reality.

It is supposed to be my moment. It is my moment. But I am not sure how present I am in that moment. I find these moments to be my most unintelligible.

A microphone is thrust in front of me, and I open my mouth to speak. It is hard to communicate in this environment. I listen to the question. I let my lips form a response, hoping that my brain will catch up later. I acknowledge my opponent, appreciate the crowd, give them a little showmanship, and try to be a little theatrical. I have no idea how the words all come out since they seem to fall out of my mouth in an incoherent jumble.

As I walk away, through the crowd with my arms around my family, back into the tunnel, after all of these fights, the feeling is always the same. There is a sense of accomplishment. There is a sense of fulfillment.

I feel safe.

Above all, there is the indisputable knowledge that I am the greatest in my role in the history of the world.

THANK YOU . . .

To Mom, for everything you've done, for everything you've taught us and for letting us co-opt some of your brilliant mom-isms for this book; to Jennifer, for always keeping it real; to Julia, for being Julia; to Dennis, for taking us in and feeling like he got the good end of the deal; to Eric, for being an amazingly supportive husband and bearing with us through this chaos; to Eva, Emilia and Calum, you are the future; to Edmond, my kyank, mentor, partner, teacher and friend; to Dana White, Lorenzo Fertitta, and Frank Fertitta, for taking the risk; to my agent, Brad Slater of William Morris Endeavor, for always believing in me; to Marina, my reality check; to Jessamyn, my favorite hug; to Shayna, Vegeta to my Goku; to Jessica Lee Colgan, you are a Godsend; to my team—Justin Flores, Martin Berberyan, Manny Gamburyan, Gene LeBell, Rener and Ryron Gracie—for (literally and figuratively) being in my corner; to Mike Dolce; to Eric Williams;

To my judo coaches Tony Mojica, Blinky Elizalde, Trace Nishiyama, Big Jim Pedro, and Israel Hernández; to my early MMA coaches Leo Frincu and Gokor Chivichyan;

To my sparring partners; to everyone at GFC, Hayastan, SK Golden Boys, Lonsdale Boxing and Gracie Academy; to Lillie

McNulty and her family; to Wetzel Parker, a friend indeed; to Dianna Linden, my healer; to Dr. Thomas Knapp; to Dr. Jake Flores; to Erin Malone at WME; to our amazing editor Alexis Gargagliano; to our publisher Judith Regan and the entire team at Regan Arts; to everyone deserving but not listed here;

To my fans, you all kick ass;

And to every asshole who motivates me to succeed out of spite.

ABOUT THE AUTHORS

Ronda Rousey is the UFC's undefeated women's bantam-weight champion and an Olympic medalist in judo. Arguably the most dominant athlete in UFC history, Rousey is responsible for the inclusion of women in the Octagon. She has taken Hollywood with her signature force, landing roles in major films and exploding onto the scene with the drive, commitment, and command that have made her a champion.

Maria Burns Ortiz is a journalist who has written for numerous publications including ESPN.com, Fox News Latino, and the Associated Press, and was named the National Association of Hispanic Journalists' Emerging Journalist of the Year. She is also Ronda Rousey's sister. She lives with her husband and their three amazing kids.